JAZZ AGE GIANT

JAZZ AGE
GIANT

*Charles A. Stoneham
and New York City Baseball
in the Roaring Twenties*

ROBERT F. GARRATT

UNIVERSITY OF NEBRASKA PRESS

Lincoln

The University of Nebraska Press is part of a land-grant institution with campuses and programs on the past, present, and future homelands of the Pawnee, Ponca, Otoe-Missouria, Omaha, Dakota, Lakota, Kaw, Cheyenne, and Arapaho Peoples, as well as those of the relocated Ho-Chunk, Sac and Fox, and Iowa Peoples.

Library of Congress Cataloging-in-Publication Data
Names: Garratt, Robert F., author.
Title: Jazz Age Giant: Charles A. Stoneham and
New York baseball in the roaring twenties / Robert F.
Garratt.
Description: Lincoln: University of Nebraska Press,
[2023] | Includes bibliographical references and index.
Identifiers: LCCN 2022034427
ISBN 9781496223715 (hardback)
ISBN 9781496235589 (epub)
ISBN 9781496235596 (pdf)
Subjects: LCSH: Stoneham, Charles Abraham, 1876–
1936. | New York Giants (Baseball team)—History. |
Baseball team owners—United States—Biography. |
BISAC: SPORTS & RECREATION / History | BIOGRAPHY
& AUTOBIOGRAPHY / Sports
Classification: LCC GV865.S864 G37 2023 |
DDC 796.357/64097471092 [B]—dc23/eng/20220826
LC record available at https://lccn.loc.gov/2022034427

Set in Fournier by A. Shahan.

To my son, Christopher,
who shares a lifelong love of the game

Contents

Illustrations

GRAPHS

Preface

And I was with him too, looking up and wondering.
I was within and without, simultaneously enchanted
and repelled by the inexhaustible variety of life.
—F. SCOTT FITZGERALD, *The Great Gatsby*

Writing about the life of Charles A. Stoneham in the Jazz Age has been a distinct challenge for me on two levels: learning about the man himself and also understanding the times in which he lived. Charley Stoneham was a secretive man and chose to live a purposefully guarded life, making the effort to fashion his biography daunting, to say the least. He made his fortune in the fast-paced, less-regulated New York Curb Exchange investment and brokerage business on Wall Street in the early twentieth century. He cut corners, took risks, and skirted the edges of lawful and ethical standards, practices that cultivated and necessitated cagey and careful behavior. Some of his business activities resulted in a number of appearances in federal and state courtrooms. For most of his sixteen years as the principal owner of the New York Giants, he preferred to remain in the background, letting others in the front office release club statements, announce policies, and handle player personnel. Stoneham's personal life was mysterious and complicated, involving affairs with mistresses and paramours throughout his married life. Rumors circulated about his ties to gamblers and crime figures.

Learning about Charley Stoneham the man encouraged me to learn about the times in which he lived, especially the decade of the 1920s. As a wealthy New Yorker, he had both the opportunity and the means to live large in the city's many speakeasies, nightclubs, restaurants, and gaming houses. The decade of the 1920s is fascinating and complicated, when high prosperity and partying were coupled with Prohibition, prompting many Americans who enjoyed urban nightlife, dance clubs, and drinking to break the law. Understanding the complexities and contradictions of the Jazz Age and the wide range of its urban culture was essential to the task of writing Stoneham's life story, adding a context to a personality.

As I learned more about the politics, economy, and culture of early-twentieth-century American life, I was struck by a sense of history repeating itself. Many of the Jazz Age writers I encountered wrote from a perspective and with an attitude that were shaped by trauma. Fresh memories of a recent horrific war (World War I) and a global pandemic of what came to be called the Spanish Flu (1918–19) prompted many American authors to see themselves disillusioned about politics and alienated from what they took to be a materialistic culture; they called themselves a "lost generation."[1] But the effects of the war and the global pandemic were felt by nonwriters as well, particularly young Americans, who wanted to turn their backs on a recent past of suffering and death to seek out and embrace an exuberant, hedonistic, live-for-the-moment lifestyle in the 1920s.

One hundred years later, events and conditions similar to those that prompted the Jazz Age shaded the writing of my biography of Stoneham. The U.S. military intervention in Afghanistan that began in 2001—called by military historians "America's longest war"—was still ongoing but winding down to a settlement and American withdrawal, raising questions about the efficacy of the nation's sacrifices and involvement in foreign countries' affairs. A worldwide outbreak of the coronavirus disease that became known as COVID-19 came on suddenly in the spring of 2020, causing countries all over the globe to tighten social and economic activities as a means to combat its spread. The dread of the global pandemic was felt throughout the nation and the world, as daily death counts were in the headlines and lead stories on the news channels.

In March 2020 I began sheltering-in-place in my home on Whidbey Island, Washington, as I worked on this book. The phrase *shelter-in-place* described one strategy of the nation's response to a global pandemic, a national "new normal," as most Americans isolated themselves from one another, took their children out of school, and worked from home. Zoom meetings were all the rage. People from across the country watched and listened every night to news reports on the spread of the virus and to experts and politicians who talked over each other with conflicting interpretations. One side explained the dire circumstances of the virus and the need to distance ourselves from one another; the other decried any danger and rejected the call for mask wearing and social restrictions, likening the virus to a common cold or the flu. As these contemporary responses played out, I was reading about how governments and societies had responded to the global pandemic of 1919. As William Faulkner famously put it: "The past is never dead. It's not even past."[2]

One of the books I read for historical background to my work on Stoneham was John Barry's *The Great Influenza*, a narrative about the progress of the virus that eventually took the lives of over 600,000 Americans.[3] Barry's description of the 1918–19 pandemic was so redolent of my own historical moment—how a virus becomes global, how governments attempt to contain the disease, how some public officials deny its severity and offer different methods of treatment—that it made for eerie reading and gave me a sense of the uncanny parallels of human lives across time: I was writing about the effects of a pandemic on a nation's cultural and social history while living through a pandemic with similar cultural and social effects. Besides giving me an insight into my own time, *The Great Influenza* also gave me a perspective on the contours of the energy of the Jazz Age—the 1920s—when America's enormous sense of relief over the end of both the pandemic and a ghastly war was manifest in the live-large, profligate attitude of the new decade, especially in and around New York City.

The sense that history repeats itself was apparent also in American politics during the time I was writing on Stoneham. The political she-nanigans of the Harding administration in the early 1920s replayed themselves in the national politics of my own moment, the 2020 pres-idential race, one that our political pundits kept telling us was the most important in our lifetime. Warren Harding was voted into office in 1920 largely because Americans wanted a return to normal times (Harding used the term *normalcy*), with an eye toward developing American interests and especially American business. Harding rode a wave of inward-looking nationalism, and "America first" thinking, a reaction to involvement in World War I and American cooperation with other nations.[4] The 2020 presidential election that took place while I was writing this book was couched by some as a continuation of the "make American great again" campaign that Donald Trump used to win the 2016 election, in many ways a reworking of issues central to Harding's campaign. Yet another connection to contemporary politics came in the scandals and illegalities of the Harding administration, the most prominent among them the Teapot Dome scandal that ensnared Hard-ing's secretary of the interior, Albert B. Fall. The Harding corruption history mirrored the legal problems and the many cabinet resignations that plagued the Trump administration from 2016 to 2020.

Writing about America in the 1920s spurred me to return to the lit-erature of that period, especially to the quintessential Jazz Age novel, F. Scott Fitzgerald's *The Great Gatsby*. Maureen Corrigan, one of *Gats-by*'s most enthusiastic readers, calls the novel "our Greatest American Novel," depicting "who we want to be as Americans." The novel's central story line—Gatsby's ill-fated attempt to reclaim the love of Daisy, a former sweetheart—is on a deeper level the yearning for something beyond our grasp yet something that nonetheless urges us forward to strive and to seek. It is this striving that makes *Gatsby* for Corrigan, as for many readers, the quintessential American novel.[5] Corrigan laments that most Americans encounter Fitzgerald's novel too early in their lives, usually as required reading in high school—

the novel is often assigned in English classes—and they miss its great significance.[6] She suggests that the novel should be read (and reread) later in life, when readers have more experience with American cultural history. Corrigan's words certainly rang true for me. As I reread the novel, I gained an appreciation for Fitzgerald's insights into Jazz Age culture and of the American dream.[7]

Rereading *Gatsby*, I was struck by its power to evoke an era and to define American values. But the novel sounded a deeper chord with me as a connection to Charles Stoneham's world and a suggestive portrayal of the man himself, a Jazz Age figure with a striking resemblance to the novel's eponymous hero, Jay Gatsby. The more I learned about Stoneham and his activities, the more I saw correlations to *The Great Gatsby*'s world of lavish parties, sporting types, flappers, drinking, nightclubs, fast cars, yachts, and shady, get-rich-quick business schemes. In thinking and writing about Charles Stoneham, I saw the novel as both a description of Jazz Age life and as a source that shines a light on Stoneham's business and social worlds.

A comparison of the fictional Gatsby and real-life Stoneham reveals striking correspondences. Gatsby stands as a true Roaring Twenties character, nouveau riche, socially ambitious, pleasure seeking, whose source of wealth is both mysterious and shady. He does his best to keep the essentials of his life to himself; his portrait emerges chiefly by innuendo and rumor. As a Jazz Age hero, his lifestyle epitomizes the extravagant consumer culture of his time, especially his accumulation of material goods, including racing cars and yachts, and his hosting of lavish parties. Gatsby is a social celebrity, connected to underworld figures and rumored to be involved in illegal activities, including selling illicit bonds and bootlegging.

In his portrayal of Jay Gatsby's character, Fitzgerald could have been writing about Charles Stoneham.[8] Like Gatsby's, Stoneham's attraction to the excesses of New York's Jazz Age culture is telling, not only in his lavish routine but also in the mysterious circumstances of his private life and the suspicious sources of his personal wealth.[9] Stoneham was also nouveau riche, coming from a modest working-class background, as Gatsby had. His lifestyle and behavior exemplified the brave new culture of pleasure seeking and living for the moment, of nightlife and drinking parties, prevalent among middle-class and upper-class Jazz Age New Yorkers. Like Gatsby, he was a generous host, often providing grand dinners and receptions at luxury hotels, both for baseball's executives and for the gambling and racing crowds in the summertime at Saratoga Springs.[10] Stoneham was connected to the notorious New York gambling kingpin Arnold Rothstein, who provides the model for Meyer Wolfshiem, Gatsby's shady business associate in the novel. In Gatsby fashion, Stoneham did his best to keep his personal life secret and mysterious. He had a reputation for avoiding publicity and for refusing to have his picture taken by reporters.[11]

These interpretive comparisons aside, there are certain direct and obvious links between Fitzgerald's novel and the life of Charles Stoneham. In Fitzgerald's first draft of *The Great Gatsby*, the novel's seminal scene of the confrontation between Gatsby and Daisy's husband, Tom Buchanan, is set at the Polo Grounds at a Giants baseball game, a clear link to Stoneham.[12] One Fitzgerald scholar identifies Stoneham as a source for the *Gatsby* character Dan Cody, a speculator in copper mining stocks, who mentors Jay Gatsby and gives him a nudge toward the world of wealth and high living.[13] A letter in 1924 from Fitzgerald to his editor at Scribner's, Max Perkins, offers another connection, confirming that Fitzgerald knew of Stoneham's business activities. Fitzgerald writes that he followed the 1922–24 Fuller-McGee bankruptcy case in the New York papers and that it provided "great material" for the novel. Both Fuller and Stoneham, who testified in the Fuller trial and whose name was in the papers as someone connected to the case, gave Fitzgerald a sense of the shady investment world in which both Gatsby and Wolfshiem are involved.[14]

But more than these established identifications and the comparisons of a real-life Stoneham and a fictional Gatsby, it was, in the end, the atmosphere of *Gatsby*—the parties, the drinking, the music, the nightlife, the reckless behavior by the principal characters—that signified for me the historical and cultural reality outside the novel. The novel's atmosphere evoked a sense of Stoneham's time and place and contributed to an understanding of him as a Jazz Age figure, someone who could fit easily into Gatsby's world of nouveau riche wealth, conspicuous consumption, lavish parties, and fast-paced lifestyle. In the end what interests me is, first, how *The Great Gatsby* and Fitzgerald's descriptions of the 1920s in his stories collected in *Tales of the Jazz Age* and the essays in *The Jazz Age* are "without" Stoneham's life, surrounding it, as it were, serving to provide a context and a backdrop to the events and personalities that shape it.[15] And second, I am fascinated by how Gatsby's character provides a sense (a means to get within) of Stoneham as a man of his time.

While I am persuaded by the precision of Fitzgerald's observations of the 1920s and moved by his elegant and captivating prose description of Jazz Age culture, I am hardly the first to assert these convictions. Almost since *The Great Gatsby* first appeared, literary historians and critics have remarked on Fitzgerald's apt portrait of 1920s social life in the novel; American historians often cite Fitzgerald as a source for capturing the essence of the era; some economists and sociologists do as well.[16] When many educated Americans think of the Jazz Age, it is largely Fitzgerald's version that is being summoned.

As an exemplary Jazz Age figure, however, Stoneham has proven to be a challenging subject. Even with the sources available to today's scholar on the internet, including newspapers and archival materials, I found many limitations. It is not always possible to be clear about certain activities or important moments—what he did exactly at a crucial occasion, with whom he associated, or where and how he traveled. It would be interesting (and profitable for a biographer), for example, to know with more certitude about Stoneham's family background and early schooling. It would help to know more completely his connections to Tammany Hall in his early days as a stockbroker, how and to what degree that association helped him build his business. It would also help deepen the portrait of a public Charley Stoneham to discover the extent of his associations with Jazz Age New Yorkers such as mayor Jimmy Walker, newspaperman and fellow gambler Herbert Bayard Swope, Broadway lawyer and personality William Fallon, and New York governor and 1928 U.S. presidential candidate Al Smith, all of whom Stoneham knew and associated with to some degree. There are aspects of his relationship with gambling impresario Arnold Rothstein that also would be useful to know. Many baseball historians and some Rothstein biographers posit that a business partnership existed between Stoneham and Rothstein, even one having to do with the Giants.[17] But I have not found any direct evidence of such arrangements.

Also, it would be helpful to uncover evidence of a more personal, emotional, and psychological nature that must have developed in a man who chose to live in such a mysterious way. Stoneham was essentially unavailable to the press, letting others in the franchise or front office speak for the ball club on most matters. He rarely sat in his front-row owners' box at the Polo Grounds—he did so only at an occasional opening day or at a World Series game, when he would have been seen by everyone, including players and sportswriters—preferring instead to see Giants home games from the seclusion and privacy of his office in center field.[18] When he was questioned about his business dealings, sometimes under oath in a court setting, he could be vague, forgetful, uncertain, and even dissembling. He also led a furtive social life, seeking out and frequenting selective and exclusive clubs rather than the celebrated, popular, and therefore more public night spots and jazz clubs. His romantic life was murky and complicated, with two coexisting families that we know of and plenty of rumors of other liaisons with women.

But Stoneham's efforts in keeping a low profile yielded only partial success. His name was often cited in the newspapers on financial matters or regarding his many legal entanglements, whose coverage by the press often revealed tawdry details that tarnished Stoneham's reputation.[19] There were occasional scandals involving liaisons with married women that would make the papers. Stoneham characteristically denied any connection or refused to discuss them.[20] As a Giants official, his name would be listed in newspapers as someone attending an important dinner or event or as a host of a baseball banquet. Reluctantly, he was forced on rare occasions to provide the press with an interview or a statement on baseball business. But this exposure provided only narrow and selective evidence of a life. Other details, especially those of a more quotidian nature, remain hidden to the biographer and must be inferred. When these moments of inference occur in my narrative of Stoneham's life, I attempt to measure and frame them with as many factual details as can be known and in line with the personality and character of the man revealed by recorded conduct and activities. I have described on some occasions, for example, what Stoneham would probably or necessarily do, based on various experiences in his life that are substantiated by evidence.[21] In these moments of approximation, I lean heavily on what I have gathered from newspaper sources, court records and testimonies, and contemporary histories, the particular social and political environment and circumstances that define the Jazz Age. Nonetheless, they remain inferences. Of one thing, however, I have no doubts: Charles A. Stoneham was a man of mystery and lived his life accordingly.

Acknowledgments

In writing about a man who spent most of his life trying to make that attempt difficult, if not impossible, I relied on many people to help me find my way.

In the early stages of thinking about this project, I presented two papers at the annual NINE Spring Training Conference. Colleagues who heard those presentation offered useful suggestions and gave me considerable encouragement. I also received helpful commentary and reactions from Society of American Baseball Research (SABR) listeners on two separate occasions when I presented on Stoneham's ownership of the New York Giants at SABR's annual meeting. The audiences at both of these gatherings are learned and informed about baseball. I am grateful for their attention, questions, and commentary, which broadened an understanding of my topic. There were others who helped me more directly, giving me considerable time, advice, and commentary. To them I want to give special thanks.

In the early stages of my research, when I was still unsure about writing a life of Stoneham, Lyle Spatz encouraged me to pursue the project; he also made helpful suggestions and provided contacts on background sources.

I consulted newspapers and archival materials at the New York Public Library, the Kenesaw Mountain Landis papers at the Chicago History Museum, and the Prints and Photographs Collection at the Library of Congress, and I thank the staff and librarians at these institutions for their courteous assistance. I worked with the Stoneham material at the

San Francisco Giants Archives, and I am grateful to Missy Mikulecky, Giants archivist, who helped on numerous occasions.

Special thanks goes to Jaime and Kim Rupert, great-granddaughters of Charles Stoneham, who shared family papers and photos that were invaluable. Jaime and Kim also facilitated my meeting and interview with Jane Stoneham Gosden, Charles Stoneham's daughter.

Once my writing was underway, a number of friends and colleagues read drafts of various chapters and offered good suggestions. I thank Barney Deasy, Cliff Bellone, Geoffrey Block, Doug Branson, John Burbage, Bill Burns, Rob Fitts, Steve Gietschier, Mott Greene, Dan Levitt, Lee Lowenfish, Bill Oltman, David Smith, Steve Treder, and Dick White.

Pat Henry, Andy McCue, and Gabriel Schechter read the entire book in different stages of development. I thank all three of them for their attention and their keen sense of narrative direction.

I am deeply indebted to Bill Lamb, who not only read the entire draft and offered critical commentary but also patiently and attentively answered my email questions on Stoneham's legal issues and on the Giants' history in New York.

I also owe a special debt of gratitude to George Wickes, my graduate school professor and mentor, whose knowledge of twentieth-century American literature and conversations about F. Scott Fitzgerald helped shape my thinking about *The Great Gatsby*. George read a number of the chapters and offered useful suggestions.

Fitzgerald scholar and American literature Professor Jackson Bryer answered questions on *The Great Gatsby* in email exchanges and read sections of the book. I appreciate his involvement in the project and his willingness to offer suggestions.

Steve Steinberg took time away from his own work as a baseball writer to help organize and select pictures for this book. Judy Cash helped with formatting problems with some of the images. Keith Andrews interrupted his business schedule to design the graphics for the book. Linda Garratt Slezak provided important genealogical information on Charles Stoneham's parents and his first wife, Alice Rafter. My thanks go out to all of them.

Rob Taylor and Courtney Ochsner at the University of Nebraska Press guided the project along the way and offered helpful direction. My thanks go out also to Elizabeth Gratch and Abigail Kwambamba who were so attentive in the final stages of the book's production.

Over the six years of working on Charles Stoneham, I was fortunate to have good wishes from a number of friends. I am grateful for their encouragement and their interest but most of all for their company: Vinni Bellone, Dominic and Paulette Carboni, Bill Cotton, Bill and Chipper Cromley, Bob Ericksen and Judith Meyer, Carmen and Kathy Gagliardi, Peggy Gilmer, Jeff Gordon and Beth McGarry, Kent Hooper, Ron and Trish Johnson, Harry and Carole McCarthy, Dan and Linda O'Connell, Duane and Nancy Oyler, Andy Rex, Roger Smith, Tony and Muriel Verdoia, Needham and Diane Ward, Louise Westling, Frances Wood and Bill Graves, and all of the Brave and Bold Spring Training group.

My entire family has been solicitous and warmly supportive along the way, and their kindness and affection have sustained me. Most of all, I thank my wife, Sally, who read every line of the book attentively and whose love and encouragement have meant everything to me.

JAZZ AGE GIANT

Introduction

> There was first the ferry boat moving softly from the
> Jersey shore at dawn—the moment crystalized
> into my first symbol of New York. . . . New York had
> all the iridescence of the beginning of the world.
> —F. SCOTT FITZGERALD, "My Lost City"

Placing Charley Stoneham within the Jazz Age requires no straining or forcing: it is an easy and natural fit. He was both a mirror and a lamp: a man who reflected the times in which he lived and who shone his own light upon them. He had the advantage of location and moment, and he lived his life in sync. The Jazz Age in New York City provided the ideal milieu for his self-expression: a Jay Gatsby type who remakes himself from humble roots to become a man of enormous wealth and reputation.[1] Stoneham grew from working-class roots to become a wealthy individual who intended to live fully and on his terms. One observer described the times as "a zany, materialistic age in which people wanted to be let alone to grow rich quickly and to have fun," two of Stoneham's paramount aspirations.[2] He was determined to make the most of what the place and the times could offer him.

The Place

According to the 1920 United State census, more Americans were living in cities than in rural areas for the first time in the country's history.[3] And the most populous of American cities was New York, with 5.6 million residents, more than doubling the second most populous, Chicago, at just over 2.7 million.[4] New York City in the early 1920s was also one of the great cultural centers of the Western world, rivaling Paris and Berlin for artistic excitement and innovation. Europe was recovering from a horrific and bloody war, and the United States was about to assume its role as a world leader, with New York playing a central role as an international city. America's cultural core, New York, was also its media center, its commercial and business hub, home to the stock exchanges of Wall Street and the headquarters of major banks. Like a bright and powerful magnet, New York City drew Americans from across the nation in the decade of the 1920s, especially young people eager to turn away from memories of a brutal world war and a horrible deadly pandemic. As the American business, finance, and entertainment capital, New York presented opportunities for those wishing for a new beginning; it also offered abundant choices for those seeking enjoyment and distraction.

Writing in the early 1920s, H. L. Mencken observed, "New York is a place where all the aspirations of the Western World meet to form one master aspiration."[5] The young with old money came to the great Jazz Age capital—like the characters in F. Scott Fitzgerald's *The Great Gatsby*, Tom and Daisy Buchanan and Jordan Baker but also the not-so-wealthy Nick Carraway, and Gatsby himself, the nouveau riche American dreamer.[6] Others came from the farms and the rural towns, leaving behind a staid and narrow traditional past to find new pleasure and, for many, a new life.[7] The city was a hive of reinvention, "attracting those who wanted, sometimes desperately, to find out not so much who they were as who they could be, those who needed the gaze of others to come alive."[8] Midway through the decade, the newly launched *New Yorker* magazine described the city as a gymnasium of celebrities and would-be celebrities; there were always "more nonentities trying to attract attention and failing than celebrities trying to avoid attention and succeeding."[9] As one New York observer put it, the possibilities seemed endless. "It was a city where you could get whatever you wanted, whenever you wanted it. There was no night, no day: only the light of the sun and the light of the electric lamps and the lush darkness, the endless rushing midnight, the true soul of the place . . . a time-seizing time of life and freedom."[10]

The Times

The Jazz Age decade of the 1920s would also be called "roaring," not just for its noisy cultural exuberance and the sound of a surging stock market but also because of its rattle of social change. Young Americans, those in their twenties and thirties, transformed existing values and lifestyles by embracing relaxed morals, risqué behavior, modish clothing, and a greater freedom for women, who first voted in national elections in 1920. Change was widespread, in the air politically, artistically, socially, and morally. Soon the example of the young spread to older generations, and the experience of change became a thing unto itself and was rampant. F. Scott Fitzgerald, the decade's chronicler, described the transition: "By 1923 their elders, tired of watching the carnival with ill-concealed envy, had discovered that young liquor could take the place of young blood, and with a whoop the orgy began."[11] Frederick Lewis Allen noted a restlessness that spread to the middle generation, whose members found themselves discontent with past values and "in a mood to question everything that had once seemed to them true and worthy and of good report. They too had spent themselves and wanted a good time."[12]

In opposition to the isolationism of previous decades, the new generation opened itself to the influence of European artistic experimentation and to the cultivation of its own homegrown sound—jazz. *Jazz*! The word described a new sound that grew from ragtime and blues and was shaped by Black musicians like Jelly Roll Morton, Duke Ellington, and Louis Armstrong and singers like Bessie Smith. Music historian Ethan Mordden believes that the word derived "from black patois (to jass: to copulate)." He stresses the tempo and rhythm of the new sound: "No matter what the intention of a composer or lyricist—no matter how chaste or sophisticated—two seconds into any song they played, every song was jazz. . . . The new music broke all the rules . . . unrelated to either popular or classical music of the past. Jazz was a dirge with an upbeat."[13] Fitzgerald then took the musical term and applied it to the decade, coining the phrase *Jazz Age*, what became known not only as an epoch but also as a description of a cultural and social lifestyle, especially one steeped in dancing, drinking, speakeasies, and nightclubs.[14] The lifestyle that was identified with the new music ushered in a bright wave of activity and interest, especially among young Americans. "Jazz, like the dances it spawned," writes Ann Douglas, "was the creation of America's Negro population, and white urban Americans wanted to go straight to the source to get more of it."[15]

Duke Ellington remarked that the new music began in the 1910s in the West Indies and drifted to New Orleans and Chicago, but "not until these musicians converged in New York and blended together did jazz emerge as a widespread and recognized art form."[16] The sounds of jazz were coming primarily out of Harlem, what some have called the "Nightclub Capital of the World," with over 125 clubs sprinkled around the neighborhood, not as big and famous perhaps as the Cotton Club or Connie's Inn but all of them capable of serving up drinks and dance music for white patrons.[17] It was a strange social and cultural phenomenon: almost exclusively Black musicians and entertainers performing for almost exclusively white audiences. By 1922 the Harlem nightlife had spread throughout Manhattan to clubs in Greenwich Village and would become centralized on Fifty-Second Street beginning in the 1930s. Paul Whiteman, a white band leader, moved his orchestra from Atlantic City to New York and played in concert halls and hotel ballrooms, promoting himself as the "the King of Jazz."[18] As jazz spread around the city, it fueled the liquor trade; the total number of speakeasies, nightclubs, and dance halls where liquor was served was estimated by the police commissioner's office to be over thirty-two thousand by the end of the decade.[19]

But there was more than jazz that was rousing the city. New Yorkers were enjoying unprecedented prosperity, with discretionary income to spend, much of it on entertainment, which flourished during the decade. There was Broadway, of course, with its history of shows and vaudeville, gaining a new life with an explosion of productions in the 1920s, not only legitimate theater with playwrights such as Eugene O'Neill but also musicals with songwriters like Larry Hart, Jerome Kern, and the team of Oscar Hammerstein II and Richard Rodgers. In the 1927–28 season alone, there were 50 new musicals and 270 theatrical productions, including blockbusters such as *A Connecticut Yankee* and *Show Boat*.[20] There was also classical music concerts and opera. And if all this did not offer enough of a rich array of choices, the city was also the center of American spectator sports, especially baseball and boxing.

A city this lively and boundless needed a political overseer whose personality and temperament matched the time. New Yorkers found such a man in James J. Walker, a debonair public figure, a trial lawyer, state senator, lyricist, and friend to Broadway, a connoisseur of night-life, a devotee of speakeasies, and mayor of New York City from 1925 to 1932. One observer pronounced it a perfect fit, dubbing Walker a playboy mayor for a playboy town.[21] Walker governed the city with a light hand, content to let business run its course, often with city contracts given out as perks to friends in Tammany Hall.[22] Known to the public as Jimmy and to his close friends as Jim, Walker was the quintessential Jazz Age politician, the ambassador of the city who would entertain prominent visitors, oversee public ceremonies, open hospitals and schools, dedicate public places, and preside over gatherings, often impeccably attired in dress suits and top hats, always ready with a dash of jaunty humor and a clever retort. A true fashionista, he was known to change his customized dress shirts three or four times a day. Invariably, he would arrive fashionably late to public events, sometimes over an hour, but he could light up the room immediately and captivate any audience. When he got moving, he kept to an active pace, especially when the sun went down, often attending more than one event in a single evening.

"Beau James," as his biographer dubbed him, was generous to a fault and magnanimous in looking after his constituents. "He could do no wrong in the Peter Pan years of his first term. He was the life of the party, the chieftain of Broadway Bedouins."[23] Turning a blind eye on reform and restraint, he pushed the city's excessive rhythms by example. Walker was the lord of misrule, until the wide-open revelry eventually caught the eye of state reformers. Pushed by the new austerity brought about by the stock market crash in late October 1929 and followed by the beginning of the Great Depression, state auditors, under the direction of Judge Samuel Seabury, began looking at the city's books and found Walker to be an ineffectual and disinterested steward and his high life manner inappropriate, bordering on the illegal.[24] He resigned from office in 1932, opening the door for the energetic reformer Fiorello LaGuardia, who was elected mayor in 1933. But Walker's time in the city's highest office reflected the great energy of the Jazz Age.

An interesting feature of the city's Jazz Age high jinks was that they blossomed and flourished despite the shadow cast over the nation with the advent of Prohibition in January 1920.[25] More and more Americans during the decade ignored the law by drinking and dancing, and nowhere was this more prevalent than in New York City, where people sought out the celebrated nightclubs and speakeasies. Indeed, some thought that Prohibition, the law of the land from 1919 to 1933, intended to curb the use of alcohol, probably increased its use with Americans of all ages. The Eighteenth Amendment made the sale, manufacture, transportation, and possession of "intoxicating liquor" illegal, although, paradoxically, not its consumption. But almost immediately after its inception, when the Volstead Act was voted in Congress to enforce the new law, Americans (especially those living in big cities) disregarded its strictures. Beginning in 1920 and continuing throughout the decade, speakeasies and jazz clubs serving drinks sprouted up all over Manhattan, catering to thirsty New Yorkers. The same was true in other cities across the country, including Chicago, Detroit, and San

Francisco.[26] The humorists Will Rogers quipped that "Prohibition is better than no liquor at all" and urged Congress to pass an amendment prohibiting folks from learning anything, remarking, "If it works as well as Prohibition [the Eighteenth Amendment], in five years Americans would be the smartest race of people on earth."[27]

A common view of the Jazz Age is that it was a child of Prohibition, engendered and nourished in response to puritanical restriction. But some close observers of the era see this view as too simplistic. Fitzgerald himself was one of the first to suggest that Prohibition was not the sole cause of Jazz Age behavior and temperament: "A whole race going hedonistic, deciding on pleasure. The precocious intimacies of the younger generation would have come about with or without prohibition—they were implicit in the attempt to adapt English customs to American conditions."[28] In his comprehensive history of Prohibition, Daniel Okrent echoes Fitzgerald, cautioning against the view that the excessive party-like atmosphere of the 1920s was solely an attempt to thwart Prohibition: "What remains dubious is the suggestion that it was the prohibition of liquor that led the young, the stylish . . . to ingest it so avidly. No one who has read the early novels of Evelyn Waugh, soaked as they are in the fizzy frolics of England's Bright Young Things, could possibly attribute short skirts, hot music and hip flasks to Prohibition, nor could anyone who paid attention to the frantic pursuit of the new and the daring in Weimar Germany. . . . It was World War I that ripped western civilization from the lingering embrace of the nineteenth century. . . . Prohibition was an accelerant, not a cause."[29] This view ignores the horrors of the Great Influenza Pandemic of 1918–19 as another reason that Jazz Age revelers might have wanted to live for the moment, but its central point holds: excessive imbibing in the 1920s was not exclusively the result of 1918 American politics.[30]

There is little disagreement that Prohibition promoted a laxness in following the law, however. During the 1920s it was fashionable among young Americans to adopt the notion about drinking that everybody was doing it. Moreover, it was chic to do so. Social behavior fostered a flexible morality, a laissez-faire attitude, and a willingness to take risks. In many cities, particularly in the Northeast, those who opposed Prohibition were ordinary law-abiding citizens whose behavior would tend to nullify the law.[31] Thus, many Jazz Age New Yorkers led double lives, respectful business professionals by day and lawbreaking, pleasure-seeking partygoers at night.[32] And as the decade progressed, according to Fitzgerald, so too did the pace of partying: "The restlessness of New York in 1927 approached hysteria. The parties were bigger . . . the shows were broader, the buildings were higher, the morals were looser and the liquor was cheaper. . . . Many people who were not alcoholics were lit up four days out of seven . . . and the hangover became part of the day. . . . Most of my friends drank too much—the more they were in tune to the times, the more they drank."[33]

In his chronicle of the decade, Fredrick Lewis Allen notes this irony:

When the Eighteenth Amendment was ratified, prohibition seemed to have an almost united country behind it. Evasion of the law began immediately, however, and strenuous and sincere opposition to it, especially in the North and East—quickly gathered force. The results were the bootlegger, the speakeasy, and a spirit of deliberate revolt which in many communities made drinking "the thing to do." From these facts in turn flowed further results: the increased popularity of distilled as against fermented liquors, the use of the hipflask, the cocktail party, and the general transformation of drinking from a masculine prerogative to one shared by both sexes together . . . the speakeasy usually catered to both men and women.[34]

There was no problem finding a drink in Jazz Age New York. Robert Benchley, a writer for the *New Yorker* magazine, once walked both sides of Fifty-Second Street between Fifth and Sixth Avenues, counting thirty-eight speakeasies.[35] In the *New York Telegram* in 1928, a tongue-in-cheek article appeared that answered the question "Where on Manhattan Island can you buy liquor?" It listed forty suggestions, including the obvious, like speakeasies, open saloons, restaurants, nightclubs, drugstores, and delicatessens, and the not-so-obvious, such as paint stores, malt shops, and moving van companies.[36]

While Prohibition did not achieve its purpose of restricting Americans from drinking beer, wine, and spirits, it did produce some results, however unintended. "It encouraged criminality and institutionalized hypocrisy," according to Okrent. "It deprived the government of revenue, stripped the gears of the political system, and imposed profound limitations on individual rights. It fostered a culture of bribery, blackmail, and official corruption."[37] This was particularly true of metropolitan police forces. Once Prohibition was underway, it was not long before the police forces of larger cities were being accused of complicity with politicians, on the one hand, and bootleggers, on the other, all for the purpose of making liquor easier to get. Many metropolitan police forces, especially in the Northeast, in Chicago, and out west in San Francisco and Los Angeles, employed a soft regulation of the liquor trade, rather than an enforcement of its prohibition. Ideally, anyone who wanted a drink could get one, but quietly and surreptitiously.[38] It soon became common knowledge to any observant citizen that the patrolman on the beat was taking cash and other favors from speakeasy proprietors, drivers of beer trucks, and all that motley crew engaged in the circumvention of an unpopular law.[39] And there were, of course, strong suspicions that sometimes the money reached higher up.

The Man
(BEAU CHARLES; OR THE GREAT STONEHAM)

As a boy, Charley Stoneham could see the towers of Wall Street across the Hudson River from his home in Jersey City, where he imagined a brave new world of prosperity. His imagination became reality a few years later when he dropped out of high school to seek a career in the investment business. He began as a clerk researching stocks and gradually moved to sales. When he opened his own firm in the first decade of the new century, he moved from Jersey City to Manhattan. A staunch urbanite, Stoneham took full advantage of urban life easily and comfortably, cultivating New York's financial opportunities and reveling in the city's lavish nightlife. He worked hard in the cutthroat investment business, and he partied equally hard at the city's clubs, watering holes, and gambling tables. He was known as a prodigious drinker and avid gambler. From the investment business, he moved to the sporting world, establishing a racing stable where he could own and train horses and then buying the New York Giants, the National League's (if not America's) most storied franchise. Stoneham lived large in a city known for its liveliness. What cultural historian Lloyd Morris said of Mayor Jimmy Walker in the late 1920s could be said of Stoneham: "The quintessence of New York, he represented its holiday mood, its vivacity and splendor, its preeminence among American cities as the pleasure capital of the hemisphere."[40]

In *The Great Gatsby* Fitzgerald portrays Jay Gatsby as the master of reinvention, a poor boy who came out of nowhere, accumulating wealth in the fast-paced, risky atmosphere of the 1920s, who chased the bright and limitless American dream, and who wanted desperately to be seen as rich and powerful. Fitzgerald could be describing Stoneham, who chased his own American dream and assumed a life of opulence and extravagant pleasure in the process. An essential Jazz Age character, Stoneham would not be hemmed in by conventional mores or a traditional lifestyle. Moreover, he would reinvent himself not once but twice. Out of a blue-collar, working-class Irish Catholic background, he would morph into a shrewd businessman. By the time he opened his own business firm, in 1911, he had acquired a new identity as a wealthy and successful Wall Street investment broker with connections to Tammany Hall, living in style in Manhattan.[41] After the war, at the dawn of the Jazz Age, he would change again, reinventing himself as a full-time sportsman who owned racehorses and a major league baseball franchise.

As a young man seeking his fortune in the investment and brokerage business, Charles Stoneham took full advantage of his Irish Catholic background, giving him an entry to New York's Tammany Hall political circles then dominated by Irish Americans. Charley, as his friends and associates called him, was known to Tammany stalwarts such as Big Tom Foley and Charles Murphy, and through them he had the chance to meet, and eventually befriend, the movers and the shakers of New York's Jazz Age politics, including governor Al Smith and Mayor Jimmy Walker. According to one source, his connection to Tammany Hall smoothed his way early on in his investment career and certainly facilitated his acquaintance with Frank McQuade, a Tammany-backed magistrate, and John McGraw, a friend to Tammany Hall, both of whom would join him in a Giants ownership group as minor stakeholders.[42] The Giants were the favorite team of Tammany Hall, and Tammany VIPs, such as Foley, Smith, and Walker, would be frequent guests in the owner's box at Giants games.

Stoneham's connections were not confined to the business and political world but extended to New York's racing crowd, gambling set, and underworld figures, other characteristic slices of Jazz Age culture. A longtime member of Arnold Rothstein's Partridge Club, Stoneham rubbed shoulders with all sorts of Jazz Age characters who frequented Rothstein's "floating crapgame," later popularized in the Broadway musical *Guys and Dolls*. Among them were business types such as oil magnate Henry Sinclair; Broadway impresario Florenz Ziegfeld; shifty gamblers like George H. Lowden, who would spend time in Sing Sing for forgery; and socialites such as Herbert Bayard Swope, the great newspaperman of the 1920s and a member of the famed Algonquin Round Table who hosted lavish Gatsby-like parties in Great Neck on Long Island.[43] Stoneham's association with these men was casual and took place mainly at the gambling tables where they would occasionally meet. Not so with underworld king Rothstein, with whom Stoneham had deeper connections. Charley was rumored to be partners with "A.R.," as Rothstein was referred to in and around Broadway, in a number of shady business deals, including bootlegging.[44] Attracted to showgirls and the Broadway nightlife, Stoneham was also a familiar guest at many of the swank jazz clubs and speakeasies, some of them financed by Rothstein, with plush carpets, upholstered booths, gilt-edged mirrors, tinkling chandeliers, and frescoed ceilings.[45] The five- or ten-dollar cover charge and the minimum drink order of a thirty-five-dollar bottle of champagne would be chump change for him.

Stoneham's reinventions of identities placed in doubt the sense of a single self—a working-class Catholic youth who moved from cutthroat broker to urbane sportsman; a habitué of the city's demimonde with a reputation for high stakes gambling, nightclubbing, and drinking, often in the company of Broadway showgirls; a family man whose complicated home life involved one wife and children in Manhattan and another with children in Westchester County.[46] Yet Stoneham's mercurial personality and tricky marital situation would hardly shock many of his contemporary New Yorkers. The propensity for furtive love lives and covert domestic arrangements among Jazz Age celebrities was understood and even condoned. Babe Ruth's many girlfriends were an open secret among members of the press; Mayor Jimmy Walker's affair with actress Betty Compton was common knowledge; screen idols like Rudolph Valentino had numerous lovers; even those with whom Stoneham kept company were complicit, including Arnold Rothstein, whose two mistresses were named along with his wife as heirs to his estate, and attorney William Fallon, a married man who lived with his mistress, the Broadway actress Gertrude Vanderbilt. Indeed, Stoneham's shadowy private life reflected a notorious slice of his times.[47]

Yet playing out this frenetic lifestyle by immersing oneself in the culture of the times could take a toll professionally, emotionally, and physically, as just a cursory look at the lives of certain Jazz Age personalities will show.[48] Stoneham's life was complicated enough without his nightlife activities. His business affairs were murky and led to years of legal entanglements and courtroom appearances, among them three indictments for criminal activity. His nightlife activities—the carousing and gambling—strained and compromised his personal life.[49] The attention given to legal affairs and a messy private life quite naturally drew his attention away from the supervision of his ball club. After a great run early in his ownership, when the Giants won four straight pennants and two World Series championships, the team never won another championship for the rest of the decade, the years in which Stoneham was engaged in multiple legal difficulties. It would not be until 1933, with a surprising championship season, that Stoneham and the Giants would enjoy, once again, a return to baseball glory. Stoneham would savor the Giants' return to the heights of baseball success, but he would only have limited precious time to do so. The years of hard drinking, late-night revelry, not to mention the stressful toll of legal complications, were catching up; his health was deteriorating. By the fall of 1935, considerably weakened, he turned over most of the ball club's business operations to his son Horace. In late December his condition was quite dire. He traveled to Hot Springs, Arkansas, for treatment but to no effect. Stoneham died on the evening of January 6, 1936, at the age of fifty-nine.

What follows is less a cradle-to-grave biography or a focus upon an individual as a baseball man. My portrait of Charles A. Stoneham stresses how place and moment are crucial to character and, conversely, how an individual contributes to a shaping of the spirit of his time. It is a narrative that looks at an epoch in American history from outside in and inside out, with an individual as the central focus. The 1920s, what came to be known as the Jazz Age, or the Roaring Twenties, has been singled out as having its own clear identity, one of high living, a pursuit of pleasure, a time of hedonism when rules were broken, years of conspicuous consumption, a decade bookmarked on one end by the horrors of war and on the other by austere economic hardship.[50] People living in the Jazz Age, in New York especially, had great opportunities to pursue prosperity, seek pleasure, embrace change, and live for the moment. Stoneham certainly did. And in the process of living that life, he became a Jazz Age prototype whose activities and personality can be understood as reflections of a specific time and place.

I

Endgames

> A little before three the Lutheran minister arrived from
> Flushing, and I began to look involuntarily out of the windows
> for other cars. So did Gatsby's father. And as the time passed
> and the servants came in and stood waiting in the hall, his eyes
> began to blink anxiously, and he spoke of the rain in a
> worried, uncertain way. The minister glanced several times
> at his watch, so I took him aside and asked him to wait
> for half an hour. But it wasn't any use. Nobody came.
>
> —F. SCOTT FITZGERALD, *The Great Gatsby*

The funeral of Charles A. Stoneham took place on a wintry morning, January 9, 1936, in Jersey City, New Jersey, the city of his birth. The location to mark his passing was the imposing neo-Gothic All Saints Roman Catholic Church, a deliberate choice to underscore a literal cradle-to-grave story; Stoneham had been baptized in Jersey City fifty-eight years earlier and brought up in the Catholic community there.[1] A high requiem funeral mass followed quickly on the heels of an agonizing death on January 6 at a Hot Springs, Arkansas, resort where Stoneham had gone a month earlier for treatment for Bright's disease, a type of kidney failure.[2]

The choice of Hot Springs as a recuperative location was an easy one for Stoneham to make even in sickness. The Arkansas spa city had a long-standing reputation as both a curative locale, blessed with natural hot mineral waters, and as a gaming center, with casinos, a racetrack, card parlors, nightspots, and saloons. In the early decades of the twentieth century, it had the potential and the ambition to become a southeastern version of Las Vegas. It was designated as a national park in 1921, the nation's smallest, and its medical waters were promoted by the locals with the motto "We Bathe the World." It attracted a colorful mélange of athletes, politicians, businesspeople, celebrities, and gangsters, some who came both to play and relax; others came just to heal and restore. Some major league ball clubs used Hot Springs for occasional spring training.

Stoneham had visited Hot Springs to gamble and take the waters, well aware of their reputation to treat everything from diabetes to epilepsy.[3] This time, unfortunately, the salubrious effects of the resort were lost on Stoneham, whose health had been deteriorating for the past year.[4] It was too little, too late, for the fast living, hard drinking owner of the New York Giants baseball team. He lapsed into a coma and died two weeks after he arrived, with only four people at his bedside, Dr. W. M. Blackshare, who had been treating Stoneham in Hot Springs; Alfred, Stoneham's African American butler; Stoneham's son Horace; and Polo Grounds supervisor Ernie Viberg. Horace Stoneham and Viberg had arrived the night before. Horace then made quick arrangements for the funeral and accompanied the body back to New Jersey by train.[5]

The large church where Stoneham was memorialized was as good as empty that cold January morning, the result of the family's wishes that a strict code of privacy surround the final arrangements, effectively wrapping the funeral mass in a shroud of mystery. Publicity and announcements of the service were monitored and even delayed by the family, making it an almost secret affair. Curiously, Giants officials were asked by the immediate family not to divulge either the time or the location of the church funeral and the burial. Heightening the sense of secrecy, the family directed Ford Frick, president of the National League, and Will Harridge, president of the American League, to request that all club owners in the respective leagues not attend. The New York chapter of the Baseball Writers' Association was asked not to send any flowers, and the local press was not informed about the events until the following day.[6]

The family's insistence that the ceremony be a private affair had its effect. Funerals are often solemn occasions, but the restrictions imposed upon Stoneham's last rites ensured a particularly gloomy outcome. The funeral mass had three priests as co-celebrants, typical for a solemn high requiem, and another priest, Monsignor Joseph Meehan, the pastor of All Saints, present as a witness. Conspicuous by their numbers, the clergy on the altar almost outnumbered the worshippers in the church, a total of eight: son Horace, Stoneham's widow Hannah, and a handful of the Giants' front-office representatives, including manager Bill Terry; Eddie Brannick and Jim Tierney, club secretaries; Leo Bondy, club treasurer and Stoneham's personal attorney; and Ross Robertson and Ernie Viberg, club directors.[7] In the setting of the huge, cavernous church, the scene of the small clutch of mourners gathered in the front-row pew accentuated the sense of solitude and intensified the somber mood.

The last rites of Stoneham, a Jazz Age figure and baseball owner, contrasted dramatically with other memorial services for the famous personalities of his era. Funerals during this period were almost always open events, reported on by the newspapers and drawing a public audience fascinated with the pageantry of the ritual. In keeping with the allure of celebrities during the Jazz Age, these occasions offered the opportunity both to acknowledge the famous and to mourn their passing. The memorials were social rituals attracting two main constituents: attending luminaries and dignitaries who wished to be seen and members of the general public who wished to see them. The funeral mass for Charles F. Murphy, head boss of New York City's Tammany Hall political machine for twenty-two years, took place on April 28, 1924, at St. Patrick's Cathedral in Midtown Manhattan, the most prominent and majestic of all the Catholic churches in New York City. Over six thousand people crowded the church from the altar rail to the entrances, while another five thousand stood outside for what the

New York Times labeled the public's "last tribute of respect" for a New York City political luminary.[8] A year later, on January 17, 1925, another Tammany Hall figure, Thomas F. "Big Tom" Foley, the Lower East Side ward boss who helped a young and aspiring Charley Stoneham make his way in the investment world, was mourned by thousands in what was described as "one of the most impressive New York City's funerals."[9]

Impressive they may have been, but neither of these funerals could hold the proverbial candle to the one held for Rudolph Valentino in August 1926. It was, as one social historian described it, "the funeral of the age."[10] Valentino, whose performance in the box office smash *The Sheik* (1921) established him as the first true American heartthrob movie star, died at the height of his fame, at the age of thirty-one. Crowds lined the streets outside as the cortege, flanked by 250 policemen, made its way from the church down Broadway.[11] Newspapers estimated the bystanders on the sidewalks numbered over 100,000, prompting one wag to remark that Valentino's funeral proved the biggest event in his career, far bigger than his ascendance in *The Sheik*, implying that Rudolph Valentino alive never drew such a crowd as Rudolph Valentino dead.[12]

Even notorious Jazz Age figures had great send-offs. Flamboyant trial attorney William Fallon died in the spring of 1927 at the age of forty-one. Fallon, enthusiastic Giants fan and an acquaintance of both Stoneham and Giants manager John McGraw, was a Broadway character known as "The Great Mouthpiece"; he gained notoriety as an incomparable and shady defense lawyer who represented over 120 criminal defendants. Reputedly, none of his clients was convicted.[13] Fallon's funeral on May 3, 1927, was a public Jazz Age spectacle: a solemn requiem mass, celebrated by three priests on the altar, attended by seven hundred mourners, many of them from Broadway society, followed by thirty-five cars in procession to the cemetery.[14] Stoneham and McGraw were among those in attendance, and it was rumored that McGraw paid for Fallon's elaborately decorated casket.[15] Underworld figure Arnold Rothstein, a Stoneham acquaintance in the horse racing and gambling worlds and the man identified by many as the one who fixed the 1919 World Series, died a violent death on November 5, 1928, shot in a dispute over a gambling debt.[16] His memorial service, a traditional Jewish ceremony, took place at Riverside Memorial Chapel at Amsterdam Avenue and West Seventy-Sixth Street. By some estimates there were two hundred guests in attendance, and another five hundred or so people waited outside for a glimpse of Rothstein's family and the other mourners.[17]

Of all the funerals honoring public figures of the era, however, John McGraw's serves as the most relevant comparison to Stoneham's own last rites. New York Giants manager from 1902 until his retirement in 1932 and Stoneham's business partner and close associate for almost fifteen years, McGraw was sent off by thousands of mourners in both New York and Baltimore, McGraw's adopted hometown. His solemn high requiem mass, held in Midtown Manhattan at St. Patrick's Cathedral, attracted baseball dignitaries, city officials, newspapermen, and average baseball fans, some of whom stood outside the church, unable to get inside, as the cathedral was filled to capacity. Newspaper coverage of the ceremony estimated the crowd to be close to four thousand.[18] The mass itself, celebrated on February 28, 1934, was part of a three-day public mourning event for McGraw, from a wake at his home in Pelham Manor in New Rochelle, where five hundred people paid their respects the night before the mass, a funeral cortege with police escort from the McGraw home to St. Patrick's, and another motorcade from the cathedral to Pennsylvania Station, where the family accompanied the body to Baltimore for McGraw's burial.[19] Stoneham attended both the wake and the mass the following morning and traveled with the McGraw family to Baltimore.

Given Stoneham's reputation as a baseball personality and a Jazz Age socialite, the expectation for his final send-off to be a public event would have been normal, especially considering the attention given to fellow baseball luminaries such as McGraw and Brooklyn Robins owner Charles Ebbets, whose 1925 funeral drew baseball dignitaries like Commissioner Kenesaw Mountain Landis, National League president John Heydler, and other baseball owners.[20] Instead, the script for Stoneham's funeral might have come right 'off the pages of F. Scott Fitzgerald's *The Great Gatsby*. In the novel Gatsby threw lavish parties in his opulent Long Island mansion, where throngs of New York's boisterous partygoers regularly took advantage of his generosity. His name was known to all New York socialites. To attend a Gatsby party was to have arrived, as it were, in society. In contrast, Gatsby's funeral, a dreary and isolated affair on a dark and rainy day, was attended by only a small handful of people, chiefly his father, some housekeepers, and two others. The description of Gatsby's funeral at the end of the novel is an eerie foreshadowing of Stoneham's last rites. The bleakness of the scene is captured in an exchange between Nick Carraway, the narrator of the novel, and one of the attending mourners, who apologized because he couldn't join the cortege from Gatsby's house.

"I couldn't get to the house," he remarked.

"Neither could anybody else."

"Go on!" He started. "Why, my God! they used to go there by the hundreds."

He took off his glasses and wiped them again, outside and in.

"The poor son-of-a-bitch," he said.[21]

In the context of Jazz Age exuberance, when even the era's funerals and memorial services were extravagant, Charles Stoneham's final send-off stands out as an aberration. While technically outside the parameters of the Jazz Age (the decade of 1920s), his funeral, like McGraw's, is defined by the life it commemorates, rather than the date of its occurrence. Stoneham was a Jazz Age figure, not in the mode of movie star Rudolph Valentino perhaps or politician Big Tom Foley or even fellow Giants personality John McGraw but a public figure and personality nonetheless. Stoneham's name was often in the newspapers, certainly in the sports pages as a figure in the horse racing world, as a baseball executive in the 1920s and 1930s, and as a promoter of boxing and soccer at the Polo Grounds. He would be known to readers of the financial pages, of course, and also to the general reader when his business activities drew him into court and stories about it would appear on the front pages and in the headlines.[22] There was even the whiff of scandal about him that the gossip columnists relished and developed, when on two separate occasions women took their lives in hotels and left suicide notes addressed to him, claiming they had been forsaken. In both cases Stoneham denied knowing them.[23]

All of this exposure would suggest that his death might be cause for some notice, one that the public at large, not to mention the inner circle of baseball luminaries, would want to acknowledge and commemorate. That they did not and would not begs an obvious question. Why did so public a man who knew so many people have such a strictly private and somber funeral? The answer turns out to be that he had something to hide.

To say that Charles Stoneham led an enigmatic life would be to state the obvious. A man with a constant public profile, he nonetheless tried to avoid publicity and struggled most of his life to maintain his privacy. As the primary owner of a storied New York sports franchise, he gave almost no interviews. He disliked having his picture taken and avoided it as much as possible. During hours of testimony in court over business matters, he offered vague answers and was unable to recall details about important transactions or daily activities. Stoneham epitomized Jazz Age culture, and he embraced the mores of his time, which prompted a double life, a public and a private self, one within and the other outside social convention. He lived in opposition, between a professional life and a party life—cutthroat businessman by day, boozy and lawbreaking reveler by night, as one Stoneham biographer, Bill Lamb, suggests.[24] Many Americans in the 1920s lived this way, of course, leading respectable and upstanding lives at the office, at institutions, and in the workplace and breaking or ignoring the law in the evening with a night on the town at clubs or speakeasies.

But Stoneham did so in the extreme. And not just as a businessman and then as a Broadway reveler and nightclub playboy. The 1930 U.S. census shows him living at two separate addresses with two different wives and families.[25]

The existence of this second family may have pressured son Horace and the Giants' front office to move, as they did with the arrangement of Charles's funeral, with haste and secrecy. What Horace knew about his father's double life could complicate and possibly even ruin his own and his immediate family's claim to the ownership of the New York Giants baseball club. It was awkward enough when Charles was alive and the children from the second family were guests at the Polo Grounds for Giants games. Russell and Jane Stoneham, both teenagers, would have box seats, be waited on by ushers, but would also be ignored by anyone from the Giants' front office. Certainly, Horace never felt any loyalty or connection to his father's second family; indeed, he never made any attempt to meet or interact with them.[26] Now, with his father gone, Horace moved to protect his claim of the ownership of the New York Giants baseball team by effectively cutting them off from any association with the ball club.[27] It also meant excluding them from the services. Horace and maybe his mother probably were less concerned about Russell and Jane and more worried that any announcement of the date and place of the funeral would precipitate a disruptive church and possibly a media appearance by the second wife, Margaret Leonard Stoneham, resulting in the revelation of a family scandal. The best way to ensure this wouldn't happen was to keep the funeral arrangements secret. In no way was Charles's second family to join the mourners.

Horace Stoneham's decisions, not only with respect to the funeral arrangements but also essentially to deny his father's second family, more than likely came in an attempt to safeguard his inheritance of the Giants. This move has had unintended consequences, however, effectively wrapping aspects of Stoneham's life in a shroud of mystery. Paradoxically, attempts at secrecy in matters of Stoneham's life have raised important questions and urged efforts of discovery: who really was this man? How did he live the life he chose? What motivated him to do so? What were the emotional costs in living his complicated life? That the answers are difficult to find is not surprising perhaps, given Stoneham's tendency toward furtive behavior and insistence on privacy and concealment. Not only did he try to avoid publicity in many aspects of his life; he also had a propensity for vagueness or forgetfulness when questioned about his behavior and undertakings. His secretive funeral was only the last and final event in a life shaped by mystery and intrigue.

2

Go East, Young Man

> Over the great bridge, with the sunlight through the girders
> making a constant flicker upon the moving cars, with
> the city rising up across the river in white heaps and sugar
> lumps all built with a wish out of non-olfactory money . . .
> "Anything can happen now that we've
> slid over this bridge," I thought; "anything at all."
> —F. SCOTT FITZGERALD, *The Great Gatsby*

In the fall of 1918, stately, plump, and wealthy Charles A. Stoneham sensed the time was right to make a change in his business pursuits. For almost two decades Stoneham had profited spectacularly as an investment broker, starting as a specialist in copper mining stocks before moving on to general securities, bonds, and portfolio funds. His success allowed him to cultivate an interest in horse racing—he played the horses regularly at most of the New York tracks—and become an owner-trainer, establishing his own racing stables. He now had an itch to leave the investment world behind and become a full-time sportsman, possibly the owner of a professional sports franchise in baseball. Now forty-two years old, Stoneham was ready for something different, a new start in another field. If he waited much longer, he reasoned, he might never move.

Stoneham's rise in the investment business was nothing short of meteoric. As a schoolboy growing up in Jersey City, New Jersey, he could see across the Hudson River the towering cityscape of New York, with all its promise and allure. At the age of seventeen, perhaps prompted by the death of his father and a sense of responsibility for his mother and the household, Charley left school and headed for the canyons of Wall Street to find work, not across a bridge but by ferry, the standard means, circa 1900, of commuting from Jersey City to Lower Manhattan. Presumably through family connections within the Irish-Catholic community and perhaps Tammany Hall, Charley secured an appointment in the Wall Street brokerage and investment firm of Haight and Freese as a board boy, one who posts up-to-date information on a stock quotation board.[1] It was a fortuitous opening for a young man on the rise in the investment business. By 1900 the Haight and Freese Company was well established, specializing in commodities and New York stocks and operating seventy branches on the Eastern Seaboard.[2] Stoneham soon moved from the board boy position to an apprenticeship as a stock salesman. Astute in business matters, with an ability in numbers and an uncanny sense of timing, he thrived in the fast-paced, chancy atmosphere of Wall Street trading and, in a few short years, became a supervisor of the sales staff, often called in to close transactions.[3] By 1903, ten years after he joined Haight and Freese, Stoneham became president of O. F. Jonasson and Company, an investment firm that traded primarily in mining stocks.[4]

It was a dream come true for the clever and ambitious young man from a working-class family. Stoneham's father, Bartholomew Stoneham, was a Civil War veteran and a bookkeeper; his mother, Mary Howells Stoneham, was a former house cleaner.[5] All indications are that Charley was close to his family, especially his mother, with whom he lived even as a married man, commuting to his work on Wall Street from Jersey City. In 1897 Stoneham married Alice Rafter, who died in 1898, giving birth to a daughter, Mary.[6] Apparently not temperamentally suited to a lengthy bereavement, Stoneham married Johanna "Hannah" McGoldrick in early 1900; this second marriage produced two sons, Charles A. Jr. in 1901 and Horace C. in 1903.[7] Charley Stoneham was making his way in the business world and raising a growing family.

In his formative years on Wall Street, Stoneham sought advice from many in the investment field, some of whom tutored him in the statistical basis of investing, while others provided a wider view of the complexities of the market. Certainly, he learned much from his mentors at Haight and Freese, a firm that had a reputation for putting profit before the interests of its customers.[8] But there were others in the business, or in the related field of marketing, who helped as well, and as one might expect from the cutthroat environment of investment trading, not all of them were choirboys. One was George Graham Rice, a rather notorious character floating through the get-rich-quick atmosphere of the pre–World War I stock market. Rice's chief interest was mining stocks, especially copper and precious metal. He was also keen on salesmanship and understood the importance of marketing to a public eager for quick returns on investment. Aggressively touting the advantages of mining stocks, he often cut corners, letting the promotional side get the better of him, committing so much to sales volume that he sold stocks that had no real worth. For his efforts Rice would spend time in Blackwell's Island prison for mail fraud. Released but unrepentant and certainly undaunted, he ventured into horse racing during the war, gambling and writing tipster sheets for bettors. He also wrote an audacious memoir, *My Adventures with Your Money*, dedicated to his avaricious customers.[9]

Stoneham's connection to Rice was seen by some as peripheral, but others in the investment world saw it as more telling. Stoneham's rise in the stock business took place in a loosely regulated market; he was drawn to the more open spheres of risky trading, some of which were, as one writer put it, of doubtful legality.[10] Rice was one of the early voices that drew the young investor's attention to that side of the market, the highly speculative, sometimes shady ventures where oversight remained light but potential profits were high. One Wall Street watchdog named Stoneham as one of Rice's protégés, not only for his penchant for the risky, highly speculative trade but also because many of Stoneham's early brokerage accounts dealt with copper and silver mining stocks, Rice's specialty.[11]

Others helped young Stoneham as well. His association with Rice would be only the first in a line of New York's movers and shakers with whom Stoneham would meet and socialize. It didn't hurt his rise in the stock business that he had the acquaintance and endorsement of Tom Foley, the Lower East Side district leader of the powerful Tammany political machine in New York City. Foley was himself a protégé of "Big Tim" Sullivan, who for twenty-five years was Tammany Hall's boss of Lower Manhattan, and second in Tammany's power hierarchy behind Charles F. Murphy, the organization's boss.[12] In the 1900 elections, Sullivan personally picked Foley to run for district leader of the Lower East Side ward, thereby ensuring an easy victory at the polls.[13] For the next twenty years, Tom Foley would remain Tammany's district boss of the Lower East Side.

Being connected to Tammany was no small advantage for any young businessman in Manhattan, and Stoneham would profit from this association. Most likely, Stoneham took advantage of his Irish heritage (his father was a first-generation Irish American, and his mother was born in Ireland) to connect with the Irish-dominated Tammany insiders.[14] Foley would steer clients to Stoneham for the duration of his time as a broker. The Tammany boss also provided access to influential players in Manhattan politics and social circles who could offer safeguards when corners needed to be cut, something that often happened in the risky, fast-paced, ruthlessly competitive atmosphere of speculative investing that Stoneham pursued.[15]

As a young investment broker, Stoneham recognized the potential of mining stocks and decided to specialize in those accounts. To gain firsthand knowledge of the companies involved in the production of copper and silver, he traveled to western mining sites, especially in Colorado and Nevada.[16] The following year, he moved the office of O. F. Jonasson and Company to 54 Broad Street in the heart of the city's investment district. He was energized and on the move. It was at this time that he gave up his residence in Jersey City and his routine as a daily commuter across the river to move to Manhattan with his wife, Hannah, a daughter, Mary, and a five-year-old son, Horace.

That year, 1909, he opened an office in Boston, specializing in the sale and promotion of mining stocks.[17] The expansion proved propitious; as the mining stocks business grew, he hired accordingly, seeking associates in these offices who touted high returns and sought out customers willing to seek greater gains by pursuing high-risk speculation. Stoneham, in turn, profited spectacularly. By 1913 he established a New York City–based brokerage business firm, Charles A. Stoneham and Company. His hunch about the profitability of the speculative mining futures was paying off. He was aware also of the growing public interest in stocks and bonds. Between 1900 and 1920 the number of Americans owning stock tripled from 4.4 million to 14.4 million, many of these investors came from the so-called middle and wage-earning class.[18] Sensing that he was in the midst of a growth industry, Charley Stoneham went all in. By the end of 1913, he had expanded his operation, opening Charles A. Stoneham and Company branch offices throughout the Northeast, in Chicago, Boston, Providence, Buffalo, Hartford, and Philadelphia.[19] He was about to become a big player in the investment game.

Attracted to gambling as a young man, Stoneham used his gaming sense to gauge and shape his business, seeking out the higher-risk markets of Wall Street investing; as one baseball historian put it, stocks and games were one coin to Stoneham.[20] Not only did he bet that the market was healthy, but he also believed that, with only a little marketing, the public would seek out investments for maximum growth and return. He joined the so-called Curb Brokerage firms (also called the Consolidated Exchange), less regulated and one of Wall Street's most volatile and speculative arenas, what business pundits called "bucket shops." Open more hours than regular Wall Street brokerage houses, bucket shops charged less commission on transactions and allowed investors to buy in smaller allotments in order to attract a wide clientele. While the standard New York Stock Exchange houses sold securities in one hundred–share allotments, the bucket shop brokerage house allowed clients to buy with as little as ten shares. Bucket shops also featured highly motivated and active sales forces to promote accounts.[21]

Stoneham guessed correctly. The lightly regulated Curb market, with its open features, attracted working-class small investors unable to meet the higher capital requirements of the more established and regulated New York Stock Exchange brokerage houses. Moreover, bucket shops often allowed their clients not only to purchase stocks with minimal deposits but also to open accounts on a margin, with the broker holding the remainder of a transaction in the form of an advance or loan. There would be a high interest rate attached to the loan, of course. Bucket shops offered easy and quick purchases, but if ever the watchword *caveat emptor* applied, it did so with any bucket shop transaction.[22] An accepted and regular practice of many "bucketeers"—the name given to those who operated these Consolidated Exchange firms—would be to promote and sell (mostly legitimate) stocks to eager customers but not transact the order. The broker would then "bucket" the order, waiting for the market to rise or fall, making a profit in either case from the transactional differences in price. In other words, brokers would speculate—that is to say "gamble"—with the customer's money, looking for an opportunity either to buy or sell at the broker's advantage. Any profit would thereby be pocketed by the firm. In a 1906 decision, the U.S. Supreme Court provided a clear definition of *bucket shop* and a description of its aims: "An establishment, nominally for the transaction of a stock exchange business, or business of a similar character, but really for the registration of bets or wagers, usually for small amounts, on the rise or fall of the prices of stocks, grain, oil, etc., there being no transfer or delivery of the stock or commodities nominally dealt in."[23] The gains, then, were clearly on the side of the broker. While customers understood that the Curb brokerage firms were playing by their own set of rules, it did not seem to detract from their interest in putting up their money. The Curb brokerage / bucket shop firms would enjoy a surge in customers after 1918 and the end of World War I, as many middle-class Americans wanted to put the austerity of the war effort behind them and take part in a growing economy that everyone knew was soon to come.[24] Investing in stocks and securities seemed a good way to profit from the development of American businesses.

In order to stay legitimate, however, the successful bucket shop brokers had to cover the clients' withdrawals or profit sharing when requested. By and large, Stoneham's firm seemed to manage this requirement.[25] But change was coming for Stoneham, and he was slowly but steadily distancing himself from the brokerage business. As the war was ending, and certainly by the winter of 1918–19, Stoneham did little bucketeering himself—this was handled by salesmen and promotors who dealt with individual clients, their investment choices, and eventually their portfolios—but, rather, oversaw his expanding company, developing investment strategies, hiring salesmen and account managers, and tending to his various branch offices as an executive director. He also had little to do with the day-to-day activities of account management. Instead, he kept his eye both on general elements of the stock market, especially its fringes, and those smaller start-up companies and commodities that were undervalued and had potential to develop. Investing in these companies also carried higher risk, something that Stoneham as an inveterate gambler was willing to accept. His oversight proved auspicious. By the end of the decade, he had become one of the most successful brokers in the investment field, a leader in this particular branch of investment. His net worth in 1920 was estimated to be $10 million, or more than $157 million in 2020 dollars.[26] And his influence and importance in this field of investing was widespread. As one Wall Street observer put it, "The largest (and most important) bucketeers in the country seemed to stem from the Chicago and New York offices of Charles A. Stoneham and Company."[27]

It is perhaps unsurprising that Stoneham made his fortune in the speculative arena of bucket shop stock trading. He took to the arithmetic aspects of investing he had developed in his early years as a board boy; he understood numbers and calculation, trading, evaluating securities, and buying and selling—he had, in other words, a conceptual foundation for the business. More crucially, however, he was attracted to the aspects of gambling that came with investing in stocks, bonds, and commodities and had the personality and character for its demands. When he opened his own brokerage businesses, he was rumored to have an interest in big-time gambling; by the end of the decade, those rumors were well established. Choosing the riskier Curb Exchange investing allowed him to follow a business career and satisfy his attraction to gambling at the same time. What is surprising, perhaps, is the extraordinary and prolonged success he achieved despite the hazardous volatility of his chosen branch of the investment business. In the prewar years of the 1910s, Charles A. Stoneham and Company had become one of the most established and successful bucket shops organizations on the East Coast, and its founder was enjoying record high returns. As some have observed, his success was a result of shrewd business acumen and a penchant for risk-taking and timing. And Stoneham had better timing than most.[28]

"Good Time Charley," as one writer called him, was a driven businessman by day but fond of the city's nightlife and its casinos and gambling houses.[29] By the war's end, in 1918, he had the resources to expand his interest and time in gambling and to cultivate the lifestyle of a sportsman. Long a regular at racetracks around New York, including Aqueduct, Jamaica, and, in the summers, Saratoga Springs, he furthered his interest in racing by buying and training several horses that raced not just in New York meets but also in Kentucky and Cuba.[30] Stoneham traveled often to Cuba, where he would winter out in Havana for both horse racing (he had some interest in local horses) and gaming in the casinos. John McGraw, manager of the New York Giants, also frequented Havana, sometimes with his ball club for spring training, sometimes with his wife for a vacation, but always as a regular visitor at the racetrack. It was only a matter of time before the two New York gamblers would meet at the Havana racetrack. So taken was Stoneham with winter racing in Cuba that in 1919 he bought the Oriental Park track, not only as a place to train and race his own horses but also as an investment, bringing in McGraw as a minor partner.[31] They also owned the controlling interest in the adjacent Havana Casino.[32]

Stoneham's reputation as a carouser, playboy, and high-stakes gambler grew in some part by his choice of associates. McGraw, who owned billiard rooms, was a regular at the racetracks, and enjoyed a drink, was one. But Stoneham's most notorious association was with Arnold Rothstein, the gambling king of Manhattan. It was probably Stoneham's interest and involvement with racehorses that precipitated his meeting and then relationship with Rothstein, whose reputation as a nefarious underworld character preceded him. Events and aspects of Rothstein's life, like Stoneham's, are often difficult to substantiate. "A.R.," the name given to Rothstein on and around Broadway, was the kingpin of New York's gambling world during the Jazz Age. He lived in mysterious and shadowy circumstances, and his lifestyle depended on deceit, cunning, and guile, traits that he perfected.

A good deal of what is known about events in Rothstein's life is based on conjecture and rumor. According to his biographers and various reports in the New York newspapers, he was an active gambler and organizer and controlled or had a slice of most gambling operations in New York City during the 1910s and 1920s. He carefully managed his public image and cultivated an air of sophistication, grace, and manners, often denying publicly that he was a professional gambler. Frequently tied to various illegal activities, including gambling, money laundering, drug trafficking, and rum-running, he was never convicted of any crime, in part because of his Tammany Hall connections.[33] Thought to be the leading force in fixing the 1919 World Series, Rothstein went to Chicago to testify in the 1920 grand jury investigation of the fix on the advice of his Broadway attorney William J. Fallon. Apparently, Rothstein made a good impression and was never charged or indicted.[34] He spent the rest of his life denying his connections to the World Series scandal, but his name would always come up with any mention of the event. It is this connection that Fitzgerald dramatizes in *The Great*

Gatsby in his portrait of Meyer Wolfshiem, Gatsby's business partner, who is based on Rothstein.

For all of the shady deals with which his name was associated, Rothstein remained a true Teflon man, who always seemed just out of reach of the law with an alibi, the right attorney, or friends in high places. On the night of November 4, 1928, however, Rothstein's past finally caught up with him, but it was one of his own who forced the reckoning. Accused of welshing on a bet, he was shot at a poker game by someone he knew. But mysterious and furtive even on his deathbed, he refused to identify his assailant to the police, taking the secret to his grave.[35]

Stoneham's association with Rothstein most likely began a few years before the war. In 1912 Rothstein was running his "permanent floating crap game," called the Partridge Club, that moved to and from many of Manhattan's fancy hotels, including the Astor, the Knickerbocker, and the Ritz-Carlton.[36] Stoneham, by then a known gambler, was invited and often played at Partridge Club games, where high rollers and upscale New York socialites were welcomed and afforded VIP treatment. While playing at the Partridge Club gatherings, Stoneham rubbed shoulders with a number of bigwigs who themselves were regulars, including oilman Henry Sinclair, celebrity journalist Herbert Bayard Swope, Broadway maestro Florenz Ziegfeld, and New York City's fire commissioner John H. O'Brien, among them.[37]

Stoneham's connection and involvement with Rothstein extended beyond the Partridge Club and became more established in their mutual love of horse racing. Stoneham's decision to own and train horses may have been precipitated by Rothstein, who began buying horses in 1916 and eventually established a racing stable called Redstone.[38] In 1917 Stoneham created CASCO Stables in Westchester County, hired a trainer, and began developing his own racing stock. He actively bought and sold enough horses to race year-round—summers at New York tracks, including Aqueduct and Jamaica near the city and Saratoga Springs in Upstate New York, and winters in Cuba at Oriental Park in Havana. Stoneham enjoyed a good deal of success in the racing game and was especially active between 1917 and 1923, with a number of thorough-breds donning the colors of CASCO Stables, often competing against Rothstein's Redstone horses. Stoneham won regularly at Oriental Park in the winter months and was consistently successful during the summer seasons. In certain years CASCO Stables dominated the New York racing scene. In 1918 Stoneham's horses finished regularly in the money at Jamaica and won the popular Colorado Stakes.[39] Yellow Hand and Dry Moon, geldings Stoneham had bought for a total of twenty-five thousand dollars in 1920, won ten handicap races between them at Aqueduct, Belmont, and Empire City during the 1921 season, easily tripling Stoneham's investment.[40] Flannel Shirt, another CASCO star, paid good dividends for Stoneham in 1923, winning the main event at Tarrytown on July 12 and the featured event at Aqueduct on September 26.[41]

Every year during August, the New York racing action shifted to Saratoga Springs, where Stoneham, like many rich New Yorkers, spent the month escaping the city's heat, taking advantage of spas, grand hotels, dining, theater entertainment, and, of course, horse racing and gaming. Stoneham's Saratoga routine would be to spend the day at the track and the evenings gambling at the various resort hotels and casinos. He was also a regular fixture at Saratoga's annual horse auction and one of the big buyers.[42] And he was also known to throw a few good parties. It was in Saratoga Springs, in August 1918, that Stoneham hosted a lavish dinner at the posh United States Hotel, reportedly providing his 250 or so guests with "all the champagne that could be found in the town" and afterward tipping all the waiters one hundred dollars each and the wine steward five hundred dollars.[43]

Stoneham was also a frequent guest at Rothstein's summer Saratoga Springs gambling casino the Brook, where both would meet annually after Rothstein acquired the resort in 1919.[44] It was at the Brook in August 1920 that two events occurred linking Rothstein and Stoneham and contributed to the legendary qualities of both men's gambling habits. One evening, concerned that a gambler was making a run on the house's holdings, Rothstein telephoned Stoneham to send away $300,000 in cash from his summer house's vault to cover the possible loss. It turned out to be a precautionary move on Rothstein's part; by the time the cash arrived, the house had won back almost all of the gambler's stake. On another occasion that August, Stoneham, who was housebound with a gimpy leg and craving some action, called Rothstein on the phone to ask what color had come up on the previous spin of the house's roulette wheel. When told it was black, Stoneham told Rothstein to bet $70,000 on red for the next spin, waited patiently on the line, and then was informed that red it was! Apparently, the extraordinary manner of the bet and its success had little effect on Stoneham. He stayed on the line and continued to bet until the house had won back its initial loss.[45]

The connection between Rothstein and Stoneham is rumored to go deeper than their interests in gambling and involved partnerships, or at least cooperation, in various business ventures. Stories circulated that A.R. was a silent partner in some of Stoneham's bucket shops and racing operations and helped broker some of Stoneham's business transactions, but no hard evidence for these arrangements has been uncovered.[46] It was asserted by some New York sportswriters that Rothstein helped broker the sale of the Giants for Stoneham; others speculated that Rothstein provided the insurance for the Polo Grounds once Stoneham owned the team. One of Rothstein's biographers claims that the gambling king and Stoneham cooperated in a bootlegging scheme in which Stoneham used his Havana racetrack and casino facilities to store a sizable shipment of Scotch whisky from Britain.[47] In many ways Stoneham's relationship with Rothstein seemed a natural fit for someone as attracted to gambling and nightlife as Stoneham was. Stoneham admitted later in life that he knew Rothstein for over twenty-five years.

It would be difficult, if not impossible, to determine the success of Stoneham as a gambler. What can be said with certainty, however, is that he was steadily at it, especially in the postwar years at the racetrack. Undoubtedly, his decision to found his own stable boosted his interest and his connection to both the sport and the wagering. It is also clear from all of this activity in horse racing that Stoneham was devoting more of his time to the "Sport of Kings," including the buying and training of horses, and less time with the frenetic daily activities of Wall Street, an indication that he was becoming more and more interested in a life as a sportsman.

The exact reasons for Stoneham's decision to leave the brokerage business where he made his fortune may never be known. Nor is it possible to understand with any precise sense when he made that decision. Some of Stoneham's observers reasoned that he believed the market was heading for an inevitable overheating and that he wanted to get out while the getting was good. Stoneham's investment strategy depended on a falling market, when he could "bucket" a customer's order and buy it back later at lower cost. For a seasoned gambler like Stoneham, timing was everything.[48] Maybe the attraction of a less volatile business, requiring less daily vigilance, seemed appealing. Or it could have been a certain restlessness tinged with a trace of jadedness over the repetitive nature of his life as a broker and businessman.

Or perhaps it was simply the allure of some other pursuit at this time in his life. It was possible that after twenty-five years in one line of business, he had become less engaged or enthusiastic. Some who knew him suggest that his interest in the sporting world became stronger after the war, so much so that he wanted it to be more than a part-time diversion. He was already a fixture in the New York racing scene and a well-known owner with his own stable of racing horses. So the itch to join the sporting world full-time was not a great stretch. Besides horse racing, he enjoyed baseball, and like many in Manhattan, he was a longtime fan of the New York Giants.[49] His involvement and success with CASCO Stables possibly whetted his appetite for further sports ownership, and with the fortune he had accumulated in the stock market, he was positioned to pursue the idea, maybe in baseball. There was a rumor that he had attempted to buy the Newark International League baseball team but could not agree on the deal. Nonetheless, he remained interested.[50]

Stoneham also sensed something about the mood of the country. A change seemed to be coming and not just for him personally. America had endured a bloody and difficult war in Europe and the terrible Spanish Flu pandemic of 1918–19. The country was eager to turn its back on horrific suffering and look ahead to better times. Perhaps Stoneham thought he could take advantage of that momentum. There was something in the air, ready to take shape. A new age was coming, led by young restless people in their twenties and thirties who were ready to look forward to a new decade and take pleasure in life. As one writer put it, the nation was poised to step out of a troubled past, one defined by suffering and dominated by traditions and outmoded manners, and step into the modern world, one epitomized by pleasure and lack of restraint.[51] As a habitué of the city's demimonde at the end of the decade, Stoneham undoubtedly sensed this momentum. He witnessed the popularity of the nightclubs and restaurants firsthand, even as Prohibition was about to take hold throughout the country. People were keen on drinking (even if it meant disregarding the law), dancing, dining, and above all, entertainment.[52] Sporting events—horse racing, boxing, and especially baseball—offered a public eager for distraction great opportunities for amusement.

Perhaps for all these reasons, both private and public, Stoneham, the inveterate gambler, felt the time was right to risk a chance, a big one even: to leave the investment business behind, move from the unsavory and volatile world of the bucket shops, and seek a fresh beginning in another field. After the war, he reasoned, spectator sports would become even more popular in the public's eye. He knew of the appeal of racing firsthand; boxing was attracting big crowds nationwide; and baseball was primed for a big comeback, having become a sport that, as one baseball historian notes, "mean[s] more to more people than any other."[53] Stoneham wanted to be part of this sporting world not only because he was a fan but also because he sensed it would be good business. He decided in the winter of 1918 to look for a buying opportunity. He would not have long to wait.

3

The House of Lords

I would have accepted without question the information
that Gatsby sprang from the swamps of Louisiana or
from the lower East Side of New York. That was
comprehensible. But young men didn't—at least in my
provincial experience I believed they didn't—drift coolly
out of nowhere and buy a palace on Long Island Sound.
—F. SCOTT FITZGERALD, *The Great Gatsby*

Charley Stoneham's desire for a change in his business life coincided
with a momentous time in New York Giants baseball history. In late fall
of 1918, Harry Hempstead, the chief executive officer of the National
Exhibition Company (NEC), the corporate title for the New York
Giants, decided to sell his family's majority holdings in the ball club.
Hempstead became involved with the Giants organization through
his father-in-law, John T. Brush, who bought controlling interest in
the ball club in 1902. When Brush died, in 1912, his Giants stock was
divided equally among his three survivors, his wife, Elsie, and his two
daughters, Eleanor (Hempstead's wife) and Natalie, with Hempstead
assuming the role of Giants club president. Although Hempstead was
corporate chairman of the NEC and unquestioned boss of the ball club,
his loyalty rested chiefly with the Brush women and their financial
interests, rather than the franchise itself; he left most of the club's
administrative affairs to club secretary John B. Foster and most player
personnel matters to John McGraw, the Giants manager since 1902.[1]
Nonetheless, Hempstead was a crafty businessman who turned out

to be an able baseball executive, seeing his organization through the Federal League challenge in 1914–15 that threatened to compete directly for territory and players on existing American and National League teams.[2] He also fended off an attempt in 1915 by wealthy oil magnate Harry Sinclair to buy enough NEC stock to control the team.[3]

All this focus and engagement shifted, however, after the 1917 baseball season. Always a portfolio-first, baseball-second financial planner, especially regarding Brush family interests, Hempstead sensed a downturn in the business of baseball and, by extension, the value of Giants stock. The United States' entry in the Great War in April 1917 quickly took its toll on the nature of the game. Fans' interest in the "national pastime" became secondary to patriotism and world affairs. Meeting in December 1917, organized baseball cut the 1918 major league season to 140 games, severely restricting team revenues. In July 1918 the government issued its "work or fight" order, calling for all able-bodied men to serve in the military or work in war-related industries. By midsummer of 1918, 124 players from the American League (AL) and 103 from the National League (NL) had joined the armed services, resulting in a dramatic falloff in the quality of play.[4] Nor was Hempstead alone in his concerns and worries about the national pastime. As public attention shifted and the nation geared up for the war effort, there were many who doubted the game's future. After a poorly attended 1918 World Series—the Boston Red Sox beat the Chicago Cubs in six games, with a total attendance of 128,483—one established sportswriter declared baseball dead in all parts of the country, except perhaps the shipyards and the army camps, where it was played recreationally.[5]

World Series attendance was only one indication of a shift in the public's interest. Beginning in 1917, almost all professional baseball teams saw a decrease in revenue as a result of shrinking gate receipts, an effect of the war. Attendance figures dropped throughout the sport, in both major league and minor league cities. Playing in baseball's most lucrative market, the Giants saw their annual gate receipts drop from the previous year, 1916, despite winning the pennant and playing in the 1917

World Series.[6] In 1918, the second year of the United States' involvement in the war, the owners shortened the season, then the Spanish Flu
pandemic broke out. Giants attendance sank even lower, to 256,618,
down almost 50 percent from the previous year. Across the East River,
Brooklyn owner Charles Ebbets remarked that, financially, his National
League club could not sustain a repeat of the dismal 1918 season.[7] Chicago, the second-best market in baseball, saw the combined Cubs and
White Sox attendance drop by almost 500,000 from 1917 to 1918.[8]

Hempstead required no further proof. Whatever sentiments he held
for the national game could not reassure his pragmatic business side.
The future of baseball seemed dismal, a poor and risky place for the
Brush family assets. The telltale signs were obvious throughout baseball nationwide. It was time to shift investment strategies and seek a
newer commodity. In the late fall of 1918, he began to seek a buyer for
the National Exhibition Company. He hoped to have the Brush family
out of baseball by the year's end.

When Giants manager John McGraw learned of Hempstead's intentions, he was both heartened and reinvigorated. McGraw had become
resentful of Hempstead's control of administrative franchise operations,
particularly the power given to John B. Foster, the club secretary, who
often cut McGraw out of business decisions and on occasion traded
players without McGraw's approval.[9] As a result, McGraw's relations
with Foster grew cold and those with Hempstead distant.[10] Under a
new owner, McGraw felt he might reclaim the more dominant role in
club affairs that he had enjoyed during John T. Brush's ownership. He
also sensed an opportunity to realize a lifelong dream, to be a partner
in the Giants' ownership. Perhaps if he were able to attract some well-
financed buyer and work out a way that he might be a minor stakeholder,
he could share in the franchise partnership. For over fifteen years,
McGraw had been the heart and soul of the Giants ball club. He knew
a wide variety of fans, from all walks of New York society and public
life. The time was right, he decided, to reach out to those who might
be interested in a possible deal for the Giants.

While the story of the 1919 sale of the Giants is beset with conflicting narratives and contradictory statements, almost all versions place McGraw at the center of the wheeling and dealing.[11] Initially, he cast a wide net. He was well-known in the city and planned to use his influence and contacts to drum up an interested buyer. As one writer shrewdly observed, "There were two 'misters' on the New York public scene, men who were seldom addressed by their first names: Charles F. Murphy, the kingpin of Tammany Hall, was one; the other was John McGraw."[12]

"Mr." McGraw let it be known that he had some influence with Hempstead and could serve as a kind of broker for ownership of the club. He also used the media to drum up curiosity about the sale, alerting the newspaper reporters that he was approached by ten different potential buyers, some of whom, he admitted, did not have the financial means to acquire the club.[13] While it is worth noting that McGraw's remarks to the press were often self-serving and somewhat unreliable, the idea of multiple interested parties, if not ten, is plausible. There was certainly interest among business types in New York who thought owning the most celebrated team in baseball would be a good investment and great publicity. With many suitors available, McGraw settled in early December on two prospects to help him make his bid for the team, one headed by George Loft, a wealthy candy manufacturer and former U.S. congressman, and another led by Broadway music star and songwriter George M. Cohan and Broadway producer Sam Harris. McGraw was working with both interested parties and with Hempstead to ensure a quick resolution but also to secure a place for himself in ownership. After the new year, rumors began to circulate around town and in the press that the Cohan group had the inside track and were in final negotiations with both McGraw and Hempstead.[14]

It came as a big surprise, then, both to an astonished George Cohan and to New York baseball fans when they opened their morning newspapers on January 15, 1919, and discovered the announced sale of the Giants to a syndicate headed by someone called Charles A. Stoneham, a Curb Exchange investment broker, that included John McGraw and New York City magistrate Francis X. McQuade as part owners and small stakeholders. Up until the announcement of the purchase, there was no mention of Stoneham as an interested buyer or even as someone vaguely connected to the team. Those in the baseball world knew almost nothing about him. The only thing that could link Stoneham casually to the Giants was his role as a fan.[15] One writer described the dilemma of the press: "Stoneham was a stranger, even by reputation, to most, if not all of the baseball writers. They discovered after consulting their morgues, files and clippings on prominent persons, that he had been a broker on the Curb Market, that he owned a small stable of good racehorses, and that, although he lived most of his life in Jersey City, was politically powerful in New York because of his close personal ties with Al Smith, Tom Foley and other leading figures in Tammany Hall."[16] Speculation that in 1918 he had tried to buy the Newark team of the International League, or at least take a substantial financial interest in the ball club, has remained unestablished.[17] Those few New York sports journalists who recognized his name could do so only because of his connection to horse racing as an owner. He was, himself, a dark horse in the Giants' ownership sweepstakes. Certainly, to the other major league owners, he was an unknown. Like Jay Gatsby, Charley Stoneham had come out of nowhere. A mystery man had become one of the biggest names in 1919 New York City sports.

The *New York Times* headline ran "Giants Change Hands in Biggest Deal in Baseball History."[18] With an eye on public relations and perhaps even damage control, Hempstead praised the new ownership group, thanked the newspapermen who had covered the team, and assured the fans that the team was in capable hands. Hempstead's greatest acclaim was bestowed on McGraw, who helped facilitate the sale and who, as a famous New York sports personality, would provide a sense of continuity: "It is fitting to say that in releasing the club that it continues in the hands of Mr. McGraw who will advance to part ownership. . . . He is entitled to much credit and praise for his untiring efforts for the benefit of the club."[19] Hempstead did not say a word about Stoneham. The selling price of the ball club was reportedly one million dollars, easily the most ever paid for a professional sports franchise, and Hempstead could sleep soundly now that he had managed two important feats: improving the Brush estate finances and getting the family effectively out of the business of baseball.[20]

The abruptness of the sale and the surprise it created among New York baseball fans, almost all of whom were unfamiliar with the name Stoneham, prompted a number of explanations of how it came to be. The precise details of the story, however, may never be known, hampered by the passage of time, the number of parties involved in the sale, and the characteristic aura of mystery that tends to surround Stoneham's activities. An oft-repeated version of the sale puts gambling kingpin Arnold Rothstein at the center of the agreement.[21] Rothstein, associate and business partner of both McGraw and Stoneham, known to many on Broadway and connected to Tammany Hall, reportedly used his influence to link the interested parties.[22] Another story contends that McGraw, impatient and tired of the negotiations and counteroffers with Loft and then with Cohan, had turned to Stoneham, someone he knew from horse racing circles who had sufficient capital to conclude a deal.[23] Yet another account suggests that McGraw approached McQuade, a city magistrate and Tammany insider who knew of Stoneham's interest in sports ownership and brought McGraw and Stoneham together.[24] Still another version, a rumor circulated around town, had a retired New York City police captain acting as intermediary, helping McGraw and McQuade contact Stoneham.[25]

But if one must have a single narrative of the sale, one might look past Rothstein, Loft, Cohan, and a New York City policemen and settle on McQuade as a primary mover. Frank McQuade was well placed in city politics as a magistrate judge and an established Tammany Hall operative. McQuade's friendship with McGraw was long-standing.[26] It is reasonable to assume that through Tammany connections, McQuade was acquainted with Stoneham, himself a Tammany insider, close to Big Tom Foley and Charles Murphy. It is certainly possible that McQuade could have arranged for McGraw and Stoneham to meet. McQuade insisted on this version, of his singular importance in finding Stoneham as a buyer for the Giants. Interviewed by a reporter at the party to celebrate the new ownership, McQuade was emphatic. "Judge, who got Mr. Stoneham into baseball?" the reporter asked him. "'I did,' he [McQuade] said. 'You may hear other stories about it, but I'm telling you the truth. I got Charles A. Stoneham into baseball. Your Uncle Dudley—and nobody else. McGraw was fooling around with dead ones. It took me to dig up a live guy. I told him, "John, you are dealing with a lot of stiffs. I've got the fellow for you. My pal, Charley Stoneham.""[27]

McQuade's self-serving blather aside, there is another strong consideration for the centrality of his role in the sale. It offers a probable explanation to a perplexing question: why did Stoneham cut McQuade into the Giants ownership? Bringing McGraw into ownership was a strategic move for Stoneham, binding McGraw, now as partner, more tightly to the performance of the ball club. But McQuade? He was not a baseball man, only a Giants rooter. Moreover, McQuade was not a wealthy man and had to borrow from Stoneham to buy the small amount of National Exhibition Company shares (seventy) to qualify as a partner. More than likely, Stoneham included McQuade in the partnership as a gesture of gratitude for his role in putting the deal together and also, perhaps, as a move to shore up political support.[28] Stoneham, as a crafty businessman, knew the importance of perquisites. And perks, in Tammany-controlled New York politics, were all-important. Stoneham's financial heft was certainly essential in securing the purchase of the team, but his willingness to expand the partnership may have been more crucial to clinching the deal. For his part Stoneham, knowing that he was entering a brave new enterprise, valued McGraw's experience in baseball and his reputation in the city enough to lend him the capital, interest free, to buy into the partnership and become a minor stakeholder. Stoneham also recognized McQuade as a Tammany player, well placed in city politics, and wanted to acknowledge his role in the negotiations. He offered him an opportunity similar to McGraw's, to buy in as a minor stakeholder but with a difference: McQuade would be charged interest on his loan, something that would vex him throughout the partnership and contribute to his break with Stoneham and McGraw a few years later.

The first item of business for the new owners was to structure the board of directors, assign duties, and allocate salaries. Stoneham, as the principal stockholder, named himself president, with an annual salary of forty-five thousand dollars. He would function as chairman of the board and arrange and approve the financials. McGraw, as vice president, would earn an annual salary of seventy-five hundred dollars, handle player personnel, and accompany Stoneham to the owners' meetings. McQuade would function as treasurer at an annual salary of seventy-five hundred dollars and would work with both Stoneham and McGraw monitoring team expenditures. As the principal majority stakeholder, Stoneham was allowed, under the joint agreement, to vote for all three at corporate meetings, giving him 53 percent control of NEC.[29] The terms of the agreement between Stoneham, McGraw, and McQuade indicated that each of the three partners had the right of first refusal on the sale of their shares of the NEC stock, an important feature of the partnership when things turned sour between the three men at the end of the decade.[30]

For Stoneham the purchase of the Giants put him on a new path and opened a new life. The Giants were an established New York institution, a favorite of Manhattanites, of businessmen, Broadway, and of course Tammany Hall. The Giants' connection to that New York City political establishment goes back to the earliest days of the club's history with former owners John B. Day and, a decade later, Andrew Freedman, both of them Tammany stalwarts.[31] As owner of the Giants, Stoneham would be thrust into the center of sports action in New York and become an instant sports celebrity, joining McGraw, the most well-known figure in baseball for the previous twenty years, and McQuade, a Tammany insider known to politicians and Broadway celebrities as one of the team's most loyal fans.[32] With the controlling interest of the Giants in hand, Stoneham could now carry out his plans to pull away from the investment business and assume the role of a full-time sportsman. Almost immediately, he began to divest himself of his brokerage business, gradually transferring his clients to other firms, a process that would take almost two years and eventually cause him some significant and expensive legal trouble.

With Hempstead's announcement of the Giants' sale, the city's press corps reacted to Stoneham's ownership initially with critical surprise, suggesting that, like everyone else, they too were caught off guard. The mention of McQuade, a Tammany Hall insider, as part of the ownership group, coupled with Stoneham's acknowledged friendship with Big Tom Foley, the Lower Manhattan Tammany boss, set some reporters on edge, bemoaning the connection of city politics and sports. Not everyone, however, saw this linkage as a liability. Responding to the criticism that the new ownership group attended Tammany events, one writer, remembering that the Brush family was from the Midwest, argued the Tammany Hall affiliation only goes to show that the owner-ship was distinctly New York.[33] Others pointed to McGraw's retention with the organization as another link to the local and to the city's past but with his position strengthened. Not only was he back as manager, but he was now aligned with an owner like Charles Stoneham, who would provide the resources needed to improve the club. Stoneham himself, in his inaugural interview with the press, sounded all the right notes. Explaining to the gathering of reporters that for him the New York Giants were more than simply a business enterprise, he stated that the new owners understood that the team has a special connection to the city and its fans, and they would do all in their power to nurture that connection.[34] With this kind of reassurance, it is not surprising that reporters would warm to the new owners and sing Stoneham's praises as a promising sportsman. One reporter wrote in the *Sun* on January 15, 1919: "As Stoneham is known in local sporting circles with a good reputation—the owner of Casco stables—never has a word of innuendo or the finger of suspicion, both so often used on the turf, been directed at Stoneham. As President of the Giants he will be quite a man in local sports."[35]

Fellow baseball owners seemed less sanguine. Exactly why they were cool to Stoneham's entry among their ranks might never be clear. Whether caught off guard themselves with the news of Stoneham's purchase or resentful about the long-standing importance of the position of the New York club in the National League, they tempered their welcome with minimal expressions of enthusiasm.[36] Stories of Stoneham's shady business activities and his reputation as a horseman and a high roller might have played into their thinking. Even the National League's approval of John McGraw to join Stoneham in voting at league meetings was taken by some as a rebuke of Stoneham as an interloper. McGraw was known to the owners as an experienced baseball insider, aware of baseball's culture and how it functions. McGraw's role in league meetings underscored the owners' sense that Stoneham was an outsider who needed help in finding his way. A day after the announcement of the sale, Stoneham attended his first meetings as a member of baseball's ruling class at which two of the motions he backed were defeated.[37] At the close of the owners' winter meetings, Stoneham hosted a party at the Waldorf Astoria in Manhattan to celebrate the new ownership, but only Garry Herrmann, Cincinnati Reds president, and Charles Ebbets, of the crosstown Robins, dropped by.[38] If Stoneham took umbrage at what appears on the surface to be a snub by other owners, there is no record of it. Perhaps because there was so much ahead for him to think about, he took little notice or at least behaved as if he had.

Charley Stoneham's next few months were suddenly framed and structured. The baseball season was only three months away, and spring training travel plans were on the horizon. There would be considerable demands on his time. He also had much to learn about the nuances of baseball culture, especially as a member of the sport's most exclusive club, the owners, or "the Lords of the Realm," as one baseball historian would term them.[39] Even with McGraw at his side at the league meetings, Stoneham knew he had to establish his own reputation among the lords. When Yogi Berra declared one can observe a lot just by watching, he could have been describing Stoneham's first year as an owner. There would be much to notice and consider. Stoneham was entering baseball at a time of unprecedented crisis, and his education would be akin to a baptism by fire. In the spring of 1919, in the wake of the Federal League settlement, attorneys for the defunct Baltimore franchise sued baseball for damages, claiming that the sport was a monopoly with unfair labor practices that restricted players' bargaining rights with the "reserve clause," which effectively allowed a club to control the rights to a player for his entire career. Baltimore won the case and was awarded damages of $240,000.[40] The lords were terrified.[41]

But the residue from the Federal League settlement was just the beginning of a new round of difficulties. Indeed, things were about to get much worse. What baseball historians refer to as the game's "darkest hour" was looming and would bring with it profound changes, especially for the owners. The Black Sox Scandal burst upon the public in the late summer of 1920, after nine months of swirling rumors that the 1919 World Series might have been fixed. After a Chicago grand jury investigation at the end of September, it was common knowledge among those in the know—baseball people, journalists, and the Chicago legal community—that in the 1919 World Series between the Chicago White Sox and the Cincinnati Reds, certain Chicago players, soon to be known as the "Black Sox," had colluded with gamblers to throw the games.[42]

The news sent shockwaves throughout baseball, especially among the lords. The integrity of the sport (not to mention turnstile receipts) lay in the balance. The public's attraction and trust in the national game were threatened, and the owners were desperate to contain the damage. In only his second year as an owner, Charles Stoneham, a risk-taker and big spender, someone who profited from his sense of timing, on knowing when to get in or get out of a stock deal or a bet, might have had second thoughts about his decision to buy the New York Giants baseball club. If he did, who could blame him? His plan was to leave the turbulent, speculative, cutthroat, and chaotic atmosphere of the investment business and join the regulated, scheduled rhythm of Major League baseball, which would provide a semblance of stability and consistency to his business life. In the fall of 1920, baseball was hardly stable. Nonetheless, Stoneham showed no signs of panic. For the moment he would adopt a manner of wait and see.

Dealing with the World Series gambling fiasco forced the owners to confront a deeper structural dilemma. As they attempted to grapple with the Black Sox scandal over the summer of 1920 and into the fall, the leadership problems that had been festering among them for months broke open. Most of them now realized that the existing authority that oversaw the game, the National Commission—a triumvirate of the American League president, the National League president, and a third person elected by both leagues—was too fraught with rivalries to be workable. Resentment and suspicion had caused friction between the two leagues from the inception of the National Agreement of 1903, which established Major League Baseball.[43] But now tensions were sprouting up within the American League, threatening its cohesion. Ban Johnson, longtime president of the AL and a dominant force in baseball for the past twenty years, was being challenged by newer owners Jacob Ruppert and Tillinghast Huston from the New York Yankees and Harry Frazee of the Boston Red Sox. As a result, as one writer put it, the owners' collective governing body was incapable of action, especially when presented with a serious challenge: "The worst part was that baseball had no leader to restore its good name. Its governing three-man National Commission was a warren of politics. The two leagues were at one another's throats again."[44]

It is common to think that the Black Sox scandal forced the change in baseball's governance that took place in November 1920, but two baseball historians caution against that view. Harold Seymour and Dorothy Seymour Mills contend that the conditions that eventually led to the election of Kenesaw Mountain Landis as commissioner of baseball existed prior to the 1919 Series mess: "The National Commission was wobbling many months before the scandal occurred, and it collapsed altogether before the Series sellout came to public knowledge. It had been stumbling along for several years under mounting difficulties and criticisms."[45] Perhaps it might be better to say that the Black Sox scandal concentrated the lords' collective minds. Their reactions to the 1919 Series sellout by the Chicago players merely brought the old grievances and rivalries into plain view, which made their existing means of addressing problems unsustainable. The recognition of this untenable working relationship led them to place the question of leadership ahead of any consideration of the fallout from the 1919 World Series. A majority of the owners decided that a new structure of governance was needed. Charley Stoneham was part of that majority.[46]

Starting in the fall of 1920, when the Black Sox scandal was unfolding, the owners started forming positions to address the core of baseball's governing process. A proposal for leadership outside of baseball to govern the sport, the so-called Lasker plan, formulated by Albert D. Lasker, a Chicago businessman and Chicago Cubs stockholder, began to circulate among the owners. Quickly, the issues of authority and control divided the owners into two camps, one for change and one for the status quo. It was a messy process and has been discussed in depth by a number of baseball historians.[47] After days of deals, plans, and brokering, the old triumvirate of power—two league presidents and one elected position—gave way eventually to a version of the Lasker plan, a single office, that of commissioner, who would control the game.[48] On November 8, 1920, Kenesaw Mountain Landis was elected by unanimous vote as baseball's first commissioner. His final and revised contract, approved by the owners and signed January 12, 1921, gave him sole authority to govern the game.[49]

Stoneham's role in the reorganization was minor, befitting an owner with limited experience, but in some reporting, the part he played was nonetheless meaningful. He was a loyal backer of the Lasker plan from the outset and part of a contingent that walked out of the November 11, 1920, owners' meeting when the five American League owners loyal to Johnson tried to circumvent a vote by procedural means.[50] He also pledged a significant amount of money to establish a new league of twelve teams (those of the owners who backed the Lasker plan) if necessary.[51] According to one source, however, Stoneham's role in the change in baseball's governance might have been more significant.

A 1919–20 diary kept by Harry Grabiner, the secretary of the Chicago White Sox, describes a ploy by Ban Johnson to oust the two New York Yankees owners at the time, Jacob Ruppert and Tillinghast Huston, who had challenged Johnson's authority in American League governance. Grabiner's entry records that Johnson approached Stoneham to force Ruppert and Huston out of their lease at the Polo Grounds. (The Yankees played all of their home games at the Polo Grounds.) Johnson, believing that Ruppert and Huston would sell the Yankees if they had no ballpark, proposed that Stoneham grant the lease to the American League. If Stoneham agreed, Johnson would then allow the Giants' boss to approve the new Yankee owners. To sweeten the deal, Johnson would nominate Stoneham as the third member of the National Commission that oversees baseball. Grabiner writes that Stoneham went to Lasker, who was proposing a new order to govern baseball, and reported Johnson's offer. Lasker then arranged for Stoneham to report Johnson's ploy to Ruppert at the next owners' meeting. The Johnson offer to Stoneham proved to be further reason for Ruppert to join with the National League owners in accepting the Lasker plan and weakening Johnson's hold on the American League in the process. Ruppert's defection from Johnson helped bring about the approval of Landis for commissioner.[52]

Although his first two years as a major league owner were turbulent, difficult times for baseball at large, Stoneham at least had the consolation of financial success with his own club during this period. In his inaugural season, 1919, the Giants finished second in the NL, with a respectable eighty-seven wins, but could not catch a good and steady Cincinnati team. They dropped four of six games in a crucial mid-August series with the Reds, which effectively ended their pennant hopes. An early September surge teased Giants fans, but in mid-September the team suffered another skid, losing six of eight games. Their run for the NL flag was over. It was essentially a two-team race between the Reds and the Giants (the third-place Chicago Cubs were thirty-three games back) in 1919, and Cincinnati avoided any big losing streaks throughout the season. Disappointed though he might have been with a second-place finish, Stoneham, as a first-year owner, still had plenty to smile about. His Giants easily ran away with the top attendance in all of Major League Baseball, drawing 708,857, doubling the previous year's home gate. With such results, Stoneham felt he could be generous. At the season's end, he announced that all Giants players would receive pay increases, much to the chagrin of some of his fellow owners.[53] The 1920 season was almost a mirror image of the previous year, a second-place finish, but with even greater results at the turnstiles, 929,609, again the best in the National League. Whatever his misgivings might have been about baseball's organizational problems, Stoneham was gratified with his own situation with the Giants. The National Exhibition Company was making money.

Despite being gratified with attendance records in the first two years of ownership, Stoneham was at heart a businessman with an acute awareness of assets and liabilities. He also had a keen sense about value. Yes, his club was making money in the short term, but would it continue? With all the turmoil of the past two years—baseball's organizational problems and the Black Sox scandal—the sport seemed as susceptible to volatility and cycles as Wall Street. This turmoil might have rekindled a shadow of doubt in Stoneham's mind about having made a long-term investment in baseball. This thinking might have led Stoneham to consider selling his interest in the Giants when its value was high.

Reports surfaced in the fall of 1922 that former Giants president Harry Hempstead wanted to get back into baseball and made Stoneham an offer.[54] News of the potential sale forced the first serious breach between the ownership syndicate, causing McGraw and McQuade to threaten legal action against Stoneham. Annoyed and angry, they insisted that the terms of the partnership agreement required the pre-approval of the others if one partner wished to sell his shares. There was also a "right of first refusal" for other syndicate members before a selling member could negotiate with an outside buyer.[55]

Whether McGraw and McQuade's legal threat chastened Stoneham or the terms of Hempstead's offer were not satisfactory, nothing came of the rumors of a deal. When questioned by the press, Stoneham dissembled and denied any interest in selling, a practice that would continue over the next few years when other rumors of Stoneham's interest in selling the club would surface. Both McGraw and McQuade remained upset with Stoneham, revealing cracks in the partnership that would expand in the coming years. Eventually, McGraw would make a separate and uneasy peace with Stoneham, but McQuade nursed his wrath. He took Stoneham's private and independent willingness to entertain an offer as a personal slight. From this moment on, his relationship with Stoneham would be strained, and he would remain highly suspicious of Stoneham's moves, even though he would profit in the next few years from the team's financial gains.

The success of the Giants on the field resulted in no small measure from the hands-off approach Stoneham took with the operation of the ball club. From his earliest days as an owner, Stoneham wasted no time in settling into an administrative style that put McGraw in the forefront of all of the baseball decisions. For one thing, up to this point in his life, Stoneham was essentially a baseball fan, not someone with deep knowledge of the game, certainly not in player acquisition and development or in the day-to-day strategy of playing the game. These he gladly conceded to McGraw. Stoneham was prudent enough, and content, to adopt a wait-and-see attitude, giving himself a chance to learn on the job. As a businessman, he also understood delegation of authority and how to oversee operations, both of which he did successfully in his brokerage firms. He studied and assessed the finances to provide McGraw with the resources he needed. The general impression among the members of the press was that Stoneham remained in the background—rarely did anyone see him on the field or in the clubhouse—with an open wallet when McGraw needed a player. It was an administrative style and formula that was to pay huge dividends in the immediate future, not only in the National League standings but also for the stockholders of the NEC.

As he looked forward to a new decade, Stoneham felt cautiously optimistic about his decision to shift careers from an investment broker to sportsman. The nation seemed poised for a great new economic run, and good times were bubbling to the surface despite (or maybe because of) Prohibition. New York City's Jazz Age was about to erupt. Nightlife flourished—jazz clubs, music halls, movies, the bright lights of Broadway—much of it fueled by the social drinking that the 1919 Volstead Act was intended to restrain.[56] The Giants would also be part of that entertainment world, with Stoneham ready to take full advantage of his ownership status and the good times ahead. It would turn out that he would be only half-right. The Giants would be atop New York City's sporting world for the early part of the decade and would draw many fans from all over the city, bringing good returns for the NEC. But clouds were gathering. The success and the revelry would be accompanied soon by difficulties, both within the Giants organization and in Stoneham's personal life. Jazz Age owner Charley Stoneham would find the next few years a bizarre mixture of highs and lows that would prove both stressful and challenging.

4

A Fresh Scent of Scandal

> We all turned and looked around for Gatsby. It was
> testimony to the romantic speculation he inspired that there
> were whispers about him from those who had found little
> that it was necessary to whisper about in this world.
> —F. SCOTT FITZGERALD, *The Great Gatsby*

Aside from the frosty reception he endured from his fellow baseball lords, Jazz Age baseball began smoothly and beautifully for Charley Stoneham. His New York Giants, who finished second in 1920, would win it all the next year and then go on to capture three more consecutive National League pennants, giving them four World Series appearances halfway through the decade. This successful run not only put Stoneham at the top of baseball's world in the Jazz Age capital; it also provided a good New York story to counter the recent Black Sox scandal that was threatening baseball's popularity with the public. The settling of the scandal, complete with public testimonies and trials, followed by the lifetime suspensions of popular Chicago White Sox players, all of which was covered extensively by the national press, was messy and put the integrity of the game in jeopardy. The reverberations of the scandal spread to all corners of baseball, triggering an overhaul and reorganization of its governance and the appointment of a commissioner of baseball in January 1921 to clean up the sport and oversee the two leagues. For Stoneham, as well as the other owners, much was riding on baseball having an exciting and compelling 1921 season.

As it turned out for the owners, and especially for Stoneham, worries were overblown about the degradation of the sport in the hearts and minds of the fans, especially in the Jazz Age capital, New York. For one thing, the game had a bigger-than-life hero in Babe Ruth, who had come to New York from Boston in 1920 and was drawing fans to see him hit home runs, not only in Gotham but in all the cities where he played. He swatted an unimaginable fifty-four homers in the 1920 season and, twenty-five years old and at the prime of his career, gave every indication that this was just the beginning. For another, 1921 was a particularly magical year for baseball fans in New York City.[1] Ruth grew in stature, if that can be imagined, exceeding his previous year's record with fifty-nine home runs while leading his team to their first American League pennant. And the Giants were beginning an incredible run, one that would establish them as the NL powerhouse for the next few years. They pulled away from Pittsburgh in the final weeks of the season to secure their seventh National League pennant.

In a true New York celebration, the Giants faced their American League cousins (and tenants at the Polo Grounds), the Yankees, in the 1921 World Series, the first of the so-called Subway Series. As well as stirring up the interest of fans throughout the city, New York Jazz Age baseball captivated the interests of the Broadway crowd, the likes of Charlie Chaplin, Florenz Ziegfeld, Fanny Brice, and George M. Cohan among them, with divided loyalties over the two New York teams.[2] Atop the city's sporting world, Stoneham, just three years in as an owner, hosted all of baseball at his Polo Grounds. Most of the other owners set aside their misgivings and attended.

The buildup to the series, created and fostered by the press, focused on territorial rivalry within the city and the contrasting approaches to the game between Babe Ruth and John McGraw, the two most powerful baseball personalities in the city. Questions about how McGraw would handle Ruth were contemptuously sluffed off by the Giants' manager, who dismissed the Yankee slugger and claimed that the Giants had faced better hitting in the National League.[3] But the writers continued with the stories, and the interest in the city grew as it never had for a World Series. The pregame hype about the two New York teams held up, as baseball fans were treated to an exciting back-and-forth series, with the Giants coming from behind, losing the first two games, to take the championship five games to three.[4] After the series the victorious and jubilant McGraw crowed that he had kept Ruth in check, holding him to one home run that was inconsequential. Ruth still managed to hit .313, with six runs batted in (RBIs), but could not lead his team to capture the series. Once again, the Giants ruled the city.

Winning the World Series gave Stoneham the opportunity to host a lavish victory bash at the old Waldorf hotel. One observer deemed it a celebration that never would be forgotten for those in attendance, especially for one young Giants player, up to that night abstemious when it came to drinking alcohol but who nonetheless had to be carried out at five o'clock in the morning, stiff as a board. In a Prohibition-be-damned, Gatsby-like style, Stoneham had pulled out the stops. Sportswriter Frank Graham described the festivities:

> There were hams and chickens and turkeys for the guests that night—or steaks for those who wanted them. And rye and Scotch and gin and champagne. Little Jimmy Flynn, a tenor much fancied by the baseball and prize-fighting mob, and a great favorite with McGraw, sang. So did Frank Belcher, once a basso with the famed San Francisco Minstrels. . . . So, too, did Lieutenant Gitz-Rice, whose "Dear Old Pal of Mine" . . . was sung by him to his own accompaniment on the piano. . . . Someone had clipped the headlines from the evening newspapers telling of the Giants' victories and pasted them across the mirrors in all the rooms of the suite. Endless toast were drunk to McGraw. The sun was high over Fifth Avenue and Thirty-fourth Street as the last of the guests emerged and tottered homeward.[5]

Stoneham's party could have provided an apt model for Fitzgerald in *The Great Gatsby*, even with the musical interludes.

The good times rolled for Stoneham and McGraw. The Giants won the next three National League pennants to give them four consecutive titles, still a National League record. They continued their mastery over the Yankees in the 1922 World Series, winning four games to none, although one game ended in a tie. McGraw was particularly satisfied with the win, giving him bragging rights in the city, but also pleased with his mastery of Ruth, who managed only two hits in five games against Giants pitching. Stoneham was happy to open his wallet for another victory celebration at the Waldorf. The revelers partied deep into the night.

The 1922 victory bash turned out to be the last Giants' World Series victory celebration for a while, although neither Stoneham nor McGraw could imagine that as the Giants continued to win pennants. But in 1923 the Yankees would finally break through against the Giants in the third straight New York World Series, the first one in which the Yankees would be in their new home, Yankee Stadium, in the Bronx. Ruth obviously liked his new environs and had a more characteristic performance, hitting .386, with three home runs and eight runs scored. The Yankees won the series four games to two. It was a pivotal moment, not only for the Giants but for Stoneham and McGraw personally. Stoneham found his attention abruptly diverted from baseball as he became increasingly involved in legal entanglements growing out of the previous sales of his investment business. McGraw, bitterly disappointed in his loss to the Yankees, tried to refocus on the coming season. But he had lost his place as the city champion. Moreover, he would not win another World Series. For the Giants their dominant command of the National League was soon coming to an end.

In late September 1924 and facing some legal difficulties connected to the sales of his brokerage businesses, Charley Stoneham was poised to find some solace in the success of the 1924 baseball season. His

New York Giants were closing in on an unprecedented fourth straight National League championship, in first place, a game and a half ahead of archrival Brooklyn and two games ahead of the Pittsburgh Pirates, with only three games left to play in the regular season for each contender. Win two of the games in a three-game series with seventh-place Philadelphia and, regardless of what either Brooklyn or Pittsburgh did, New York would claim the pennant. The odds looked good for the Giants, and visions of hosting other owners and league officials for a World Series at the Polo Grounds and perhaps a victory party after the Series danced in Stoneham's head. These thoughts would take his mind off New York City courtrooms, where it seemed he had been spending all his time.

The pennant race was settled on September 27, when the Giants beat the Phillies and Brooklyn lost to the Boston Braves, effectively eliminating the Robins from the race. Stoneham had little time to celebrate and relish the Giants' triumph, however. Only a few hours after the Giants clinched the pennant, a messy bribery scandal broke, involving an alleged attempt by Giants players and personnel to bribe a Phillies player in order to ensure the Giants' chances of a win. Close on the heels of a joyous clubhouse victory celebration, Stoneham and Giants manager John McGraw found themselves in the midst of another baseball hearing with the commissioner, raising questions, yet again, about the integrity of the game and their role in the scandal. Before things could be settled, the story and subsequent accusations would open old wounds among baseball officials. Old rivalries surfaced among the owners, with a call from Ban Johnson, president of the American League, that the World Series should be canceled. Stoneham would find himself thrust into the middle of old grudges and the subject of rumors, the last thing he wanted heading into the festivities of a World Series.

There are so many loose ends about what baseball journalists term "the O'Connell-Dolan affair" that a complete understanding of what happened may never be possible. The incident began on September

27, 1924, when Philadelphia Phillies shortstop Heinie Sand told his manager, Arthur Fletcher, that he was approached before the game with New York by Jimmy O'Connell, a young bench player for the Giants, who said that it would be worth five hundred dollars if he, Sand, eased up "and not bear down on us too hard today."[6] O'Connell, a naive rookie from the San Francisco Seals ball club, was urged to do this by the old Giants bench coach Cozy Dolan. As it turned out, the Giants won the game without any assistance from Sand, who made three putouts at shortstop and committed no errors. Nor would the outcome of the game have mattered; the second-place Brooklyn Robins lost to Boston, mathematically assuring the Giants of their fourth consecutive league championship. Nonetheless, Fletcher reported the O'Connell incident to National League president John Heydler. Fletcher's quick move was no doubt motivated by what he knew of the 1919 Black Sox scandal investigation and the penalties doled out to those who had knowledge of the fix but who kept it to themselves.[7] Heydler, in turn, telephoned Commissioner Landis in Chicago. Landis thought the incident significant enough to probe the matter firsthand and left immediately for New York.

On Monday, September 30, five days before the scheduled start of the World Series, Landis called in Stoneham and John McGraw and informed them of the incident and of his intentions to question everyone involved. What they heard did not go well with either of the Giants officials—not only the incident itself but also the way they were brought into the investigation. Both Stoneham and McGraw expressed their displeasure that they had not been informed first, that it was a matter of their ball club and their personnel. They were annoyed with Landis but most of all with Heydler, who, in their view, should handle league matters in house before involving the Commissioner's Office. It is unknown what effect Stoneham and McGraw's complaints had on matters—probably very little, given that once Landis informed the Giants owners of the situation, he decided to pursue the O'Connell-Dolan matter with all due diligence and call in the principals for questioning. Nonetheless, what both Stoneham and McGraw perceived as a slight stuck in their respective craws for some time, and their resentment, especially against Heydler, was the cause of friction between the Giants and the National League office for the next few years.

After listening to both Fletcher and Sand, Landis decided to go forward with the investigation and brought in O'Connell to get his version of the incident. O'Connell was candid and admitted everything to Landis, who was taken aback by how forthcoming the young player was: O'Connell declared that he had indeed approached Sand and offered him five hundred dollars to throw the game. To make matters more difficult for Landis and Heydler, O'Connell implicated others as well. He said that he was "put up to it" by Cozy Dolan, the Giants coach, who told him he would somehow find the money, and that Giants star players Frank Frisch, Ross Youngs, and George Kelly all knew about the plan. Landis was perturbed and on edge. With recent baseball scandals fresh in his mind, he feared another discovery of bribery to throw a game would pull baseball back into the muck of controversy and threaten the public trust in the sport. He immediately summoned Frisch, Youngs, and Kelly to hear O'Connell's story and get their reaction; all three, in O'Connell's presence, denied talking to him about approaching Sand. Landis was convinced by the sincerity and consistency of their statements and cleared them.[8]

Cozy Dolan, however, proved to be a more difficult and cagey character. During the questioning by Landis, Dolan was consistent in his answer, a singular one as it turned out, "I don't remember," driving the commissioner to aggravation.

Landis asked, "Did you tell O'Connell to offer Sand $500 not to bear down against the Giants?"

"I don't remember," Dolan said.

"You don't remember!" Landis said.

"No, sir," Dolan said.

"This is Monday," Landis said slowly. "Do you mean to sit

there and tell me you don't remember whether or not you told O'Connell to offer a bribe to Sand on Saturday—two days ago?"

"Yes sir," Dolan said.

"'Yes sir' what?" Landis roared.

"I don't remember," Dolan said.⁹

In the end Landis ruled that both O'Connell and Dolan would be placed on baseball's permanent ineligible list. A brokenhearted and disillusioned Jimmy O'Connell, feeling that he had been betrayed by his teammates, nonetheless accepted the ruling and left for San Francisco, never to play organized baseball again. Dolan, however, would not be so compliant in his reaction to Landis's decree.

Landis issued his ruling on the O'Connell-Dolan case three days before the World Series and signaled the matter was over, hoping for an end to the affair. National League president John Heydler followed suit, announcing that the case was closed and the issues settled. They both soon discovered that any attempts at closure were nothing more than wishful thinking. Indeed, their words had the opposite effect as interest in the story began to grow. Initially, the O'Connell-Dolan hearing was wrapped in secrecy, with only the principals involved. Once the rulings were made public, however, the story gained momentum, especially among national sportswriters. For a few days, interest in the fate of O'Connell and Dolan, and the involvement of other Giants players, became front-page news and took precedent over the usual buildup to the World Series. In the eyes of many of the sportswriters, the case raised more puzzling and worrisome questions, despite Landis's declaration that the scandal was a closed matter. Where did O'Connell, a young bench player, come up with the money? How could Dolan, a rather dull and simple fellow, be the brains behind a bribe? Who was the real source of the attempted fix? Given the close pennant race, was there big New York money that wanted to secure a Giants win? Why was Landis in such a rush to judgment and to claim the matter closed and settled?

Nor was it only members of the press who had questions. Some among baseball's higher-ups felt there was more to the story than Landis was willing to make public. Stirring the pot by grandstanding with the press, American League president Ban Johnson, an old enemy of John McGraw and someone who resented the commissioner's power, wanted Landis to call off the World Series or, short of that, disqualify the Giants from playing in the fall classic. Pittsburgh Pirates owner Barney Dreyfuss joined Johnson in a public disagreement with Landis. Dreyfuss also called for a cancellation of the World Series. The Pirates owner was outspoken in his criticism of McGraw, implying that there always seemed to be unseemliness with the Giants, due to McGraw's leadership.[10] This meddling coming from baseball officials rankled Landis, especially when he was feeling some heat from members of the press who thought he was moving too quickly to quash the incident.[11] Nonetheless, Landis and Heydler held firm, and the World Series between the Giants and the Washington Senators began as scheduled on October 4 in Washington DC, the first time in four years that it would include a city other than New York.

Once the Series was underway, it looked as if both Landis and Heydler would be prescient about the finality of the O'Connell-Dolan story and its grip on both the sportswriters' and the public's imaginations. The 1924 fall classic was both thrilling and dramatic, pushing the O'Connell-Dolan story off the front pages, with the Senators, playing in the World Series for the first time in franchise history, pitted against the National League powerhouse Giants. Led by the great Walter Johnson, who, at the age of thirty-six and after seventeen seasons, would finally get his chance to pitch in the postseason, the Senators were sentimental favorites. The Series was tight and went seven games (four of them decided by one run and two of them in extra innings), finishing in dramatic fashion in the twelfth inning, when a routine ground ball to third baseman Fred Lindstrom hit a pebble and bounced over his head, allowing the winning run to score , giving the Senators the championship. The nation's capital went delirious with parades, celebrations into the night, and neighborhood gatherings. The Giants headed back to New York deflated and down; even Stoneham's post-season celebration at the Commodore Hotel couldn't shake them out of their gloomy mood.[12]

After the World Series concluded, the chief spokesmen on the scandal were nowhere to be found. Landis took a golfing holiday to Havana, Cuba, and Heydler left for a family holiday, both of them putting the 1924 season in the rearview mirror. McGraw left for Europe on a preplanned exhibition tour in Ireland and England with the Chicago White Sox. Stoneham remained in town but was unavailable to the press. He had become occupied with various bankruptcy cases resulting from failed brokerage firms that had absorbed his clients after the sale and closure of Charles A. Stoneham and Company. But sportswriters nonetheless remained focused on the O'Connell-Dolan story as new developments about the affair surfaced, broaching fresh considerations.

With the time provided him by the World Series, Cozy Dolan drew his breath and considered his options, ultimately deciding to sue Landis for defamation of character. Advised by some contacts in New York, he sought out Manhattan attorney William J. Fallon to represent him. Dolan's choice of counsel was in itself newsworthy and raised suspicions among New York writers that either Stoneham or McGraw was behind the move.[13] For one thing, Fallon was a famous, if not notorious, Broadway lawyer whose clients included Arnold Rothstein and John McGraw and, as a great Giants fan, had a friendship with Charles Stoneham.[14] For another, everyone knew that Dolan could not afford Fallon's fees. The press pondered who was really behind Fallon's representation, and speculation arose that it must be someone from the Giants.[15] Eager for publicity, Fallon gave a number of interviews to the press about his intentions to get Landis in court in order to have him testify under oath and thoroughly grill him. Fallon let it be known that he was no fan of Landis and considered him someone who administered decisions with a personal agenda. Fallon commented that he wanted to have a little fun with the judge on the witness stand in the form of payback: "I was in court one day when he got awfully tough with a bootlegger, and sentenced him to two years in the penitentiary."[16] If nothing else, Dolan's action and Fallon's pontificating provided great post-Series theater.

The gravitas of the O'Connell-Dolan affair intensified when New York district attorney Joab H. Banton informed the Commissioner's Office that he was prepared to pursue criminal charges against O'Connell and Dolan under a state law passed in 1921, in the wake of the Black Sox scandal, making the offering of a bribe a felony.[17] Banton's decision stirred new interest among the New York press. Fallon took advantage of the district attorney's move to inform the reporters that his client would look forward to any chance, under oath, to clear his name. Back in San Francisco, O'Connell responded through an attorney that he would not cooperate with any New York legal proceeding or any court summon without a promise of immunity. Landis's and Heydler's hopes that the affair was out of sight and out of mind seemed more and more like a pipe dream.

After only a few weeks, Dolan's suit languished, partly out of Fallon's growing disinterest in the case due to what he saw as Dolan's lack of resolve. For his part, Dolan grew increasingly hopeful that Landis might reinstate him and did not want the suit to go forward, fearing that it might provoke Landis's ire and ruin any chance with the commissioner. That reinstatement never came, however, and Dolan, like his coconspirator O'Connell, drifted away from baseball. There was some speculation that Dolan's decision to abandon any legal battle with Landis might have prevented a big rift in baseball. One writer claimed that a thoroughly miffed Landis was prepared to go after the Giants' front office, especially after he learned that Fallon's fees were most likely being covered by Stoneham or McGraw.[18]

Eventually, even the district attorney's office lost interest in the case, but the publicity that grew out of the initial announcement caused more musings in the press. Circling back to the quick resolution of the case, writers raised questions about a cover-up. Reacting to the criticism that he had not been forthcoming about the details of the case in an effort to save baseball from another scandal, Landis released the full transcript of the hearings to the press, and they were published in January 1925.[19] But the release of the transcript caused more confusion. Intended to bring transparency to the case, it merely muddied the water. The actual "confession" by O'Connell was missing from the record since the stenographer was not present in the room for that part of the hearing.[20] The effect of second-guessing among the press (and some baseball officials) raised more concerns about the position of the Giants, who often had seemed to be on the dark side of baseball over the past few years. Writers recalled the escapades of Hal Chase and Heinie Zimmerman in 1920, Benny Kauff in 1921, and Phil Douglas in 1922, all of them scandalous to different degrees but each resulting in an expulsion from baseball.[21] Some wondered about the culture of the ball club, implicating management and owners.[22]

Despite the availability of the transcript of the interviews with O'Connell and Dolan, the attention given to the details of the case from contemporary newspaper sources, and the work of baseball historians, questions remain even to this day. The O'Connell-Dolan scandal, as many have now dubbed it, conjures up descriptive characteristic markings: "mysterious," "puzzling," "curious," "murky."[23] There are also dangling strings that remain untied. If Dolan knew the story to be false, why didn't he come forward with details? Was there a possibility that he was paid to be silent? And if so, by whom? What about the gamblers? Days after the O'Connell-Dolan hearings with Landis, a story broke in the *New York Mirror*—a newspaper devoted to sensationalism—that Broadway gambling interests had big money tied to the Giants winning the pennant and might have been behind the attempted fix. But when Landis and other journalists tried to verify the claim, they could find nothing. Moreover, the way the story developed, O'Connell's measly offer does not seem to reflect big-time Broadway gambling money.[24] But the gambling twist only reinforced the sense that there must have been more to this business than simply a clubhouse prank with O'Connell as the goat.

Landis probably thought so. One of his biographers speculates that he suspected others but could not connect the dots.[25] A number of contemporary journalists and writers felt that O'Connell was an unfortunate dupe and was doing the bidding of others, whether he knew it or not. Damon Runyon, for one, certainly held that view, and a few years later, during a World Series, he approached Landis informally to ask if O'Connell could get a reconsideration, that he had been just a young, naive kid and was taken advantage of by others. Landis was sympathetic but remained resolved in his response: "Damon, I'm just as sorry for that young man as you are. But what can I do? O'Connell confessed his guilt, namely that he tried to bribe another player to throw a game. I couldn't let him back. You know that. Every ball player we expelled would be in my office seeking reinstatement. As for the great bulk of other players, what would they think? They know now that any action seeking to throw, or otherwise tamper with a game, means expulsion. And it has to stay that way. Damon, no, I can't do it."[26]

Scrutiny of the Dolan-O'Connell case also occasioned speculation about both Stoneham and McGraw, not only into their involvement as Giants officials but also about their personal lives in general, as gamblers and habitués of nightlife. Old stories recirculated about Stoneham, himself no stranger to the innuendos of scandals, and his place in the game. His alleged involvement in shady business deals had caused the owners in the fall of 1923 to find a way to ease him out of baseball, "for the good of the game."[27] Rumors persisted about his philandering, his attraction to Broadway showgirls and nightclubs, and his gambling habits, which had him playing in big games, some of them organized by Arnold Rothstein, the notorious gambling king of New York.[28] Stoneham's association with Rothstein already had become the subject of league discipline. In 1922, after hearing reports that Rothstein was a frequent guest at Giants games in Stoneham's personal box at the Polo Grounds, Landis called Stoneham and got the Giants owner to promise that Rothstein would no longer be his guest at games.[29] A number of newspaper accounts of Stoneham's associations, gambling life, shady business ventures, bucket shops, and bankruptcies raised questions about his propensity to be always on the edge of legality.[30] Might he be more involved in the O'Connell-Dolan story than previously known?

Rumors about Stoneham's connection to the Dolan-O'Connell case resurfaced a few years later, when Frank McQuade sued Stoneham and McGraw for breach of contract after being forced out of his position as treasurer of the National Exhibition Company at a directors' board meeting in May 1928. During the trial and under oath, both Stoneham and McGraw testified that McQuade had threatened to reveal "certain facts" about Stoneham's and McGraw's involvement in O'Connell and Dolan being permanently banned from baseball. But Stoneham and McGraw claimed, separately and under oath, that they had no involvement in any decisions about either Dolan or O'Connell, and, as it turned out, McQuade let the threat drop, probably an indication that he had no information on either man's involvement with Dolan-O'Connell affair.[31] Nonetheless, the testimony added to both the mystery of the case and the rumors piling up about both Stoneham's and McGraw's unseemliness.

All of the rumormongering added to accusations and insinuations, but Stoneham was always ready with denials and refutations. In response to a story that he was selling the team to get out of baseball, he was blunt: "The story is all bunk. It makes its annual appearance just before the opening of circus season at Madison Square Garden. I will not sell my stock in the Giants now or at any time."[32] Nonetheless, the persistent rumors had their effect. Stoneham's constant brush with the shady side—the latest being that the Giants were back in the baseball scandal business—kept a whiff of scandal circulating around him. The whispering, the conjecture, the innuendos, contributed to views of his business profile, already under scrutiny because of his connections to bucket shops, and since he was the owner of the Giants, added to the sense that the ball club was in the midst of some murky business.[33] Most of it was conjecture, designed in some way to sell newspapers, but an impression was created, nonetheless, that Stoneham was a nefarious character.[34]

Within baseball itself, however, comments on Stoneham were mostly muted. It was widely known that he faced legal problems connected to his former investment business. Some fellow owners expressed concerns about adverse publicity for the game that came with Stoneham's situation, but overall the owners' complaints were in the main half-hearted. With five years to judge him as an owner, his fellow lords had grown to accept him and even admit his contributions. "As far as the sport is concerned," one owner remarked, "Stoneham was a good and decent owner." This view was seconded by Commissioner Landis, who reminded baseball's inner circle that Stoneham had been convicted of nothing as yet and remained a responsible and reliant owner.[35] Buoyed perhaps by the backing of the commissioner and most baseball insiders, Stoneham followed the path he always took in the wake of guesswork and gossip. He brushed rumors aside and pushed forward with a ruthless focus on getting through, relying on an impervious determination and his deep pockets to see him through any crisis.

5

See You in Court

"Why isn't he in jail?"
"They can't get him, old sport. He's a smart man."
—F. SCOTT FITZGERALD, *The Great Gatsby*

Long before Charley Stoneham jumped feetfirst into baseball's politics as a member of the House of Lords ownership group, he was actively pursuing the swanky life of a sportsman in the horse racing world. The draw of the sporting world became stronger with the purchase of the Giants in January 1919. There is every evidence to suggest that Stoneham was both happy and optimistic about the decision to reinvent himself as a true sportsman with baseball ownership and connections to the horse racing world. This new identity prompted his transition from the volatile investment world of the Consolidated Exchange in the winter of 1920. By March 1921, well into his third year of baseball ownership, he was ready to withdraw formally from the brokerage business; he sent letters to all of his clients and customers, informing them of the liquidation of Charles A. Stoneham and Company and advising them of the transfer of their accounts to other investment firms on the exchange. Once the accounts were settled, Stoneham's personal fiduciary ties to his clients on Wall Street and the Curb Exchange would be severed completely. Then he would be ready to give his full and undivided attention to horse racing and, especially, baseball.

It was with some shock, then, only one year later, that the brokerage world he thought he had left behind began to ensnare him in its complicated and messy business. For the next six years, Stoneham would find himself entangled in complex legal matters involving the firms that took over the accounts of his former clients. He would spend countless hours in court or in meetings with his attorneys defending his every business decision. Even as he attempted to enjoy the phenomenal success of the Giants playing in four straight World Series between 1921 and 1924, he was continually distracted by depositions, court appearances, and indictments over his connections to various Consolidated Exchange brokerage firms that had failed, costing their customers most of their holdings.

When he left the brokerage business in early 1921, Stoneham did so for two chief reasons. The first had to do with his change of career paths: he wanted to devote full-time attention to the sporting life and baseball ownership. There was also another reason, a strategic business move, involving a calculation that the stock market was heating up and would no longer favor Stoneham's style of investment. As a firm that traded in the less regulated Consolidated Exchange, Stoneham's company depended on a falling market to maximize its profits. As one analyst explained it, in brokerage houses like Stoneham's, stocks would be purchased but then immediately sold. When a customer demanded the certificate of sale, the firm would go back into the market and purchase the stock but at a cheaper price, pocketing the margin.[1] In Stoneham's thinking, the early 1920s American investment climate seemed too positive and buoyant, showing no signs of slowing down. With a rising market, his former practice of buying and selling would be too risky. Moreover, timing was everything in this type of investment practice, and Stoneham felt it was time to get out when the getting was good. This business assumption, as much as the change in his career choice, motivated him to close his investment company. But as he would discover, his transition from the brokerage business to full-time sportsman would not be a smooth one.

Stoneham's first serious difficulty arose in January 1922 with the collapse of E. D. Dier and Company, the successor to Hughes and Dier, a firm that took in many of the clients from the now closed Charles A. Stoneham and Company.[2] In the course of one year since receiving the Stoneham clients, it was apparent that Dier was severely undercapitalized and could not cover the liabilities of its customers, an amount totaling more than four million dollars.[3] The scandal about Dier's collapse made the papers in dramatic fashion when it was revealed that Ben Franklin Shrimpton, the head of Dier, had cashed out some of the holdings and in a hasty overnight trip fled to Canada.[4] As the shock spread among Dier clients, many sought legal help to recover their losses. At a bankruptcy hearing on March 14 before U.S. Commissioner Alexander Gilchrist, receiver attorney Manfred Ehrich announced the establishment of a settlement fund to help compensate Dier creditors.[5] After various negotiations with the creditors over the next three months, Ehrich presented a compromised plan of a $500,000 restitution fund, which was confirmed at a bankruptcy hearing in July by federal judge Julian Mack. Under the negotiated agreement, a fund of $500,000 was established, with Charles A. Stoneham the largest single contributor, at $200,000.

While Stoneham was on record expressing concern over his former clients' losses, his contribution to the Ehrich fund was not motivated solely by empathy or largesse.[6] It had a big string attached that would provide Stoneham some conditional protection; those former clients who accepted the settlement would release him of any future liabilities concerning their Dier accounts. Commenting on his portion of the fund, Stoneham stressed that the liabilities were more widespread. He explained that Charles A. Stoneham and Company did not operate as a member of the New York Stock Exchange or the Consolidated Exchange but independently, doing business through exchange houses, paying the usual fees and commissions in the transfer of accounts. Therefore, he reasoned, other firms involved in business dealings and transfers from Stoneham and Company to Dier also should be held accountable and contribute to the restitution settlement fund.[7]

At the same time, another group of Dier creditors intent on investigating the firm's business methods organized a Creditors Protective Committee, headed by chief counsel Daniel W. Blumenthal, who, in time, would be a major nemesis of Charley Stoneham.[8] Blumenthal's clients rejected Ehrich's negotiated settlement, preferring instead to sue Stoneham in civil court. In addition to the civil filing, Blumenthal also pursued criminal charges against Stoneham over the next few months and in May filed a misdemeanor complaint alleging irregularities in stock transfers. Moreover, Blumenthal was clear in his animus toward Stoneham, calling him the "mastermind" behind the operations of E. D. Dier and Company.[9] This complaint was subsequently dismissed because Blumenthal had selected the wrong Stoneham client; Stoneham was in Cuba when this particular client's transaction took place and had no knowledge of it.[10] Nonetheless, Blumenthal's actions were pulling Stoneham deeper into a legal morass.

As the Dier bankruptcy negotiations with creditors dragged on for months, various complexities began to cloud the clients' claims. Some of the issues had to do with records and paper trails of security transactions among various brokerage agents. Attorneys representing some clients wanted to know if Charles A. Stoneham and Company held or had under its control the securities involved in the transfers. Blumenthal's criminal complaint was one example. In another, proceeding, attorney L. Barton Case produced a letter announcing the transfer of Stoneham's customers to Dier in which Charles A. Stoneham and Company assures its customers about Dier's financial health, "We have investigated Hughes and Dier and believe them to be financially responsible and fully capable of carrying out any obligations they assume in the taking over of this business." When questioned under oath by Case, Stoneham stood by the claims in the letter.[11] The question of Stoneham's prior knowledge about Dier's solvency before clients were transferred to that firm would prove to have serious legal consequences.[12] (This claim would be disputed two years later, when the Dier case moved to criminal court.)[13]

As the general investigations of the Dier transfers moved forward, Stoneham found himself in other courts contesting individual damage suits involving those clients who did not join the bankruptcy settlement and who claimed Stoneham mismanaged transfer of their accounts, including some who alleged that Charles A. Stoneham and Company had withheld details of the sales or did not provide certificates of securities. Most of these Stoneham settled, but they added to his already pressing legal concerns.[14] If these were not vexing enough, he was soon to find out that his problems with the courts would get considerably worse. Just as the Dier hearings were reaching a settlement agreement, a second brokerage house with Charles A. Stoneham and Company connections collapsed, adding another messy layer to Stoneham's ongoing legal troubles.

In June 1922 the firm of E. M. Fuller and Company failed and filed for bankruptcy, unable to meet the claims of customers, which were estimated to be as high as $5.8 million.[15] E. M. Fuller and Company had been a member of the Consolidated Exchange for eight years. While it was known that Fuller was one of the companies receiving clients when Charles A. Stoneham and Company closed its books, Stoneham became more deeply involved in the case when the Fuller owners, Edward Fuller and William McGee, testified in court hearings that Charley Stoneham was a silent partner in the firm, something Stoneham had denied on at least two separate occasions. During a Fuller-McGee bankruptcy hearing before bankruptcy referee Harold P. Coffin, Stoneham was asked directly by attorney Carl Austrian about his "real" relationship with E. M. Fuller and Company.

AUSTRIAN: Mr. Stoneham, do you realize you are under oath?
STONEHAM: I do.
AUSTRIAN: Then you say that you were not a special partner of E. M. Fuller and Co.?

STONEHAM: I do. If I wanted to continue in Wall Street, I would have remained in business. I had a better business than E. M. Fuller.[16]

At a July hearing before Referee Coffin, Stoneham was asked about checks from the National Exhibition Company totaling $147,000 that made their way to E. M. Fuller and Company through Tammany boss Big Tom Foley. Foley testified in court that he wanted to help the brokerage house stay solvent. Stoneham was explicit in his own testimony that the money he gave Foley was a loan and not a payment for interest in the Fuller firm: "I borrowed money from the National Exhibition Company and put up my own securities with the company (as collateral). . . . Foley said he would like to befriend Fuller by trying to stop the run then going on. . . . I would not have loaned the money had not Foley requested me to do so."[17] The federal grand jury, with the confessions of both Fuller and McGee in hand, did not accept Stoneham's denials about a silent partnership and indicted him for perjury on August 31, 1923.[18]

The Fuller-McGee legal proceedings would drag on for more than four years, involving numerous bankruptcy hearings, criminal trials that included three mistrials, and both Fuller's and McGee's jailing for contempt of court charges for failing to disclose documents to the trustee in the Fuller bankruptcy, all of which provided great copy for New York newspapers and tabloids. In addition to ensnaring Stoneham, the Fuller-McGee proceedings would expose the sensational exploits of a number of Broadway's personalities. The principals themselves, Ed Fuller and William McGee—described by one of their attorneys as likable roughnecks who lacked moral scruples, ready for any racket that would bring in "jack"—would be involved in four bankruptcy trials, three of them ending with hung juries, largely due to the courtroom shenanigans and legal antics of their primary defense attorney, William J. Fallon, known throughout the city as "the Great Mouthpiece."[19] Other famous and notorious characters swept up in the hearings included

Big Tom Foley, gambling kingpin Arnold Rothstein, and William S. Silkworth, the president of the Consolidated Stock Exchange. The parade of witnesses, depositions, and examinations in court, along with the mistrials and hung juries, extended the proceedings from weeks into months. The Fuller-McGee proceedings were delayed further by attempts from lawyers representing creditors to audit accounts in order to determine the value of the holdings. Fuller and Company paid out some money but felt it would be better off in the hands of the court for the protection of the remaining creditors.[20]

As it worked its way toward a conclusion, the reverberations of the Fuller-McGee hearings were widely felt. Fuller and McGee, in addition to spending time in Ludlow Street jail in May 1923 for contempt charges, pleaded guilty two years later to mail fraud and served time in Sing Sing.[21] Silkworth resigned his post as president of the Consolidated Exchange in June 1923, was indicted on mail fraud charges by a federal grand jury in May 1924, and was convicted in a Manhattan federal court on November 29, 1924.[22] After its negative exposure in the Fuller-McGee case, the Consolidated Exchange ceased operations in 1926.[23] Rothstein was indicted for hiding one of Fuller's assets from the bankruptcy court—a Pierce-Arrow sedan—but the case never went to trial.[24] Fallon was charged with bribing a juror in the third Fallon-McGee bankruptcy trial in 1924, hid from the police for three weeks with his mistress, was captured, and defended himself in court successfully, although after the ordeal, he was a broken man and died on April 29, 1927, at the age of forty-one.[25] Foley died in 1925 while the bankruptcy proceedings were still ongoing. Stoneham's continued involvement in the Fuller-McGee bankruptcy would eventually play out in criminal court.

That the Fuller-McGee trial swept up a number of Jazz Age celebrities was not lost on one discerning reader of the New York press. Jazz Age chronicler F. Scott Fitzgerald paid particular attention to the case, especially when he learned that Edward Fuller was one of his Great Neck Long Island neighbors. Fitzgerald had moved to Great Neck in 1922—the year that the Fuller-McGee trial began—just as he was beginning to draft his ideas for *The Great Gatsby*. In a 1924 letter to his editor, Max Perkins, at Charles Scribner's Sons, Fitzgerald states that he followed the Fuller-McGee trial closely and it gave him considerable material for the novel.[26] That Fitzgerald based the character of Jay Gatsby's business partner Meyer Wolfshiem on Arnold Rothstein is well known. What is less known about the Fuller trial's influence on *The Great Gatsby* is that Charley Stoneham and Edward Fuller also find their way into the novel, although less directly than Rothstein. According to Fitzgerald scholar Henry Dan Piper, Fitzgerald borrowed heavily from the newspaper accounts of Fuller's business affairs in creating Gatsby, especially the character's murky business connections. Piper categorizes Stoneham as "another mysterious Gatsby-like figure" whose rise in the shady stock brokerage business added to the backdrop for Fitzgerald's main character. Moreover, Stoneham's paternal interest in Fuller, who was much younger than Stoneham, was revealed in courtroom testimony. It was this relationship, Piper asserts, that piqued Fitzgerald's interest and is paralleled in the novel in Dan Cody's friendship for Gatsby.[27]

The demands of the Fuller-McGee proceedings were pulling Stoneham away from any attention he might give his baseball team, frustrating him. It was just the beginning. He would soon see those frustrations intensify as his legal problems deepened. Pushed to the background by the pace and exigency of the Fuller-McGee bankruptcy trials, the Dier case would suddenly and dramatically reemerge and demand Stoneham's immediate attention. On January 11, 1924, a Manhattan federal grand jury indicted Stoneham for mail fraud in the transfer of accounts to E. D. Dier and Company.[28] For the foreseeable future, Stoneham would find his world turned upside down. His daily routine would involve regular attendance at the court; he was only an occasional visitor to the Polo Grounds. In a matter of six months, Stoneham was now immersed in fighting two criminal charges stemming from a business practice he thought he had placed behind him. An unfavorable outcome in either case not only could threaten his place in baseball but would likely send him to prison.

The sporting world took notice, of course, questioning Stoneham's place in his newly chosen field. *The Sporting News*, the national news source on baseball, called attention to Stoneham's plight in the fall of 1924. Commenting on the charge of mail fraud in the Dier case, the editorial speculated on Stoneham's future in baseball: "If by any chance Stoneham should escape conviction of that [the Dier indictment], another ordeal awaits him: a perjury charge with the bankrupt firm of Fuller and McGee. . . . In the event of conviction on either charge, or both charges, it will be interesting, as well as illuminating to see what Commissioner Landis, or the National League, will do about Mr. Stoneham further representing officially the New York club."[29] *Collyer's Eye*, a Chicago weekly with a taste for scandal and gossip, claimed that circus impresario John Ringling and former Yankees owner Colonel Tillinghast Huston offered to buy the Giants as a consequence of Stoneham's legal troubles.[30] New York newspapers reported various rumors about Stoneham's interest in selling the Giants, a story he consistently denied.[31] These reports continued to circulate despite the resounding faith that the National Exhibition Company had shown at the annual stockholders meeting in November 1923, reelecting Stoneham to the presidency of the organization by acclamation.[32]

The Dier jury trial, before Judge Francis A. Winslow, began in federal district court in January 1925 and lasted seven weeks. The proceedings were bitterly contested, as both sides were determined to exhaust every legal avenue, often provoking the ire of the court. The complaint against Stoneham made references to irregularities and even illegalities in the transfer of securities to Dier, but the essence of the indictment was the implication by Charles A. Stoneham and Company in letters to customers that Dier was solvent when it was not.[33] In the weeks that followed, objections, interruptions, and bickering slowed the proceedings, prompting Judge Winslow to threaten to hold night sessions to move the case forward. In a statement from the bench, he admonished both sides: "I regret the court has found it necessary to fill the record with so many remarks. I have no use for a talking judge, but you have made it necessary."[34] Even matters of evidence proved contentious, sometimes due to its limitations. Subpoenas for records and transactions of security transfers produced only the final letter announcing the closure of Charles A. Stoneham and Company. All of the other records, including certificates of ownership, securities, and accounting files, went missing or were absorbed into the records of other agents and firms that handled the various transfers. Stoneham's lawyers explained that Charles A. Stoneham and Company was not a member of the Consolidated Exchange but an independent agent and worked cooperatively with different brokers and firms in transfers.[35]

The prosecuting assistant U.S. attorney Victor House stated that he "intends to prove Charles A. Stoneham as a thief" and that Stoneham knew Dier was insolvent.[36] In his zeal to expose Stoneham, House expanded his accusation to include an allegation that Stoneham (and Dier) had operated bucket shops known for playing fast and loose with clients' money. This turn in House's prosecutorial strategy proved ineffective, not only because in responding to questioning about bucket shop practices, Stoneham proved to be an unaccommodating witness, forgetting some details and denying others, but also because bucketing was not yet regulated by the Securities and Exchange Commission and as such was under state jurisdiction. Judge Winslow was quick to notice. He rightly insisted that House confine his prosecution to the charge in the indictment, specifically that there was a scheme to defraud by mail: "I have never in my life before had such difficulties in keeping counsel within the limits of the issue."[37]

Led by his attorney Herbert Smyth, Stoneham took the stand in his own defense, testifying that he had relied on Hughes & Dier's reputation among brokers as a reputable firm, with an impressive volume of business and substantial real property holdings. On cross-examination, House grilled Stoneham but made little headway. House had almost no firm records—Charles A. Stoneham and Company destroyed its files after the 1921 tax return—and Stoneham gave vague answers, unable to recall the specifics of most transactions and clients.[38] After closing arguments from both sides, Judge Winslow instructed the jury that there had to be proof beyond a reasonable doubt that the defendant had devised a scheme to defraud Dier firm investors and that the mail was used to further this scheme.[39] The jury reached its verdict in relatively short order and acquitted Stoneham of mail fraud charges on February 27, 1925.[40] Commenting on the case, one writer conjectured that the prosecutor's zeal for conviction, prompted by his undisciplined display of contempt for Stoneham, may have swayed the jury to rule for the defendant.[41]

One historian suggests that the acquittal in the Dier case "saved the Giants for Stoneham."[42] This view might be somewhat exaggerated, but there can be no doubt that it eased the pressure on Stoneham and, for that matter, on Commissioner Landis and some of the National League owners who had called for Stoneham to step down. Landis had come into his leadership role by taking a broom to the gambling mess in baseball, most famously in the Black Sox scandal, banning the eight Chicago players who had cooperated with the gamblers to throw the 1919 World Series. He punctuated that action by putting a number of other players on the ineligible list for even a slight tinge of connection with gambling, most recently Jimmy O'Connell and Cozy Dolan, establishing his reputation as a no-nonsense commissioner. One decision in particular resonated with Stoneham's legal troubles. Benny Kauff, a Giants player from 1919 to 1921 had been indicted in a case involving auto theft but was later acquitted. Landis nonetheless put Kauff on the permanently ineligible list, claiming that "an indictment charging felonious misconduct by a player certainly charges conduct detrimental to the good repute of baseball."[43] Some in the press wondered if Landis, given his zealous pursuit to clean up baseball, would be as hard on Stoneham, stuck as he was in the muddle of the Dier case. If Kauff's mere indictment (rather than conviction) was enough in Landis's mind to ban him from baseball, one writer reasoned that Landis must do the same with Stoneham, "whose indictment and whose record as a bucket shop man make his presence in baseball deeply offensive to the public and injurious to the good repute of the game."[44] Another writer thought that in ignoring Stoneham, the commissioner was guilty of a double standard: "For Commissioner Landis . . . the Stoneham case has proved to be both puzzling and embarrassing, That high official, who has made a humble player, Kauff, permanently ineligible on 'moral' grounds, though acquitted in court of theft charges . . . can find no grounds for eliminating Stoneham from the old league as he has done nothing whatever in contravention of baseball pending his conviction of the criminal charges against him is a double standard."[45] Stoneham's acquittal in the Dier case put some of the questions about Landis' judgment to rest, at least with respect to Stoneham's place in the game, although there was still the Fuller-McGee case ongoing. And with a wait-and-see posture on Stoneham's fate, most of the commissioner's critics concluded that consistency was not one of Landis's hallmarks.

The commissioner's inconsistency with Stoneham, or, to be more precise, the commissioner's silence, seems even more remarkable in light of how sternly and unequivocally judgment was passed on various players. Akin to the famous silent, inactive dog in the nighttime in one of fictional detective Sherlock Holmes's famous cases, Landis made no remarks or references, preferring strict silence about Stoneham's ongoing legal problems.[46] Yet curiously, not all of Stoneham's gambling activities or associations went without some notice from the Commissioner's Office, another gauge of Landis's inconsistency. Stoneham and McGraw's ownership of the Oriental Park and casino in Havana provoked an ultimatum from Landis that the Giants' owners make a decision: either divest themselves of the Cuban property and business or get out of baseball. Stoneham and McGraw complied and sold their interest in the Havana racetrack and gambling house in the summer of 1921.[47] Stoneham also drew a stern rebuke from Landis when it was reported that gambling king Arnold Rothstein was a regular guest in the owner's box at the Polo Grounds in 1922 and 1923, prompting Stoneham, in the interest of harmony with the Commissioner's Office, to cut off any future passes for Rothstein.[48]

With the Dier acquittal behind him, Stoneham could claim some respite, but he was not out of the legal woods just yet. Residue from the Dier case remained. For one, he had to contend with various nuisance civil lawsuits filed by disaffected investors claiming damage due to Charles A. Stoneham and Company's transfers of accounts and security mismanagement. While these were nagging, Stoneham appeared to have settled them without much fanfare.[49] For another, the district attorney of New York, Joab Banton, thought seriously about charging Stoneham with operating a bucket shop (a state offense) but decided that with the Stoneham firm's books gone, it would be a difficult charge to sustain.[50] Banton's decision not to go forward effectively ended Stoneham's peril from state law enforcement authorities.

A more serious difficulty was still pending in federal court, however: the perjury indictment stemming from the Fuller-McGee bankruptcy. In this proceeding Stoneham was the beneficiary of a serendipitous organizational change and focus in the U.S. attorney's office. In March 1925 Emory Buckner was appointed the new U.S. attorney for the Southern District of New York. Buckner decided to turn his efforts into a conscientious enforcement of Prohibition laws in the city and had little enthusiasm for prosecution of stale holdover cases.[51] As a result, Buckner was content to let the Stoneham perjury charge languish. Two years later, on his last day in office, April 6, 1927, Buckner administratively dismissed Stoneham's indictment.[52] The only thing left for Stoneham to settle would be bankruptcy proceedings against him filed by a few Fuller creditors, which would be finished by the year's end. New York Giants historian Bill Lamb concludes: "There is little reason to suspect that the Fuller creditors got much, if anything, from Charles A. Stoneham. His soft outward appearance was deceptive. The deep-pocketed Stoneham was brazen, tough-minded, and determined when it came to seeing his enemies in court."[53] After more than five arduous and taxing years, Stoneham could leave the New York courts behind.

Having run the grueling legal gauntlet that effectively put his brokerage business behind him for good, Charley Stoneham finally could give his undivided attention to important issues regarding the New York Giants. He was eager for this new focus. For the past few years, in what could be described as a part-time effort at best, he had been dealing with a crucial problem confronting his team: the Giants were losing ground in fan popularity to the New York Yankees. Stoneham was keen to restore the Giants' place as New York City's team and to win back the city's fans who had embraced New York's American League team. Almost every year since 1920, the Yankees outdrew the Giants in attendance, despite the Giants' dominance of the National League, winning four straight pennants (1921–24) and beating the Yankees twice in the World Series (1921 and 1922). It would require concentration and effort to get his team back to its accustomed position as the toast of the town, but after so much time in New York's courtrooms, Stoneham was both relieved and eager to take on the challenge.

Fig. 1. Charley Stoneham as a young man, ready to make
his way on Wall Street. Rupert Family Collection.

Fig. 2. Stoneham benefited from his Irish American connections with Tammany Hall leaders such as Al Smith and Charles F. Murphy. Steve Steinberg Collection.

Fig. 3. (*opposite top*) Charles F. Murphy and Big Tom Foley, Tammany Hall figures known to Stoneham, at the funeral of Tim Sullivan, another Tammany leader. Grand public funerals were common during the Jazz Age. Library of Congress, Prints & Photographs Division, LC-DIG-ggbain-14320.

Fig. 4. 1920's movie star Rudolph Valentino and designer-actress Natacha Rambova, a flamboyant Jazz Age couple. Valentino's funeral in 1926 was witnessed by thousands in New York. Steve Steinberg Collection.

Fig. 5. F. Scott Fitzgerald's *The Great Gatsby* was published in 1925, depicting the pace and glamour of the Jazz Age. Fitzgerald drew on the activities of Stoneham and some of his acquaintances, including Arnold Rothstein and Edward Fuller, as background for the novel. Cover of the novel, *Celestial Eyes*, by Francis Cugat. Charles Scribner's Sons.

Fig. 6. Stoneham at the beginning of his career as an
investment broker. Steve Steinberg Collection.

Fig. 7. (*right*) Hannah Stoneham at the beginning of the Jazz Age. Rupert Family Collection.

Fig. 8. The triumvirate partners Francis X. McQuade, Charles A. Stoneham, and John J. McGraw at the beginning of their ownership of the Giants, January 1919. Steve Steinberg Collection.

Fig. 9. The Polo Grounds when Charley Stoneham took over the National
Exhibition Company. The Giants and the Yankees would play there
in the early 1920s, sharing the facility. In 1921 Stoneham gave the Yankees
a two-year notice to find their own home. Yankee Stadium opened
in 1923. Dennis Goldstein Collection.

Fig. 10. Stoneham (*third from the left in the middle row*) was a new member of Major League Baseball owners and executives in 1919. Dennis Goldstein Collection.

Fig. 11. (*top*) Judge Kenesaw Mountain Landis signed an agreement to become commissioner of baseball in January 1921. Stoneham (*fifth from the right in the back row*) stands with the group of owners present in Landis's chambers. *Chicago Daily News* Collection, Chicago History Museum, sdn-062284.

Fig. 12. (*right*) Jimmy
O'Connell became
permanently ineligible
because of his involvement
in an alleged bribery scandal.
Michael Mumby Collection.

Fig. 13. Giants coach
Cozy Dolan (*standing*),
who was connected to
O'Connell in the bribery
scandal, sought to clear his
name by hiring William
J. Fallon, a flamboyant
Broadway attorney. Michael
Mumby Collection.

Fig. 14. (*above*) Stoneham, Elmore Dier (*standing*), and Ross Robertson were tried in U.S. District Court for mail fraud in connection with their investment businesses. Rupert Family Collection.

Fig. 15. While the Dier trial was ongoing, Stoneham also faced perjury charges in the bankruptcy of E. M. Fuller and Company. Stoneham is shown here in 1923 with his attorney in the Fuller trial, Edward McCall, former state supreme court justice. Rupert Family Collection.

Fig. 16. Stoneham, Dier, and Robertson were acquitted in February 1925. The celebratory group shot was taken after the verdict was read. May Boylan (*center*) was identified by the newspaper as an assistant attorney, but she was actually Stoneham's secretary assistant and a key witness in the Dier hearings. Rupert Family Collection.

Fig. 17. Arnold Rothstein, Broadway gambling impresario and New York City underworld king, was Stoneham's acquaintance for over twenty years. Library of Congress, Prints and Photographs Division, *New York World-Telegram and the Sun* Newspaper Collection, LC-USZ62-116745.

Fig. 18. Jazz Age mayor Jimmy Walker throwing out a ceremonial first pitch in 1927, with Stoneham in the background. Michael Mumby Collection.

Fig. 19. One of the most famous plays in baseball history, Rogers Hornsby, tags Babe Ruth, attempting to steal second base, for the final out of the 1926 World Series, giving the St. Louis Cardinals the championship. National Baseball Hall of Fame Library, Cooperstown NY.

Fig. 20. Stoneham and McGraw signed Rogers Hornsby to play for the Giants in 1927 in the hopes that he would challenge Ruth as a New York fan favorite. Steve Steinberg Collection.

Fig. 21. Frankie Frisch was a favorite of John McGraw in the early 1920s. In 1926 McGraw soured on Frisch, making it possible for Stoneham to trade Hornsby for Frisch in late December of that year. Steve Steinberg Collection.

Fig. 22. The Giants organized a John McGraw celebration on July 19, 1927, to honor his twenty-five years as a Giants manager. Mayor Jimmy Walker presented McGraw with a silver trophy, with Judge Landis *in the background*. Commander Richard Byrd, in his white dress uniform, *is standing next to* Charley Stoneham. Steve Steinberg Collection.

Fig. 23. The Giants and Brooklyn Robins team executives, circa 1929.
Robins president (and manager) Wilbur Robinson is *seated in the front
row* with Stoneham and McGraw. Dennis Goldstein Collection.

Fig. 24. (*top*)The National League owners, circa 1933, one of the last meetings Charley Stoneham would attend. Rupert Family Collection.

Fig. 25. Stoneham with McGraw at the 1933 World Series. Charley's expression suggests that he is no longer troubled by any legal problems with McQuade and can give full attention to the game of baseball. Steve Steinberg Collection.

Fig. 26. McGraw congratulates the new Giants manager, Bill Terry, on the team's great success in the 1933 season. Steve Steinberg Collection.

Figs. 27. and 28. (*opposite*) Terry's teams in the mid-1930s benefited from great pitching, especially from Carl Hubbell, and timely hitting from Terry and Mel Ott, Jo-Jo Moore, and Lefty O'Doul. Courtesy of the Boston Public Library, Leslie Jones Collection.

Fig. 29. Stoneham in 1935, one of the last photographs
taken of him. Dennis Goldstein Collection.

6

The Battle for New York

There must have been moments even that afternoon
when Daisy tumbled short of his dreams—not through her
own fault, but because of the colossal vitality of
his illusion. It had gone beyond her, beyond everything.

—F. SCOTT FITZGERALD, *The Great Gatsby*

By the late autumn of 1926 and in his eighth year as owner of the New York Giants, Charley Stoneham sensed that his baseball team was entering difficult and, up to this moment in its history, unfamiliar territory. Although he had ceded almost all of the baseball operations to John McGraw and despite his legal distractions over the past four years, he followed the progress of the club closely. And what he sensed about the Giants and the New York market disturbed him. Over the past few years, he had witnessed firsthand the steady surge of affection among the city's fans for his American League rival, the New York Yankees, and the corresponding decline of his Giants as the town's favorite sports team. What confounded Stoneham about this turn of events was that it came in spite of the Giants' phenomenal success on the field. Although 1926 was a down year—the Giants finished in the league's second division for the first time since 1915, with a losing record of 74–77—it stood in stark comparison to the results of previous Stoneham years: four pennants, three second-place finishes, and two World Series championships, both of them against the Yankees.[1] The 1926 attendance, the lowest in the postwar era, suggested the fickleness of New York baseball fans.

Giants manager John McGraw was also concerned by this shift in fan interest, but his reaction would be driven by personal resentment. McGraw had been New York's premier baseball personality for years. The rise of the Yankees threatened that status. Moreover, his resentment of the Yankees was also driven by his dislike of the junior circuit. Never someone who believed the American League equal to National League clubs nor who admired American League president Ban Johnson, McGraw held the Yankees in contempt, chiding them as a team without a home, dependent on the Giants as their landlords in order to play at the Polo Grounds, an agreement that, for McGraw at least, symbolically implied the Giants' superiority. It was particularly annoying to McGraw when he learned midway through the 1920 season that the Yankees were outdrawing the Giants and would do so for the remainder of their stay in the Polo Grounds.[2]

The 1920 attendance figures got under McGraw's skin. In a sense of pique, he suggested to Stoneham that the Giants cancel the Yankees' lease. Stoneham, who may have felt the same, nonetheless thought the better of immediate eviction. He raised the Yankees' annual rent instead and gave owners Jacob Ruppert and Tillinghast Huston a two-year notice to find a new home, which they did, moving across the Harlem River to the Bronx and opening a new ballpark for 1923 season.[3] Continuing his Yankee bashing, McGraw shrugged off the move, suggesting that the Giants' former tenant had given up Manhattan, the heart of New York City, to go up to Goatville.[4] When the 1923 World Series again featured the matchup of the Giants against the Yankees, McGraw's simmering resentment toward his American League rival boiled over into what one McGraw biographer terms genuine hatred, "not just as intruders into his world, but as potential heirs to it."[5]

Despite his bitterness and air of superiority McGraw understood he had a public relations struggle on his hands. So did Stoneham. They knew that the recent attendance losses had less to do with the Giants' performance—only in 1926 did they not finish either first or second in the league—and more to do with the emergence of Babe

Ruth as a baseball superstar. Ruth had arrived in New York for the 1920 season and dominated his sport as no one ever had. In his first season as a Yankee, he hit fifty-four home runs, nine more than the entire Giants team managed that year. He was big both on and off the field, with a winning, outgoing personality and a huge appetite for the city's restaurants and nightlife, pushing everyone and everything off of the city's sports pages. He had become an instantaneous city personality, gathering fans wherever he went and taking the Yankees to new heights. The Giants had no such personality; even McGraw, who often commanded headlines in the city's newspapers, couldn't match the flamboyant Ruth.

The Babe's timing could not have been better; he dropped onto the New York scene at precisely the optimal moment. This was, after all, the Jazz Age, when Americans everywhere craved heroes, bigger-than-life celebrities—movie stars, daredevils, sports figures—to show them it was possible to excel, break barriers, and enjoy life. Jazz Age Americans also were dreamers, striving for something great. The fictional Jay Gatsby, the quintessential Jazz Age dreamer, strives to reclaim the love of Daisy Buchanan, a girl from his past. In the end Gatsby fails, primarily as a result of his excessive imagination. The object of his longing—an ordinary woman, after all, insecure and self-doubting—had, in Fitzgerald's wonderful phrase, "tumbled short of his dreams."[6] But it is Gatsby's effort that characterizes the drive of the Jazz Age, as young Americans, especially, strove for a brighter future and a happier life. Eager to forget the horrors of a world war and an even more deadly flu pandemic, they conjured up a new life of prosperity, improvement, glamour, and joy. The lifestyle was to spend quickly, live large, and let tomorrow take care of itself. Business was booming, young people were seeking out new freedoms, and New York City seemed to be the center of the new vitality and upbeat energy.

McGraw and Stoneham were also Jazz Age dreamers, perhaps not in the extreme Gatsby mode but close enough. Their dream to return the

Giants to their rightful place as New York's preeminent team echoes what some readers identify as the central theme in *The Great Gatsby*: "the attempt to recapture a lost vision of happiness."[7] McGraw and Stoneham's yearning to restore the Giants' prestige was shaped by an obsession to solve their Ruth problem, that is, to find their own superstar who could match and compete with the "Bambino." They decided on Rogers Hornsby of the St. Louis Cardinals, who many believed was the greatest hitter in the game, better overall than even the power-hitting Ruth. The choice of Hornsby would require the Giants' owners to exercise their imaginations, exaggerate his value as a clubhouse presence and personality, and overlook unattractive aspects of his character. Moreover, their effort to acquire Hornsby would not be a swift or easy proposition, extending over seven years and involving a number of failed attempts. The full story of Hornsby's year in New York—how Stoneham and McGraw pursued him, what happened to him as a Giants player and personality, and how he would not measure up to both McGraw's and especially Stoneham's dreams and aspirations—epitomizes a Gatsby-like Jazz Age tale, especially in its disappointing results.

For both Stoneham and McGraw, getting Rogers Hornsby into a New York Giants uniform was motivated by a deep conviction that the Giants needed their own superstar. That idea was born out of a desperation to counter Babe Ruth as both a player and a personality, in the hopes that starstruck fans would consider the Giants once again as New York's team. Initially, McGraw and Stoneham were caught off guard by Ruth's popularity and drawing power, but they soon took notice. For many in Jazz Age New York, the Babe proved the perfect hero for an era characterized by extravagance. His popularity with fans extended even to road games, for which the Yankees drew better than any club in the American League.[8] As baseball historian Peter Williams put it, Ruth was colossal, even in a decade of excess: "His appetite, whether for home runs, hot dogs, women, steaks, or beer, was immense. No public figure of any kind in the mid-1920s better symbolized the mercantile gluttony of the American people."[9]

But for McGraw and Stoneham, their take on Ruth was not personal; it was strictly business. In 1925 they watched a Yankee team slide in attendance, drawing fewer fans in the team's new state-of-the-art ballpark that season than the Giants did in the older Polo Grounds. It would be the only year in the decade when the Giants would outdraw the Yankees. But Stoneham and McGraw could hardly take solace. They knew the reason that the Yankees were drawing poorly—they would finish in the second division of the American League that season—had to do with Ruth, or rather his absence, as he was ill or injured for most of the year.[10] In fact, the small success the Giants had that year in outpacing the Yankees only drove the point home more clearly to both Stoneham and McGraw: the importance of a superstar to a franchise. After the 1926 season, brutal reality set in. With Ruth back from his injuries and illnesses, both he and the Yankees surged. He led the league in home runs, runs batted in (RBIs), and runs scored, and the Yankees won the American League pennant. Stoneham and McGraw took notice. A comparison of the two seasons left no doubt for the Giants' front office. To reclaim supremacy in New York's baseball world, they would have to counter Ruth.[11]

For McGraw, Ruth's presence posed a more complicated challenge than just attendance figures. While the Giants' skipper had managed to neutralize the Ruth-led Yankees in the 1921 and 1922 World Series contests, he came to a troubling realization that the game he knew so well and had mastered was changing. Ruth had introduced a new style of play, away from the small ball, base-stealing, pitching-dominated game to one of power, a big inning, with emphasis on the home run. Fans now wanted to see Ruth hit the ball out of the park rather than watch the low-scoring, strategic matchup that McGraw favored. It was Ruth the player rather than Ruth the personality who pushed the Giants to consider adapting their style of play to favor more offense—something Stoneham would leave to McGraw. They would need their own big hitter to effect that change, one who could, coincidentally, compete with the big Yankee slugger as a box office attraction. In short, they needed to find a player with a great deal of fan appeal.

Their remedy came into focus during the 1926 World Series matchup featuring the Yankees against the St. Louis Cardinals, pitting the power-hitting Ruth against the perennial National League batting champion Hornsby. Stoneham, in particular, was excited about the chance to concentrate on baseball matters, having been tied up for three years in legal problems that were now, for the most part, behind him. As guests of the Cardinals at Yankee Stadium, both he and McGraw would have every chance to see the matchup of the two marquee players. But if the Giants bosses hoped to watch Hornsby excel at the plate or see some significant difference between these stars, they were disappointed. As it turned out, the two headliners had muted World Series performances, Hornsby with seven hits and four RBIs, Ruth with six hits—although four of his were home runs—and five RBIs. One dramatic moment might have offered a keen insight, however. On the last play of the series, the final out, Hornsby tagged Ruth in an attempted steal of second, giving the Cardinals the World Series championship, the only time in baseball history that a World Series would end that way. It is tempting to think that for both Stoneham and McGraw, that final out held great symbolic importance, its image signifying perhaps a new possibility in New York baseball, with Hornsby if not nullifying, then at least neutralizing Ruth. What is certain, however, is that during that winter, Stoneham and McGraw resolved to contact St. Louis and acquire Hornsby for the Giants.

It should be remembered that Stoneham and McGraw's decision to act on Hornsby in December 1926, while motivated by their sense of the recent slide in Giants' attendance, was the culmination of a concerted effort over the years to gain a player whom respected sportswriter John P. Sheridan termed "probably the greatest hitter of all time."[12] McGraw had long coveted Hornsby, going back to 1919, the first year of Stoneham's ownership. McGraw had an eye for talent and recognized the greatness in Hornsby; he considered the Cardinal infielder the best hitter in the National League. It is also important to note that this early interest in Hornsby had nothing to do with Ruth—he was still a Red Sox pitcher at the time—and everything to do with Hornsby's potential as a star player.

The Giants' first attempt to wrest Hornsby from the Cardinals came in September 1919. McGraw convinced Stoneham that an investment in Hornsby would be shrewd. Stoneham, still learning the ropes as a first-year owner, took McGraw's advice. They contacted Branch Rickey, the Cardinals' club president and field manager, and set up a meeting for late September, when the Cardinals were in town for a series. In a famous encounter, the Giants owners lured Rickey to a Manhattan tavern, where, according to Rickey biographer Lee Lowenfish, they thought they could make the Cardinals boss an offer that he couldn't refuse.[13] Stoneham and McGraw were drinking men and perhaps imagined the atmosphere of the tavern would aid their persuasive powers, an odd idea considering Rickey was a teetotaler. The meeting came to nothing, as Rickey would not surrender Hornsby unless the Giants included the young hot prospect Frankie Frisch in the deal, something McGraw would not agree to. This would be only the first in a series of attempts to pry Hornsby loose from the Cardinals with Frisch as a key factor in the deal.

The interest in Hornsby was rekindled with a bit more urgency at the end of the 1920 season, Ruth's inaugural year as a Yankee. The Babe burst onto the scene and took the baseball world by storm, becoming an instant sports celebrity. Having assumed that their Giants were the toasts of the town, Stoneham and McGraw had to appreciate that they suddenly faced stiff competition for the New York sports public's attention.[14] With Ruth's effect on attendance now obvious, their need for their own star power became more apparent. In the fall of 1920, they tried again for Hornsby, this time with Stoneham taking more of a lead in the negotiations, offering $200,000 in cash. Once again, Rickey said that he would consider a trade only if Frisch were part of the deal. Once again, the Giants refused.[15] Yet the urgency for Hornsby's talent grew, with the Ruth phenomenon never far from McGraw's and Stoneham's minds. Preparing for the 1921 World Series against the Yankees, McGraw was asked by a reporter about how the Giants would pitch to Ruth. McGraw erupted: "'Ruth!' he went on scornfully. 'Why all the excitement about Ruth? We've been pitching all along to Hornsby and he's a three-to-one better hitter than Ruth.'"[16]

In the 1923 World Series, the Giants lost convincingly to the Yankees, with Ruth hitting three home runs. Both Stoneham and McGraw realized that changes needed to be made sooner than later for the Giants to best the Yankees at the turnstiles. In November they renewed their negotiations with Rickey, driven by the fact that they had failed in two previous attempts to get Hornsby, which made his star appeal seem somehow even more alluring. In remarks to the press about his plans for the future, McGraw said he had been trying for several seasons to land Hornsby, whom he considered the greatest right-handed hitter in the game, and "was willing to offer more money than any player in history had commanded."[17] Stoneham, familiar with the hard edge of business negotiations, was particularly eager for a return engagement with Rickey, thinking the Giants might break through this time. But it was not to be. The meeting followed the same script, involved the same two players, and ended with the same results. The only difference in the outcome came in McGraw's reaction. Usually accustomed to having his way with player acquisition and having grown tired over years of Rickey's horse-trading tactics, especially this latest display of inflexibility, McGraw threw in the towel, once and for all. A November interview with the *New York Times* recorded his frustration: "So far as I am concerned the proposed deal for Hornsby is off for all times. St. Louis insisted that if Hornsby was to come to New York, Frisch would have to go to St. Louis. That ended the matter right there. I wouldn't trade Frisch alone for Hornsby or any other player in baseball."[18]

It took only two seasons and a Giants slide in the standings to show

the tenuous nature of McGraw's resolve. The disappointing 1926 season provided the impetus Stoneham and McGraw needed to remake
the team. Everything that could go wrong for a ball club in a season
had just done so. For one thing, a number of Giants players collec-
tively had subpar performances. Injuries and even illness played a
role. Future Hall of Famer and McGraw favorite Ross Youngs was
diagnosed with Bright's disease in 1925 and played only intermittently
in the 1926 season, leaving in early August to check into the hospital.
He would never play another game and died in October 1927 at the age
of thirty.[19] Stalwarts Art Nehf and Heinie Groh were dealt midseason
when McGraw decided that both were on the downside of their careers.
Former NL home run and RBI leader George Kelly was released at the
end of the season.

The greatest disappointment in the 1926 season, certainly for McGraw
personally, was the rebellion of Giants captain Frank Frisch, who tem-
porarily quit the team in August during an away series against St. Louis.
Fed up with McGraw's tyrannical control of team play and his consistent
criticism, especially over the past two seasons, when McGraw would
single Frisch out for lack of effort whenever the team lost, Frisch left
the team in St. Louis and took the train back to New York, informing
no one. Once home, he tipped off the press about his general fatigue,
both physical and mental, keeping him from playing at a competitive
level. While Frisch rejoined the team in mid-September and played
the remainder of the season, he never regained McGraw's confidence
or good graces.[20] The Giants finished the season mired in fifth place
and their first losing season in eleven years, while the Yankees, with
a healthy Ruth returning to lead the team, won the American League
pennant and once again outdrew the Giants.

So it was that in the winter of 1926, with renewed determination, the
Giants were back on the hunt to find their own superstar. The dream
and the illusion were strong for both Stoneham and McGraw. Hornsby
floated back into their minds; his star power might do wonders for the
team, give them a big name to compete with Ruth, propel them upward

in the standings, and maybe bring in more fans. Moreover, the blow-up between McGraw and Frisch had made the Giants infielder expendable, giving the team a new option in what was previously a chief stumbling block to any trade talks. This time Stoneham decided to take the lead. Perhaps he sensed that the stress of McGraw's recent disappointing season had made him less effective in brokering a deal or that an owner-to-owner negotiation would produce quick results.[21] Whatever his thinking, Stoneham worked directly with Sam Breadon, the Cardinals owner, who had reached his limit of patience with Hornsby, whose prima donna behavior was irksome (his nickname, "the Rajah," reflected his imperious disposition as much as it was a play on his first name).

Hornsby had always been a difficult personality. In his time with the Cardinals, he bickered constantly with manager Branch Rickey, criticized the front office, and disparaged most of his teammates. St. Louis sportswriter John P. Sheridan summed up what most felt about Hornsby: "He impressed many people as being distant and preoccupied, if not downright unfriendly. . . . distinctly aloof from his teammates, he insisted on rooming by himself . . . hard to approach, difficult to understand, he seemed to have nothing but contempt for the usual likes and dislikes of the average player."[22]

Certainly, Breadon knew firsthand his star player's prickly arrogance. Hornsby, in his role as the Cardinals' player-manager, had a number of disagreements with ownership over the 1926 season, complaining to the press that the Cardinal front office kept interfering with the day-to-day management of the team, despite not knowing how the game was played. Hornsby's public complaints led to more testy exchanges that offended Breadon so much that he was determined not to bring his player-manager back for the 1927 season, despite the team's success as 1926 World Champions. In early December he purposefully offered a salary that did not match Hornsby's demands. When Hornsby officially refused the contract, Breadon immediately got on the phone to

Stoneham, who agreed to a trade.[23] The decision was rather easy for the Giants front office. They finally landed the player they had been chasing for seven years.

The reaction to the trade rippled through the columns of the nation's newspapers. "The biggest deal in modern baseball history," wrote James R. Harrison of the *New York Times*.[24] On the West Coast, the Hornsby trade made headlines in the *Los Angeles Times*.[25] Much of the coverage focused on Frankie Frisch, the player who only a few years earlier McGraw had said he would never give up "for Hornsby or any other player in baseball." Always a Cardinal priority in the discussions about giving up Hornsby, Frisch had become expendable after his estrangement from McGraw. To secure Hornsby, the Giants gave up Frisch and pitcher Jimmy Ring, with no cash involved. According to one New York Giants historian, the inclusion of Ring was apparently McGraw's idea, a final swipe at Frisch, lest he think that the trade was a one-for-one deal and he was the equal of Hornsby.[26]

So eager were the Giants to rid themselves of Frisch and gain Hornsby that they were prepared to settle a financial complication that threatened to scuttle the trade. Hornsby owned stock in the St. Louis Cardinals corporation and needed to sever all ties with one National League club before joining another. Breadon and Hornsby disagreed over the value of the stock, holding up the settlement. Eventually, feeling the pressure of both the deadline of opening day and the need for Hornsby's presence in the Giants' lineup, Stoneham took the lead. He formulated a price that both parties accepted and then convinced the other National League owners to pay a modest surcharge to Breadon so that matters would be resolved. To that end, the Giants also paid a disproportionate amount of the surcharge and covered Hornsby's attorney fees so that his eligibility would not be subject to question.[27] With all the contractual wrangling behind him, Hornsby opened the season as the Giants' second baseman on Tuesday, April 2, 1927, and would play the entire season.

Things looked rosy for both the Giants and Hornsby at the beginning of the 1927 season. The Giants had their man, and Stoneham and McGraw named him as team captain. Hornsby was all smiles as he met the local press and obliged them with favorable reflections on his New York situation and took a final swipe at his former team: "I'm tickled to death. I'm glad to play ball in the greatest baseball town in the country for the greatest manager in the world . . . the way I like to do it—yes or no, without any hagglin' or moanin'—no small town stuff."[28] Once the season began, Hornsby settled in to his role as the club's leader and met his end of the bargain on the field. He played in 155 games, a league record (one game was a tie and had to be replayed), led the league in runs scored and walks, batted .361 (second in the league), hit 26 home runs, and drove in 133 runs. Filling in as field manager when McGraw took ill in midsummer, Hornsby led the Giants to a 45–12 record, pulling them out of their slow start to challenge for the pennant in September. The team finished 92–62, two games behind Pittsburgh. All in all, despite missing out on the pennant, 1927 was a good year for Rogers Hornsby the player.

Yet 1927 turned out differently for Stoneham and McGraw; things did not go as they hoped for the Hornsby-led Giants. Ruth set a home run record, the Yankees won the World Series (some scribes call the 1927 Yankees the greatest team of all time), and the Giants, despite a furious finish in late August and September, finished third in the National League. In the crucial New York attendance contest, so important to Stoneham and McGraw, the Yankees outdrew the Giants 1,164,190 to 858,190.[29] Moreover, Hornsby was no answer to Ruth, especially as an off-the-field personality. A loner who had little time for his teammates or the press, he was the antithesis of the gregarious and boisterous Ruth, who was popular with everyone—his teammates, the public at large, and especially the press. Ruth was the perfect figure for 1920s New York journalism, what Ruth biographer Jane Leavy terms "jazz journalism"—a sassy bouquet of sex, money, and gossip, heavy on illustrations and photographs. Ruth was perfect for this genre, Leavy asserts, because he was bigger than life, both on the field and especially off of it, with his flashy, brash, Rabelaisian lifestyle.[30] In comparison, the solitary, private, and, by Jazz Age standards, boring Hornsby attracted no interest from the tabloid writers. In the off-the-field personality contest, so important for fan interest, Ruth completely overshadowed Hornsby.

In hindsight it is surprising to think that the Giants imagined that Hornsby could compete with Ruth as a box office attraction given the differences in their temperaments and personalities. Ever since his arrival in New York in 1920 to join the Yankees, the Babe was a fan favorite. By 1927, as baseball historian Jules Tygiel suggests, "the colossus that was Ruth prevailed not just in baseball, but throughout the national culture."[31] He was seen more broadly by some as the embodiment of the age, whose athletic prowess mirrored the pace, speed, and extravagant pursuit of pleasure in the Jazz Age. Ruth's off-the-field activities matched his oversized athletic persona.[32] His appeal had as much to do with his personality as his baseball talent, observed sportswriter John Kieran: "Fortunately, the Bambino does not have to step out of character to be what he is—an appealing swashbuckling, roistering, boisterous figure who is as natural a showman as the late Phineas T. Barnum."[33] There was no way that the taciturn, private Hornsby could match this kind of blustery star power. Lee Lowenfish notes that the Giants front office probably understood this deep down in their collective thinking but decided to acquire Hornsby anyway, with the hope that "the acquisition could take away some of the attention on Ruth and the Yankees."[34]

It didn't happen, however, primarily because Hornsby could not help himself. The change of scenery had no effect on his actions and conduct. He behaved in New York the same as he had in St. Louis: outspoken, abrupt, cantankerous, aloof, judgmental of both his teammates and ownership, and solitary when he was off the field. In spring training he criticized Giants regulars for their style of play. He remained a loner when the club traveled, often sitting by himself in hotel lobbies. In midseason, filling in as player-manager for an ailing McGraw, Hornsby banned card games and drinking and imposed a curfew on road games, causing a rift in the clubhouse. One New York writer characterized Hornsby's managerial style as blunt and ruggedly honest and his manner as frank to the point of being cruel and subtle as a belch.[35] But it was his brusque criticism of ownership that sealed his fate with the Giants.

After an opening game loss in a crucial mid-September series at Pittsburgh in the heat of the pennant race, Giants club secretary Jim Tierney suggested to Hornsby that the Giants might have won the game if infielder Travis Jackson had not been playing out of position on a crucial play. Hornsby exploded and told Tierney to do his job with hotel rooms, meals, and travel arrangements and let those who know the game manage it. When Stoneham arrived in Pittsburgh the next day for the last two games of the series, Tierney reported his run-in with Hornsby, and Stoneham was livid.[36] The Giants boss had also heard reports about Hornsby publicly denigrating the club's front office, spouting off to the press that if he ever considered full-time management of the Giants, "there would have to be a change in ownership."[37] The next day Stoneham had his own encounter with Hornsby about pinch-hitting, which drew a sharp rejoinder from the thin-skinned and tactless Hornsby: "Are you telling me how to run the ball club? If you don't like the way I'm running the club, get somebody else to do it."[38] For good measure, Hornsby, a teetotaler, added some insulting remarks about Stoneham's drinking.[39] Stoneham took notice. At the season's end, Hornsby would find out how prescient his advice to Stoneham would be.

So determined were Stoneham and McGraw to supplant the Yankees in the minds and hearts of New York fans that in their pursuit and signing of the Cardinal's star they were willing to ignore the realities of Hornsby's character to imagine him to be someone other than he was. But even a willing suspension of disbelief has its limits, and the year of Hornsby in a Giants uniform made that clear. Once Hornsby criticized Stoneham publicly, things changed utterly. Moreover, as provoked as Stoneham was by Hornsby's public display of his arrogant contempt for the front office, it is easy to suppose that Stoneham might have been more deeply disgusted by his star player for another important reason. Hornsby, known throughout the game as an inveterate gambler on horse racing, had a reputation as a welsher on his betting loses. Stoneham, himself a keen player of the horses and someone who believed in honoring one's debts, must have known this about Hornsby and may have overlooked it due to the allure and the promise of Hornsby's box office appeal. But Hornsby's attitude toward the Giants front office tested the limits of Stoneham's patience and tolerance. Moreover, recent reports of Hornsby's welshing came to light just as the 1927 season was ending. His gambling debts would make the papers as a result of a lawsuit in St. Louis in which he was accused of owing a bookie forty-five thousand dollars. Reporting of the subsequent trial in December 1927 appeared in both St. Louis and New York newspapers.[40]

By January 1928 Stoneham had had enough. Without even a word with McGraw, he abruptly traded Hornsby to the Boston Braves for a journeyman outfielder, Jimmy Welsh, and a prospect, James "Shanty" Hogan, a catcher. The trade caught all of the sports journalists in New York off guard. Many said it didn't make sense, given Hornsby's great 1927 season.[41] Others commented that the Giants got nothing out of the deal that would improve the club for 1928, and they would be right about that. But a small group of writers, digging deeper into the story, guessed that this turn of events had less to do with game day performances and more to do with personality, clubhouse presence, and team chemistry.[42] This small group would be only half-right. While Hornsby was unpopular with his teammates, some of whom apparently stated they would quit rather than play under him, his departure had more to do with Stoneham's pique at being publicly challenged by a "mere ballplayer" and his disgust with Hornsby's want of gambling etiquette.[43]

For Stoneham, it was no longer business; it had become personal. But either way, Hornsby's fate was fixed. In January 1928, he was off to Boston and the Hornsby-based challenge to Ruth (and the Yankees) was over, lasting only one year. The McGraw-Stoneham 1927 gambit to bring in "Hornsby the Hero" to win the hearts and minds of the New York sporting fan base had failed, and, for the moment at least, the Giants had to accept their secondary status as a New York City baseball team.

The connection to *The Great Gatsby* is helpful to understand Rogers Hornsby's year as a Giant, but it is not an exact literary exemplum of McGraw's and Stoneham's disappointment. Hornsby did, after all, become a Giant and performed well as a player during the 1927 season. Rather, the Gatsby theme helps elucidate the "Hornsby in New York" story more as a parallel tale, especially in shedding light on the two Jazz Age owners and their failed aspirations. Certainly, Stoneham soured on Hornsby, seeing him as arrogant, aloof, and self-centered, a detriment to the team. But Hornsby's stay in New York was brief to a large degree because of the expectations that grew from Stoneham's and McGraw's fantasy that Hornsby would somehow take Ruth's measure. Like Daisy for Gatsby, Hornsby "tumbled short" of Stoneham's and McGraw's dreams, not just through his own fault, but, in Fitzgerald's apt phrase, "because of the colossal vitality" of their illusions.

7

Götterdämmerung

They were careless people . . . they smashed up things and
creatures and then retreated back onto their money or their
vast carelessness or whatever it was that kept them together,
and let other people clean up the mess they had made.
—F. SCOTT FITZGERALD, *The Great Gatsby*

When Frank McQuade burst into Charley Stoneham's office in 1923 with
a profanity-laced demand for a higher salary for his role as the National
Exhibition Company's treasurer, Stoneham took it in stride as another
of McQuade's rants. McQuade had an aggressive way about him and
could be pushy and rude in his manner. But this latest outburst carried
a bit more heat and signaled to Stoneham that McQuade was becoming
a problem in the Giants front office. Even John McGraw, who normally
attended to players and game strategy rather than intraoffice politics,
was complaining about McQuade's antics and advised Stoneham to
give McQuade a raise to keep the peace in the organization. But the
raise was just the thin edge of the wedge, and it didn't take long for
Stoneham's hunch about McQuade to play out. A few months later
McQuade aggressively criticized Stoneham about a personal loan the
Giants president took from NEC funds, punctuating his criticism with
threats that he would "knock Stoneham's block off" and that Stoneham
could "go to hell." Stoneham knew there and then that he was in a
fatal power struggle with McQuade. Stoneham's control of the Giants
organization hung in the balance.

Charley Stoneham became a baseball man in January 1919 with the help and support of John McGraw and Frank McQuade. Stoneham put up the purchase price, buying 1,306 shares, making him the largest single stockholder of the National Exhibition Company and, as such, the chief executive officer of the New York Giants baseball team. He then sold McGraw and McQuade 70 NEC shares each, giving them an ownership share in the ball club as minor stockholders. As part of the purchase agreement between the three men, they formed a partnership as directors of the company, with Stoneham serving as president, McGraw as vice president, and McQuade as treasurer. Under the terms of the partnership, majority stockholder Stoneham would be authorized to vote the shares of all three at the annual NEC stockholders' meetings. The agreement also contained a provision regarding any future sale of the club: each partner would have to agree on the proposed sale, and each would have the right of first refusal on buying the shares of the partnership member wishing to sell. There was also an important clause in the agreement, effectively guaranteeing each of the three partners his position as an officer of the corporation in perpetuity.

> The parties hereto will use their best endeavors for the purpose of continuing as directors of said company and as officers thereof the following:
>
> Directors:
> Charles A. Stoneham
> John J. McGraw
> Francis X. McQuade
>
> With the right of the part of the first part (namely Stoneham) to name all additional directors as he sees fit:
>
> Officers:
> Charles A. Stoneham, President,
> John J. McGraw, Vice-President,
> Francis X. McQuade, Treasurer.[1]

When the partners had a falling-out a few years later, the agreement mandate requiring each to use his "best endeavor" to secure the incumbency of the other two as corporate officers proved to be a thorny issue of contention.

Initially, though, it was a fortuitous and even happy arrangement for the Giants organization and for the partners themselves. Stoneham had wanted to leave the investment business behind and become a baseball owner; McGraw, the longtime manager of the Giants, had always coveted becoming an owner of the ball club; McQuade, a lifelong Giants fan, magistrate judge, and well-connected Tammany Hall insider, relished being a part owner of Manhattan's favorite team. The agreement was hatched among the convivial group in bibulous fashion at one of Stoneham's favorite Manhattan haunts, Jack's restaurant, in late December 1918.[2] Two weeks later, on January 15, 1919, it was a happy occasion for all three men at their first press conference as owners, all smiles, friendly with the reporters, aware of the legacy of Giants baseball to the city, beaming with optimism about the future of the team, and confident in their ability as an ownership group to move forward with success. Even though Stoneham served as spokesman—a rarity for him as he disdained speaking to the public—he did so on behalf of the partnership and stressed the idea of cooperation among the three principals.[3]

But the friendly bond between these men was more fiction than reality. Barely one baseball season was in the books before their relationship began to unravel, beset by rancorous quarreling and squabbling with one another behind closed doors. In retrospect this discord should hardly have come as a surprise, given that all three men had what psychologists term "type A" personalities.[4] Stoneham, McGraw, and McQuade were each driven to take charge and accustomed to having his own way in problem solving and matters of day-to-day business. Each man acted in a presumptive manner, confident about the suitability or relevance of his behavior, and paid little heed to what others thought. This mix of strong personalities ensured that the relationship among the partners was often fraught with tension, if not ill will. One could easily provoke the other two simply by behaving in his characteristic manner.

To make matters worse, the Giants partners were given to intemperance in their personal lives, with each in his own way taking full advantage of Manhattan's Jazz Age nightlife, living large in a city known for its restaurants, speakeasies, and nightspots. Sometimes the three men would conduct business in drinking establishments such as Billy the Oysterman's or Moore's Midtown diner, where boisterous behavior, disagreements, and occasional rows could readily be witnessed by other late-night revelers. Alcohol would escalate petty disputes into rancorous arguments. On one occasion at Moore's, McQuade punched Harry Frazee, the president of the Boston Red Sox, requiring Stoneham to intervene.[5] Too often the behavior of the three men, especially McQuade, was unruly and profligate. They were, in a phrase, careless people.

The interactions and tensions among the partners fluctuated, of course. Knowing the limitations of his knowledge of the game, Stoneham deferred to McGraw on most baseball matters early in the partnership, especially on player personnel. As a result, he got on reasonably well with his manager, with one small caveat. Stoneham made it clear that it was his wallet that provided McGraw the resources he needed to acquire players. Even within these tacit boundaries, the two still had their differences, differences that sometimes degenerated into heated arguments. On one occasion early in the partnership, when both men were in Havana and drinking together, a dispute between the two of them evolved into a fistfight.[6] But this was an extreme case and was quickly downplayed by the Giants organization.[7] Although Stoneham and McGraw would occasionally disagree over the years, for the most part their professional relationship was civil and productive. Over the course of his time with Stoneham, McGraw generally felt accepted by his boss and took some comfort in their working arrangements. As his biographer Charles Alexander points out, McGraw would always be grateful to Stoneham for giving him a stake in club ownership, and as a result, McGraw would remain loyal to Stoneham.[8] The feelings of both men toward third partner McQuade, however, took a different route.

With a background in law and his position as a New York City magistrate, Frank McQuade was accustomed to evaluating competing interests and then, as a judge, exercising unilateral power to resolve the controversy. He brought this sense of authority to his role in the Giants ownership. While he lacked McGraw's deep knowledge of the game—McQuade came to baseball primarily as a fan—and could not by any stretch match the financial means that Stoneham brought to the ownership group, McQuade did not defer to either of his partners. Rather, he deemed himself an equal in matters of club business, especially when it came to the stewardship of NEC finances—this despite the fact that he held only a small stake in the club and that the shares that he possessed were entirely the result of Stoneham's largesse. But on one important matter at least, his sense of self-worth was earned: Frank McQuade had made a significant and singular contribution to the operation of baseball in New York, one that led to major improvements in the financial fortunes of the ball club.

Before he entered the partnership, McQuade took advantage of his position on the New York City bench to help legalize Sunday baseball. In August 1917 Magistrate McQuade dismissed charges of blue law violations brought by the Manhattan Sabbath Society against McGraw and Cincinnati Reds manager Christy Mathewson for staging a Sunday exhibition game at the Polo Grounds to benefit the war effort.[9] McQuade's ruling was motivated by a long-standing conviction that New York City, like Chicago, St. Louis, and Cincinnati, among others, should have Sunday baseball. But Judge McQuade couched his decision in statutory terms, ruling that the Sabbath's traditional day of rest had not been disturbed by the playing of a war benefit baseball game. Two years later McQuade worked with politicians to push through a bill to sanction Sunday baseball through passage at both the state and city levels.

On April 28, 1919, the New York City Board of Aldermen approved a Sabbath baseball plan on condition that Sunday games not start before

2:00 p.m. (so as not to interfere with morning church attendance) and that Sunday ticket prices be the same as for weekday games. An enabling ordinance was quickly signed by Mayor John Hylan.[10] Sunday baseball proved a huge hit with Gotham fans and provided a great boost for the bottom lines of all three New York teams, which saw their 1919 ballpark attendance figures surge. By June the Giants had surpassed their total gate from the previous year and by the season's end had drawn 708,857 fans, exceeding their 1918 season's total by more than 450,000.[11] For his part in stimulating this economic benefit to baseball, McQuade was given the title of "Father of Sunday Baseball in New York" and hailed by Governor Al Smith, with the pen used to sign the Sunday games bill given to McQuade at a heavily attended city banquet. Appropriately, Frank McQuade would throw out the first pitch at the inaugural Sunday game for the Giants, played on May 4, 1919, before 37,000 fans.[12]

His role in establishing Sunday baseball in New York certainly stands as McQuade's finest hour as a Giants partner and also perhaps as the pinnacle of his relationship with Stoneham and McGraw.[13] All three men were agreed that Sunday baseball was a great achievement, and all three benefited financially from it. But in a clear example of what the theologians and philosophers might categorize as a *sic transit gloria* moment, things soon began to deteriorate between McQuade and his partners.[14] It may have been that McQuade saw his contributions to Sunday baseball as testimony to his stature as a New York power broker; or it may have been that he thought that his connection to the Giants organization would solidify his importance as a public figure. Whatever the reason, McQuade tried to make the most of his celebrity status and frequently provoked his partners in the process. He often behaved independently, as if untethered from any obligations to consult with the other two, enjoying the prestige that his connection with the Giants granted him with friends and associates outside of baseball. Scattering free passes to Giants games as favors and swag among his

Tammany Hall cronies, McQuade assumed the role of "hail fellow, well met" personality and player in New York social circles. Nor was he deferential to Stoneham or McGraw. On the contrary, he consistently pushed his partners for greater recognition of his worth as NEC treasurer, demanding that his annual director's salary be made equal with McGraw's. In McQuade's estimation his contributions to the ball club were equal to, or even exceeded, those of the Giants manager. Playing one against the other, McQuade would huddle with McGraw and complain of how inept or difficult Stoneham was and how the two of them should unite against him to protect their interests.[15] He would then turn to Stoneham and grumble about McGraw. It would not be long before Stoneham and McGraw, separately, saw through McQuade's machinations and grew tired of his antics.

Things came to a head in early 1925. Stoneham was preoccupied dealing with his various legal entanglements, some of which involved criminal charges. To help defray the expense that attended defending himself against an indictment for mail fraud in the Dier case, he borrowed $125,000 from the NEC coffers without consulting treasurer McQuade and instructed club secretary James Tierney to sign off on the loan instead. When McQuade approached Stoneham about this, he did so antagonistically, threatening to go before the stockholders unless Stoneham provided security on the loan and paid interest on it. McQuade justified this confrontation with Stoneham as protection for the shareholders. But the manner of McQuade's actions grated on Stoneham, who was not accustomed to being questioned about club money. Although Stoneham agreed to secure the loan and pay the interest, words were exchanged, accusations made, and before long the two partners were locked in a power struggle. What had been previously a prickly relationship between them now became deeply acrimonious. When Stoneham responded in kind, first by telling McQuade to "lay off" and then by rebuking him about abusing the policy of free passes to games, McQuade told Stoneham he could "go to hell," adding that he intended to continue keeping an eye on club finances and doing what he wanted about passes. As a parting shot, McQuade threatened to "knock the block off" Stoneham if he tried to stop him.[16]

The relationship between McQuade and McGraw was also turning sour. Some years later McGraw would testify that early in the partnership McQuade hounded him about lining up against Stoneham and then verbally abused him when he refused to join McQuade's opposition, calling McGraw a "weak son-of-a-bitch." McGraw also pointed out that when McQuade was drinking, he was unpredictable and abusive. Once he had struck his own wife when she couldn't produce the key to their hotel room after an evening on the town in New Orleans, where the Giants were playing an exhibition game. On another occasion McQuade publicly insulted McGraw's wife, Blanche.[17] McGraw also took exception to McQuade's slippery maneuvering within the partnership. At one point during Stoneham's 1925 trial for mail fraud, McQuade sounded gleeful about the possibility that Stoneham might be sent to prison. "If that guy goes to Atlanta, we will get the ballclub," McGraw reported having McQuade said.[18] McQuade also approached McGraw about signing a private agreement that placed the two of them in opposition to Stoneham. Wary of McQuade's volatile personality and tired of his persistent quarreling, McGraw went in the opposite direction and aligned himself with Stoneham, all in the best interest of keeping the Giants as a functioning organization. McGraw reported McQuade's maneuvers to Stoneham in the hope that together they might isolate McQuade and move the ball club forward.

Stoneham, for his part, had had enough. Fed up with McQuade's irksome oversight over the advance of NEC funds and with the fractious partnership drama created by McQuade, Charley struck back. In May 1928, at the annual meeting to elect NEC board members, he orchestrated the nomination of club attorney Leo A. Bondy for the post of club treasurer and for McQuade's seat on the board. Seven directors were eligible to cast election ballots: club president Stoneham; vice president McGraw; treasurer McQuade; and four at-large board members—Bondy; Stoneham's business partner Ross Robertson; longtime Stoneham friend Dr. Harry A. Ferguson; and Stoneham's younger brother, Horace A. Stoneham. When the vote for treasurer was tallied, McQuade received only one vote (his own). Five electors voted for Bondy (including McGraw), and Charley Stoneham abstained. In a matter of minutes, McQuade lost his position as club treasurer, his annual club salary, and his board seat as well. In addition to restructuring the slate of officers, the momentous vote by the NEC board set in motion a tangled and intricate legal squabble that eventually played out in courtrooms from New York to Albany. For the next six years, Stoneham's defrocking of McQuade, while personally satisfying, proved to be a consuming distraction for the Giants organization.

Outraged by the outcome over the NEC election results, McQuade pursued legal means to undo his ouster as club treasurer and board member. His first stratagem was indirect. On November 6, 1929, a lawsuit was filed in the Supreme Court of New York in Manhattan by wealthy New York building contractor and Giants stockholder William Kenny, alleging improprieties by Stoneham as president of the franchise. Kenny was seeking over $400,000 in damages. While McQuade was not a party to the Kenny suit, he was identified as its behind-the-scenes instigator in press coverage of the litigation. Not to be outdone or cowed in any way by McQuade's maneuvering, Stoneham responded by filing suit against McQuade, alleging a misuse of the position and privileges of club treasurer and seeking damages of $250,000. The press duly noted that Stoneham's suit against McQuade was in retaliation for the one instituted by Kenny.[19] In an affidavit, Stoneham accused McQuade of instigating the Kenny suit, of using of club resources inappropriately, and of attempting to conspire with Kenny to buy a controlling interest in the NEC. But Stoneham's sworn statement did more than seek damages. It put McQuade on notice that Stoneham would not take any legal harassment lightly. Moreover, Stoneham took the opportunity in the affidavit to present a withering portrait of McQuade as a violent and unstable character: "After one of his violent stretches McQuade came to my office and got on his knees, encircled my legs with his arms and asked for forgiveness. Mr. Bondy was present, saw him on his knees and said, 'Don't you think this has gone far enough?' As Bondy was leaving the room McQuade jumped up, rushed behind Bondy and struck him in the face, breaking his glasses. At Bondy's request, no issue was made of this attack."[20] The Kenny and Stoneham suits were simply the beginning of what became a long, torturous battle in courtrooms at various levels of the New York judicial system, involving public character assassinations among the three partners.

McQuade fired the next round. In spring 1930 he filed his own lawsuit in the Supreme Court of New York, alleging that both Stoneham and McGraw had not performed according to the foundational NEC agreement of 1919. The essence of the McQuade complaint was the defendants' failure to "use their best endeavors" to retain McQuade as club treasurer. While separate from the previous legal actions initiated by both Kenny and Stoneham, McQuade's suit was not filed in a vacuum. It was clearly in response to the previous suits. Stoneham reacted immediately and moved to dismiss the McQuade complaint, but his motion was denied by the trial court. Undaunted, and obviously determined to flex his own legal muscles, Stoneham then appealed the ruling to the Appellate Division. Here, too, he suffered a setback. In a unanimous decision rendered on May 29, 1930, the Appellate Division denied Stoneham's appeal, setting up McQuade's lawsuit for trial.[21]

The trial began on December 14, 1931, before Justice Philip J. McCook of the Supreme Court of New York, and for the next four weeks, Stoneham was in a familiar setting: a New York courtroom where his reputation as a businessman was once again under fire. The trial featured testimony by the three principals, McQuade, Stoneham, and McGraw, plus a string of minor lights, including club secretaries, Polo Grounds workers, and other officers of the NEC. Each day provided juicy material for the tabloids as lurid accusations bounced back and forth in the form of a mudslinging contest, with McQuade giving an acrimonious account of his dealings with his partners and Stoneham and McGraw lobbing back.

McQuade was the first party to testify. Under the direction of his attorney, Isaac N. Jacobson, McQuade expounded on the contractual dictates of the partnership agreement pertaining to the election of club officers and how both Stoneham and McGraw had violated them by failing to support his retention in the May 1928 NEC election. McQuade also testified about the irregularity of Stoneham's dip into NEC funds, drawing loans that were not secured and without interest. Whenever he could, McQuade denigrated Stoneham and McGraw, characterizing both defendants as devious or selfish. He was particularly hostile toward Stoneham, portraying him as dictatorial and having little regard for anyone challenging his actions.[22]

Under questioning from the lead defense attorney, Arthur Garfield Hays, Stoneham repaid the slander, describing McQuade as irascible, impulsive, self-centered, and a detriment to the partnership. The Giants boss recounted a number of incidents in which McQuade had come into his office, banged on the desk, cursed, shouted, and bellowed, insisting that he be given more salary or a bigger cut in the club's profits and that the organization should follow his lead in business matters. Stoneham repeatedly gave details about McQuade's insults, his use of profanity around the office, and his threatening outbursts, McQuade telling him more than once that he would "knock my block off" or "punch me in the nose." Often McQuade would conclude these encounters by telling Stoneham he could "go to hell."[23] Stoneham's description of McQuade's belligerence revealed a concern (and a paradoxical sense of respect) that both he and McGraw held about McQuade, that McQuade was formidable with his fists and a man to be avoided when he was angry, or drunk, his slight build notwithstanding. He would be more prone to fight and prevail than Stoneham, who, overweight and out of shape, never initiated fights, and McGraw, an aggressive but harmless brawler who usually took his lumps.[24]

When his turn came, McGraw was no less critical of McQuade, point-ing out how toxic McQuade was for the organization. McGraw deplored McQuade's propensity for drink and the effect it had on his behavior, citing McQuade's abusive conduct when under the influence—striking Mrs. McQuade in public, insulting McGraw's wife, threatening to get rid of Stoneham by "putting a pill" in his soup, abusing players on the field and in the dugout, and using profanity around the office and acting uncivilly to secretaries—as illustrative of McQuade's erratic and distempered personality. On the contractual issue central to the case, McGraw bluntly testified that he did not vote for McQuade as treasurer because he did not think McQuade was holding up his end of the partnership. McGraw also mentioned that months would go by without his speaking to McQuade. And when he did, it was entirely on matters of business. McGraw made it clear that after 1922 he had ceased being friendly with McQuade.[25]

The derogatory tenor of the court proceedings continued in the closing remarks of the attorneys for both sides. Defense attorney Arthur Hays pulled no punches in accusing McQuade of perjury; Hays then went on to describe McQuade's incompetence and his disloyalty to his fellow directors. McQuade's lawyer, Isaac Jacobson, in a curious defense of his client, said McQuade, Stoneham, and McGraw were "of the same ilk and none was an angel. They were all drinking men, all cursing men, all fighting men." Jacobson went on to say that it was common knowledge that the Giants ownership was in the hands of "a rough element."[26] Coverage of the trial by local newspapers gave the public a view of what had been concealed behind closed doors for the previous ten years: the Giants front office was a place of great hatred, little room.

Although Stoneham's, McGraw's, and McQuade's characterization of one another as impossible and unruly partners delighted the press and the reading public, it made no headway with Justice McCook. Commenting that quarrels, insults, and arguments between corpo-rate partners were not unusual and that McQuade's behavior might be disagreeable and uncivil, McCook stated that neither had bearing on the contractual issues pivotal to the case. On the merits the court found that Stoneham and McGraw had in fact breached their original NEC election agreement. But Justice McCook was not disposed to grant the remedy sought in the complaint that McQuade be reinstated as NEC treasurer. In the court's view McQuade was entitled to $42,827 in damages, but his restoration as NEC treasurer was detrimental to good corporate governance. As the McCook decision explained, "The court infers, and plaintiff has not shown the contrary, that were he restored in either capacity (i.e., NEC board director and club treasurer), the bitterness accumulating since January, 1925, which now has become public property through the preliminary motions and the trial, would prevent harmonious functioning by the board of directors and create, there and at meetings with stockholders, an atmosphere inconsistent with efficiency."[27] In effect, Justice McCook's decision gave McQuade something of a Pyrrhic victory—although it did not appear so to Stoneham, who took the ruling as a bitter rebuke.

McQuade's award was a devastating prestige loss for Stoneham and not one that he was prepared to accept. With his deep pockets, his considerable personal experience with the courts, and his now fervent desire to best McQuade on all matters, including litigious ones, Stoneham resolved to challenge the court; he could not abide McQuade having any success. On behalf of McGraw, although clearly making this a personal decision, Stoneham appealed the McCook decision to the Appellate Division. But to no avail. On March 17, 1933, the Appellate Division affirmed the trial court judgment and McQuade's award of $42,827.[28] This outcome was no less of a disappointment for Stoneham than the trial had been and only deepened his resentment of McQuade.

This latest loss did little to quash Stoneham's determination to deny McQuade victory, however. Indeed, as the biblical plagues did to the Egyptian Pharaoh, the event hardened Stoneham's heart. Without any hesitancy, Stoneham decided to appeal the decision to the state's highest court, the New York court of appeals, seated in the state capital at

Albany. His prospects were not high, as the granting of appeals by the high court is discretionary and confined to a limited number of cases each year. But Stoneham's ire toward McQuade was considerable and his determination strong. He went ahead and filed the appeal, and in June 1933 he received favorable news. Against the odds, the court of appeals had decided to review the McQuade judgment.

It turned out that the third time was indeed the charm. On January 18, 1934, the high court ruled in Stoneham and McGraw's favor and reversed the lower court's action. In a majority decision written by chief judge Cuthbert W. Pound, five members of the court determined that the Giants partnership agreement was contrary to public policy regarding the governance of corporations and hence unenforceable.[29] The rulings were, therefore, vacated and the McQuade complaint dismissed. The court denied McQuade's contractual claim for holding office, something the lower courts accepted. But the more compelling reason for reversal involved McQuade's role as a magistrate judge: "At the time the contract was made the plaintiff was a city magistrate. No city magistrate shall engage in any other business, profession, or hold any other public office."[30] It may have been a technicality, as some have insisted, but the effect was the same. After five years of litigation throughout the various levels of New York's legal system, McQuade lost his claim against Stoneham and McGraw.

Stoneham's battle with McQuade did not confine itself to the courtroom. It extended into the arena of the marketplace as well. In the process of dealing with the Kenny suit against him, Stoneham had learned that it was McQuade who persuaded Kenny, in the spring of 1928, to pay almost a half-million dollars for shares that would give him 20 percent of NEC stock. With Kenny as an ally with a significant stakeholding, McQuade intended to form a group, with himself and Kenny as principals, that might eventually control the NEC board. But Kenny soon realized that he had bitten off more than he could chew. After only a year and much to McQuade's disappointment, Kenny, having grown tired of the squabbling and the political maneuvering among the NEC board members, sold his interest to Harry McNally, another wealthy contractor. It was now Stoneham's turn to pounce. Knowing that McNally was not particularly close to McQuade, Stoneham moved to limit McQuade's ambitions to control the NEC board. In late 1930 Stoneham approached McNally with an offer to buy half of his holdings at a favorable price that would give McNally a nice gain on his investment. McNally was happy to sell Stoneham 230 shares, giving the Giants boss enough stock to control 69 percent of the company and a stronger position with the NEC board, effectively reducing any other threat from McQuade.[31]

The high court's ruling and the additional accumulation of NEC stock marked the end of Stoneham's battle with McQuade, undoubtedly giving the Giants president great personal satisfaction. There were, however, some lingering costs. The partnership's dissolution had brought to public view the unsavory elements of the ball club's ownership, particularly the individual partners' carelessness, causing some personal embarrassment to all three men, despite their claims to be impervious to the opinions of others. McQuade was the biggest loser, of course, saddled with a total defeat. He had no chance at reinstatement to the NEC board or as club treasurer, and his monetary award of $42,827 had disappeared. To add to his sense of loss and disappointment, he had resigned from his magistrate position in 1930 in anticipation of the Seabury investigations of corruption that eventually would cause Jimmy Walker to step down as New York City mayor.[32] No longer an owner of the Giants nor a city magistrate, McQuade was isolated.

For McGraw the high court ruling signaled a definitive end. He was happy to have the McQuade legal matter behind him, as, by his own admission, he had ceased being on friendly terms with McQuade for the past ten years. Like Stoneham, McGraw regarded McQuade as a distraction and detriment to club business. But something else about the ruling signaled a change for McGraw, or perhaps more of a recognition. The high-profile litigation over the past five years established beyond a doubt that Stoneham was the single most important figure in the organization. McGraw's days of sharing partnership and being Stoneham's equal in matters of baseball were over. Moreover, while all the legal wrangling was ongoing, McGraw had begun to do some soul searching. He was feeling somewhat out of touch with the game; his small ball style of play having given way to power and hitting, especially home runs. He also sensed that his managerial manner might be out of mode and that he had lost his effectiveness with his players. In June 1932 all of this, in addition to considerable ongoing health problems, pushed McGraw into having a conversation with Stoneham about stepping down as manager. Stoneham concurred, and at midseason star first baseman Bill Terry was appointed player-manager. After almost thirty-five years with the Giants, McGraw retired from active duty, to remain as a consultant to the team. He died in April 1934, only a few months after the court of appeals' decision.

As for Charley Stoneham, the high court's decision brought great personal satisfaction and a sense of enormous relief. Might this be the time in his life, he may have wondered, when he was truly free of the courts and litigation? That now he might be able to turn his attention fully and completely to his beloved ball club? If so, he would have to do so alone as the last remaining partner. McGraw was gone and McQuade vanquished. The old tri-partnership that ushered in his time with the Giants was finished and merely a memory. The dispatching of McQuade from his place in the organization had taken its toll, however, and exposed the Giants front office, warts and all. Stoneham's task was now to try to put all that behind him and move forward to the events of the next few years. Sadly, as it turned out, he would have precious little time to enjoy the change.

8

Crash Time

> It ended two years ago, because the utter confidence which
> was its essential prop received an enormous jolt, and it
> didn't take long for the flimsy structure to settle earthward.
> And after two years the Jazz Age seems as far away as
> the days before the War. It was borrowed time anyhow—the
> whole upper tenth of a nation living with the insouciance
> of grand ducs and the casualness of chorus girls.
> —F. SCOTT FITZGERALD, "Echoes of the Jazz Age"

The end of the great American Jazz Age came not with a whimper but
a bang. It was hastened by a collapsing stock market and punctuated
by dramatic plunges on two days that economists and historians designated as "Black." On the first, Black Thursday, October 24, 1929, a
record 12.9 million shares were sold on the New York Stock Exchange,
sending shock waves throughout the financial institutions in New
York City and then the nation. The second occurred five days later, on
Black Tuesday, October 29, with an unprecedented sale of 16.4 million
shares. At the end of the day, the Dow Jones Industrial Average closed
at 230.79 from an opening of 305.85, a decrease of 25 percent.[1]

There had been rumblings and some warning shouts two weeks
earlier, when things began to look shaky. On Monday, October 14, the
market began to sag, but many interpreted this as a temporary slip, even
a correction to the spectacular bull market of the past two years. Some
were even suggesting that this momentary drop might signal the time

to find some bargains. In other words there was no panic . . . yet. The week played out with prices of shares bouncing back and forth. On the following Monday, October 21, the slide from the previous week caught the glamour stocks—AT&T, General Electric, Standard Oil, and U.S. Steel among them—and for the next two days, the slump continued. On Thursday a worried crowd who had come to the exchange to watch the trading witnessed what one observer described as utter chaos:

> People watching could not understand more than a wild word or two as men charged from one post to another, hands waving and faces contorted, while others stood besieged, trying to cope with a hundred petitioners at once, like men who had meat to distribute to a pack of ravening dogs. Then, at three o'clock, the gong sounded and there was instantaneous stillness. . . . After this breath of silence, a sudden spontaneous cry arose of mingled cheers and boos, with an undercurrent of moans. Men everywhere threw up their hands, scattering bits of papers and small notebooks, and a few laughed in half-hysterical relief. Some men jumped off their feet a few times and beat their hands together, their shirt collars ripped and their ties dangling free. A few men stood dazed.[2]

The sell-off produced a nightmare for stockbrokers and a headache for traders on the exchange floor, where bedlam had broken out.[3] The next day the city banks that had some skin in the game—those that provided loans to stockbrokers—jumped in to help prop up the falling prices. But as one historian of the period observed, "It was like bailing Niagara Falls with a bucket."[4]

By the end of the month, President Herbert Hoover and his secretary of the Treasury, Andrew Mellon, strove to provide reassurances, both adamant that American business was sound and that investors should stay the course. The public thought otherwise, however, and people began selling their securities. Into the next few weeks of November, stocks were falling to the bottom like stones tossed in a lake. The rout

was on, as anxious sellers were caught flat-footed with securities certificates in their hands and buyers nowhere in sight.

Banks were also suffering, caught up in a collapsing credit market.
Some Wall Street investors paid only nominal amounts to buy shares,
relying on bank loans to fund the remaining costs. As the market fell,
banks demanded more money to secure their loans, cash that their debt-
ors didn't have. Conditions were spiraling downward quickly. One of
the major banks, National City Bank, led by Charles A. Mitchell, lost
half of its value during the plunge. Mitchell tried to calm the jitters of
Wall Street by saying that the sell-off was a normal correction and that
he was prepared to buy some of the now underpriced stocks and have
his bank pump some $25 million into the market; he urged others to
do the same. A Wall Street fat cat, Mitchell had an ulterior motive. He
planned to offer stock in a holding company he was putting together that
combined Hershey's Chocolate and Kraft Cheese, a move that would
require a stable economy, hardly the condition of the October 1929
market.[5] Mitchell's advice to feed the beast fell on deaf, and nervous,
ears of investors. The market kept falling. Major companies saw big
losses in value: United States Steel fell from 261 to 150; AT&T from 310
to 193; General Electric from 403 to 168; Standard Oil from 83 to 48,
even after John D. Rockefeller plunked down $50 million to buttress the
company's common stock.[6] The city's newspapers were obsessed with
stories of both corporate and individuals' losses. Even the Broadway
newspaper *Variety* broke from its traditional role of covering the city's
theater schedule and musical productions with its Wednesday, October
30, 1929, headline: "Wall Street Lays an Egg," a sharp appraisal of the
disastrous sell-off on Black Tuesday, the day before.

While economists will disagree over the role the crash of the 1929
stock market played in the Great Depression of the 1930s—was it the
cause of the Great Depression that followed or merely an early signal
of a weakened economy?—there is no argument that the 1929 October
massacre was only the beginning of a hardship and struggle that would
play out over the next several years.[7] At the end of December, stock

prices were back at early 1927 levels, having lost all the gains of the 1928–29 bull market. By the fall of 1930, less than a year after Black Thursday and Black Tuesday, the economy was reeling. Banks now held worthless notes that had been loans to brokers. Jittery depositors were threatening withdrawals, forcing banks to call in other loans and severely curtail new ones, effectively restricting credit and the flow of capital.

A seismic shift in everyday life was underway from the carefree days of the 1920s, when Americans had taken advantage of an abundance of credit to give them purchasing power. Now the topsy-turvy direction of American businesses had ordinary folks tightening their purse strings and passing on that new car, that new appliance, or that new coat. With the crash and the subsequent ripples throughout business that caused a rise in unemployment, those families that were carrying a burden of debt felt vulnerable and wary of accumulating more debt. They stopped spending. The slump in spending then caused companies to cut back severely on workers, triggering a sharp rise in unemployment. Those fortunate enough to keep their jobs held onto their earnings as a safeguard against the possibility that they, too, might be out of work in the near future. This decrease in consumer spending exacerbated the recession and pushed it into a depression. As Robert S. McElvaine explained, it was a shift in mass psychology: "When the outlook had been sanguine [in the 1920s], large numbers of American had been willing not only to spend most of their incomes, but to commit future income through installment plans. Once the Depression was underway, this psychology reversed itself completely."[8]

The result was felt throughout the general economy. Sensing the drying up of consumption and the subsequent loss of demand, corporations scaled back production. This in turn led to less need for labor, triggering payroll cuts. Corporations also cut back on investment and growth so that by 1933 that sector of the American economy was down to $800 million, from a 1929 level of $16.2 billion. The nation's gross national product fell from 15.2 percent in 1929 to 11.2 percent in

1930. Unemployment rose from 1.5 million to 4.3 million; the lucky ones who kept their jobs saw their salaries reduced by more than $4 billion.[9] The prosperous and carefree days of the Jazz Age were over, and the hard times of the 1930s had begun. As one New Yorker put it, the music had changed, and the night rhapsodies of jazz had given way to "Brother, Can You Spare a Dime?"[10]

Oddly, the crash and the subsequent recession-depression had little effect on baseball, at least in the short term, and on Charley Stoneham as a baseball owner. Overall attendance for the 1930 Major League season topped 10 million for the first time in baseball history, and profits rose to $2 million, tripling the 1929 figures, all this despite the country's clear economic woes.[11] The Giants drew over 800,000, second highest in the National League.[12] The standard explanation for such an anomaly was to situate the sport into the narrative of a sinking economy: "Poor business years are good baseball years." Baseball games, it was argued, served as a kind of escapism, giving the unemployed a place to go and something to watch.[13] But this theory was short-lived. The 1930 season proved to be an outlier, and the following year in baseball reflected the grim reality of the overall economy. When even a bleacher seat for a game was deemed a luxury by the growing numbers of unemployed and when the cost of that ticket for those out of work could be used to purchase a loaf of bread, attendance fell by more than 15 percent during the 1931 season, and baseball's income sagged. And over the next few years, it would only get worse.

At the winter meetings in December 1931, a few major league owners, feeling the pinch of dwindling revenue that season, nonetheless refused to admit how difficult things were. Disdaining any Cassandra-like views of a national economic disaster, they preferred instead to blame other factors for the drop in attendance, citing a runaway pennant race in the National League or cold weather.[14] Charley Stoneham was not among them. He was convinced of the reality of a weak and uncertain market and the dire circumstances of the Depression and urged other like-minded owners to find solutions to the immediate economic circumstances. Rather than tinker with the product—the game itself—they settled on a business decision, cutting their labor and operating costs. They pruned the player rooster from twenty-five to twenty-three per club, reduced coaching staffs, and trimmed front office employees. A few clubs turned to player-managers as a further cost savings. The owners also voted to restrict free passes to the games.[15] But their efforts proved to be a small Band-Aid on an open, gaping wound. Attendance dropped again during the 1932 season, almost a third from the previous year.

At the 1932 winter meetings, nervous and edgy about yet another year of continued loss in revenue, the owners again searched for more ways to confront the downturn. This time they decided to shave players' salaries. Babe Ruth, the game's highest-paid player, took a cut of $23,000 to sign for $52,000. Teammate Lou Gehrig agreed to a $23,000 salary, down from $25,000 in 1932. Bill Terry, the player-manager of the Giants, begrudgingly accepted a 40 percent reduction in his 1932 salary and signed for $30,000. Even Commissioner Kenesaw Mountain Landis took a pay cut, voluntary in his case, from $65,000 in 1931 to $40,000 in 1933.[16] Some of these measures undoubtedly helped, but more to reduce losses rather than promote earnings: baseball's overall profits plummeted during the early years of the 1930s.[17] Despite Commissioner Landis's rosy outlook that "Americans loved baseball" and his hopeful view that attendance will improve when the economy recovers, most clubs faced austere times for the next five or six years.[18]

The situation was not as dire in New York as it was in other major league cities. Teams in what was termed the "old Northwest"—Michigan, Illinois, and Ohio—suffered at the gate beginning in 1931.[19] The Giants, on the other hand, drew a surprising 812,163 fans in 1931, almost the same as they had in the previous year. The Yankees and the Brooklyn Robins also did well: the Yankees drew 912,437; the Robins drew 753,133, despite finishing fourth in the National League—giving New York City a total of 2,477,733 in attendance at baseball games in

1931, exceeding the next closest major league city, Chicago, by almost a million.[20] Only in 1932 and 1933, the years most economists term the nadir of the Great Depression, did the attendance in New York City begin to mirror the economic conditions across the country. In 1932 the Giants drew 484,368, their lowest since World War I.[21] Beginning in 1933, however, attendance rose slightly at the Polo Grounds and improved modestly over the next few seasons. The 1933 season marked a turnaround for the Giants, not only at the gate, where they drew 604,471 (first in the league), but also in the standings, winning both the National League pennant and the World Series, beating the Washington Senators, four games to one. For the rest of Stoneham's ownership (through 1935), the Giants were the top drawing team in the National League. The Yankees, too, held steady throughout this period, as did Brooklyn, although the Dodgers (so named by the ball club after the 1931 season) fell off a bit in the 1934 and 1935 seasons.[22]

The uptick in the Giants' attendance that started in 1933 was a boon for Charley Stoneham, whose main source of income came largely from the revenues of his ball club. A former wheeler-dealer in the stock market, Stoneham sold his brokerage business in 1921 to devote his time to being a baseball owner and head of the National Exhibition Company which also sponsored other athletic events such as boxing and college football.[23] Leaving the investment business when he did—the market was surging in value at the time—not only assured him of a significant profit but also contributed to his reputation as a shrewd, cutthroat businessman with an uncanny sense of timing, establishing a linkage between Stoneham the gambler and Stoneham the businessman—knowing when to hold them, when to fold them, and when to walk away.[24]

But he didn't cut himself off completely. As one writer put it, even as the owner of the New York Giants, Stoneham was at home in the canyons of Wall Street; his base was the financial district and that world of paper and profits in which he was knowledgeable and savvy. His shrewdness prompted him in late 1927 to gauge the market and offer a dour prediction of a coming downturn in the price of stocks that was reported on by Bill Corum of the *Evening Journal*, though it obviously fell on deaf ears.[25] It mattered not to Stoneham if others agreed with his investment insights and decision. As someone who was once thoroughly connected with Wall Street, Charley Stoneham knew the general effects of the market and its role in the general economy. With his income from the National Exhibition Company, he could follow a more prudent investment strategy. He did not liquidate his holdings, but he cut back on his personal stock portfolio even as the market rose. And once again, his timing was remarkable.

Stoneham's financial hunches worked, in the main, because his ball club was phenomenally successful, especially in the early years of his ownership, on the field, winning four pennants and two World Series championships, and at the gate throughout the decade, all of this generating a healthy bottom line with over two million dollars in profits, two-thirds of which went as dividend payments to stockholders.[26] As the largest shareholder in the National Exhibition Company, Stoneham gained significant financial reward from team profits, giving him plenty of means to sustain his exuberant and lavish lifestyle. Any misgivings about missing the itch of gambling on the market, of leaving the brokerage business and reducing his personal holdings in the market, surely were assuaged by profits from the Giants throughout the 1920s. As the decade drew to a close, his financial decisions looked inspired and prescient. More than likely, with the sales of his brokerage companies, his concurrent purchase of the Giants, and his reduction of personal holdings in the market, Stoneham may have breathed a sigh of relief more than once and perhaps experienced a tinge of schadenfreude as he watched the New York Stock Exchange go to pieces as the decade closed. With his ownership of the Giants and his utilization of the Polo Grounds as a venue for other sporting events, he may have felt sufficiently secure to weather any Wall Street stock market storm.

With the downturn in the economy at the end of the decade, however, prospects for the immediate years ahead seemed shaky and ominous, certainly unsettling and giving pause to one used to a high-rolling Jazz Age lifestyle. Even with his changes in business practice, he had to worry. Questions of the general economy prompted consideration of the effects of the crash and downturn on baseball. How would fans react? Would the public consider the sport frivolous and inconsequential? Moreover, despite his moves and adjustments, Stoneham, like many of his ilk, was still hurt by both the crash of the market in 1929 and the economic downturn of the Great Depression that followed. While he was no longer a brokerage businessman tethered to the day-to-day activities on Wall Street and had reduced his personal stock investments, Stoneham still held some investments in stocks and commodities. The crash undoubtedly weakened those holdings, causing Stoneham significant financial pain. And the subsequent weakening of the general economy following the crash would affect the Giants' bottom line. Indeed, all of baseball was hit hard, especially between 1931 and 1934, when both the American League and the National League showed declines of $1.6 million each in collective operating incomes.[27]

But again, Stoneham's luck held. Playing in baseball's largest market, the Giants were more fortunate than other franchises and drew better crowds than other teams. This advantage offset somewhat the effect of Stoneham's losses in the stock market. Moreover, whatever financial blow he took was softened by his management of resources. Even for a quintessential and practiced Jazz Age playboy, he had enough business sense to know that he had to readjust to the financial realities of this brave new monetary world. And for someone with a complicated personal life—running at least two households and families as well as carrying on an extravagant lifestyle in New York—Stoneham faced a necessity both to govern his means and pare back on luxuries. Costly and extravagant items were let go, among them a yacht, a car, and some horses. There was even some modest belt-tightening with household costs (for both families) and personal expenses.[28]

He was hardly destitute, however. Considering the plight of many who had fortunes tied to the stock market, he came through the 1929–30 ordeal rather well. He still managed to keep two expensive addresses—one in Jersey City with his wife, Hannah, and another, a country home in Westchester County, with his second family, paramour Margaret Leonard Stoneham and their young children, Russell and Jane. He also may have forgone some of the attractions of New York's restaurants and nightlife, although this would be hard to know precisely. Indeed, as appearances go, he continued to play the role of the generous host, springing for celebratory baseball dinners and gatherings for baseball officials and executives. He was a regular attendee at the New York Baseball Writers' annual dinner, where he sat at the head table. And he continued to open his checkbook for player acquisition in the early 1930s. Nonetheless, with aging, gradual health problems, growing family demands, and the need to curb expenses, it is not difficult to imagine Stoneham scaling back on his Jazz Age playboy lifestyle.[29]

This weighing and shifting of his financial position took place during a period of immense turmoil in Stoneham's life, demonstrating, again, his ability to manage (rather astonishingly, one must say) a number of important tasks concurrently. Just as he had done in the early years of the 1920s, when he was leaving a brokerage business, learning the ropes of baseball ownership, contending with a number of legal issues, including indictments for criminal activity, and living what one might call a spirited social life, Stoneham met the challenges of the early 1930s with the same energy. Fighting with Frank McQuade in court, becoming increasingly more involved in the day-to-day business of the ball club as John McGraw receded into the background, overseeing a managerial change with Bill Terry replacing McGraw, adjusting to the country's economic woes, and somehow performing as head of the household to two separate families, Stoneham behaved and operated as one who is described in current parlance as an efficient multitasker. That this multitasking took some toll on him seems obvious enough, but for the remaining few years of his life, he stayed his newly modified course, leading as active a life as possible, both as a baseball owner and a New York personality.

9

The Last Hurrah

I have an idea that Gatsby himself didn't believe
it would come . . . he must have felt that he
had lost the old warm world, paid a high price
for living too long with a single dream.
—F. SCOTT FITZGERALD, *The Great Gatsby*

For many Americans, 1933 was a dismal year, what one American histo-rian called "unprecedented in its magnitude, the worst thing to happen to the American people since the calamitous Civil War."[1] Economists would write later that 1933 was the trough of the Great Depression, the nadir of the struggling economy, when unemployment was rampant, manufacturing was down, banks were folding, and the stock market languished.[2] In early March, Franklin D. Roosevelt had just taken up residence in the White House, promising a "new deal," something that most Americans were hoping for, but in the spring of 1933, things were gloomy around the country. He projected optimism and told Ameri-cans in his inaugural address that the only thing they had to fear was fear itself, but for the working public and the farming communities, it was difficult not to be afraid in such a grim time.[3] Millions were out of work with no prospects in sight. With the drop in production, the need for workers lessened. There were long lines of unemployed in New York City, as well as other cities around the country, queuing in breadlines or to get into soup kitchens. As Roosevelt took office, millions of Americans were hoping for better days ahead.

Although he hardly feared for material comfort and well-being, Charley Stoneham also hoped for better days ahead. But his hopes were focused on the fortunes of his New York Giants baseball team. And his wait would be a short one, unlike the rest of the country, which would need most of the decade to find better times. For the Giants, 1933 was a banner year, a return to the glory years of the early 1920s, when they won four straight National League pennants and were the toast of the town twice, with two World Series championships over the Yankees. Playing their first full season under manager Bill Terry, the 1933 Giants once again reached the pinnacle of the baseball world, capturing both a National League pennant and a World Series championship. Attendance, too, improved, even in the depths of the Depression; the Giants lead the National League, with over 600,000 fans at home games, more than 200,000 above the previous year. It had been a long wait for Stoneham to see his Giants as world champions, and he savored the moment, knowing that such times in baseball are rare and fleeting. He was right to think so. It was a great and joyous release from all the friction and front office squabbling that had gone on in recent years. He could enjoy the game of baseball completely, in and of itself.

The great achievement of the 1933 Giants season started the year before with a momentous change in Giants history. While the details vary somewhat depending on the perspectives of various narrators, the essential event that happened in early June 1932 was clear: after thirty years, John McGraw stepped down as the team's manager. In consultation with Stoneham, McGraw agreed to retire midseason, and Bill Terry was appointed player-manager. In every sense it was a watershed moment for the Giants organization. For over three decades, McGraw had been the face of the franchise, its leading personality and its driving force. He was the most famous National League personality and a living baseball legend. Almost all New York Giants fans, certainly those under the age of forty, had known only McGraw as the head of the ball club. Giants baseball without McGraw was truly the beginning of a new era.

Around the 1932 Memorial Day weekend, it became apparent to McGraw that he was at the end of his time with the Giants. Two weeks earlier, he returned home early during a road trip to recuperate from an illness, leaving assistant coach Dave Bancroft in charge of the team. Although his health had been a troubling issue for the past few years, it was becoming more debilitating. McGraw's sinuses were bothering him, and he suffered from prostatitis, causing him severe discomfort. Once home, the thought of going on the road again seemed daunting. He did not think he had the energy to endure another round of train travel, hotels, and meals out as well as attending to the details of the ball club. Besides his health, something equally troubling was nagging him. He began to doubt his effectiveness with the team and wondered if his style of managing could work with a new generation of younger players, who seemed to bristle at his leadership style. Even veterans like Bill Terry, Fred Lindstrom, and Carl Hubbell complained that McGraw was hurting players' initiative with his micromanaging: calling every pitch, repositioning players, and constantly giving batters signs to take or swing at pitches.[4] The mood on the ball club was also noticed by the writers, one of whom observed that "the players had developed a deep resentment of McGraw's rigid, strained, almost neurotic leadership . . . the unreasonable disciplinary methods . . . the violent tirades."[5] And despite all McGraw's emotional efforts, the Giants were mired in last place in the National League.

During a late May–early June home stand, McGraw made his decision. On June 2, when the game with the Phillies was rained out, McGraw called Terry into his office and asked him if he wanted to manage the team. Stunned, Terry nonetheless gathered himself together and, with little hesitation, answered yes, he would. McGraw told Terry that a meeting would be arranged with Stoneham to settle things. Before he left for home, McGraw posted a message to his players on the club bulletin board, announcing his resignation. By chance and despite the rain delay, Tom Meany of the *World-Telegram* had wandered over to the Polo Grounds on June 2 in search of a story. When he noticed

McGraw's announcement on the players' bulletin board, he knew he had more than a simple baseball story—he had a blockbuster. McGraw had been the heart and soul of the Giants forever; suddenly that was over. Meany frantically called in the story to his news desk in time for the evening edition.

The Giants had hoped to structure the story with their own press release, but Meany's scoop beat them to it. To control what was left of the narrative, the Giants invited reporters to Stoneham's office at noon the following day, where club secretary Jim Tierney read McGraw's statement. Those from the Giants front office in attendance were Stoneham, Tierney, Terry, and Leo Bondy, club treasurer and attorney. Conspicuously absent was John McGraw, who had left the ballpark earlier and was at home in Pelham when the reporters gathered. The meeting with reporters was essentially a rehash of an earlier private discussion that morning with Terry and Stoneham during which the Giants boss formally had offered Terry the job of manager. Terry had accepted with one caveat, that it would be his club, that he would have complete control. When Stoneham assured him that would be the case, Terry made his first symbolic move. He said he wanted to fire "Doc" Knowles, the club trainer but really McGraw's "spy," who reported back to McGraw on the players' whereabouts and behavior. Stoneham said that would be fine. With that move, Terry had sent notice that he would do things differently, and Stoneham had given his permission. The time of the "Terrymen," the team nickname invented by the sportswriters, had begun.

Once the shock waves died down among the New York press corps over the news of McGraw's resignation, the head scratching began. New York baseball writers began to dig into the story and raise questions. Was McGraw's decision to resign his alone? Was the resignation something that had been brewing, or was it a recent event? Was any pressure put on McGraw to resign? How much did the Giants' poor standing in the National League affect McGraw's decision? How did Terry rise to the top as a managerial candidate? Rumors spread even among the national press that McGraw might have been forced out of his job.[6] A few New York writers speculated that McGraw had lost the clubhouse and his players were in revolt, especially infielder Fred Lindstrom, who was the latest in a long line of McGraw's whipping boys.[7] Others speculated that McGraw's bad health had affected his command of the game and that Stoneham agreed and suggested that McGraw should take time off and get healthy. One national writer, J. G. Taylor Spink of the *Sporting News*, learned that a "major stockholder" (Spink did not name Stoneham, but it could hardly be anyone else) had decided that 1932 "was to be either make or break with McGraw, that he either win the pennant—or at least make a stout fight for it—or he would have to resign and let someone else try."[8]

The exact details behind this seismic shift in Giants history may not ever be known. McGraw's statement was the main source of the central narrative that appeared in most of the city's papers. This version has McGraw as the central actor, the decision maker, the one who pushes the action, not surprising, perhaps, since it was McGraw himself who wrote the statement. Advised by his doctor not to travel with the team, McGraw had decided to resign and reported that decision to Stoneham, suggesting that another manager be appointed, that it should be Bill Terry, and that Stoneham had agreed. McGraw had also advised Stoneham that Terry must have "full and complete charge and control of the club and will have to assume entire responsibility therefore," and Stoneham had approved.[9]

Bill Terry's own version is slightly different, not in the main story line but in certain details, suggesting nuances. Stressing that there was little love lost between him and McGraw—they hadn't spoken in almost four months—Terry remembers that the initial conversation about the manager's job was very brief. McGraw had asked if Terry was interested, and Terry had responded quickly that he would take it. McGraw then told Terry to shower (Terry was still in uniform, expecting to play before the game was officially called off), dress, and meet him in Stoneham's office, "upstairs." The meeting took place between

Stoneham, Terry, McGraw, and Jim Tierney; Stoneham had nothing to say to the press, who joined them a bit later. According to Terry, most of the conversation about the job had occurred between Terry and Stoneham, since, according to Terry biographer Peter Williams, Stoneham had lost confidence in McGraw. McGraw was present in the room when Terry asked to fire Knowles, a signal that McGraw's "influence was not only diminished as he sat meekly in Stoneham's office that afternoon, it was gone."[10] Williams heard this story from Terry late in Terry's life and thinks there were probably other versions that Terry told to others. Nonetheless, Williams asserts, "one element remains consistent: Terry accepts on the spot, without hesitation, surprising McGraw, who is puzzled that he needs no time to think about it."[11]

McGraw's biographer Charles C. Alexander offers yet another and somewhat different version. The meeting between Stoneham and Terry took place on June 3, a day after McGraw's initial conversation with Terry in McGraw's office. McGraw was conspicuously absent from the June 3 meeting, preferring to stay home, while Jim Tierney, the club secretary, with Stoneham, Terry, and club attorney Bondy present, read and then distributed a statement signed by McGraw, indicating that he was stepping down and that he and Stoneham had agreed on Terry as the new manager.[12] The newspapermen invited to Stoneham's office for the announcement did not have the luxury of directly questioning McGraw or, for that matter, other Giant officials. The biggest change in Giants baseball in thirty years had taken place with little organizational commentary aside from the distributed statement. For his part, following his usual practice, Stoneham had nothing to say to the press. Terry gave interviews much later at his own apartment. At home in Pelham, McGraw instructed his wife that afternoon to tell anyone calling for an interview that "I am not here."[13]

Spink's conjecture that McGraw was under some pressure to resign points to what is the most probable explanation of the change in Giants managers. While not differing in the main from details of most newspaper accounts, Spink nonetheless presents a new twist by putting

Stoneham as the main force in McGraw's resignation. This hunch is not far-fetched. Beginning with the Rogers Hornsby's trade to the Boston Braves in 1928, Stoneham had become more engaged in club business, however gradually and sporadically, especially when it involved personal matters. Prior to the Hornsby trade, Stoneham, while consulted on player acquisitions and trades, was content to take a back seat to McGraw on personnel issues, even on player salaries. Shuffling Hornsby off to Boston, however, was Stoneham's doing and his alone. In fact, it even caught McGraw by surprise, since he was out of town and was not informed until the decision was made. Stoneham also had taken the lead in what would be the last of Terry's continual contract disputes and holdouts. In early spring of 1932, when Terry returned his contract unsigned with a demand for a higher salary or to be traded, it was Stoneham, not McGraw, who stepped in, sending Terry a sharp and pointed ultimatum to accept the terms of the contract or quit baseball. And from 1928 through 1933, in what seemed to be the never-ending legal standoff between Stoneham and McGraw against Frank McQuade, Stoneham took the lead in the various appeals, all the way to the state's highest court, with McGraw clearly in the background. Given all of Stoneham's growing involvement in the Giants organization and business matters, his role in the McGraw resignation seems obvious enough, even without any clear and definitive evidence or record.

In these examples of Stoneham's having taken the lead role in major club decisions, one motivating factor stands out: that it was personal and not strictly business. When Charley Stoneham felt his authority was being challenged or that he was being disrespected, he acted decisively, usually with an eye toward some sense of retribution. With Hornsby, there were the Rajah's public affronts and insults aimed at Stoneham; there was also Hornsby's known tendencies to welsh on bets, behavior that Stoneham, a gambler himself, could not personally abide. In the Terry contract dispute, annoyed about Terry's presumptive dictation of club business—Terry, as a player, demanding a certain salary or a trade—Stoneham decided to handle the contractual negotiations personally, something that usually fell to McGraw.[14] Stoneham's lead in the McQuade lawsuits was also deeply personal, fueled by his resentment of McQuade that grew into a bitter obsession to best him on every contested legal issue. And the situation with the Giants' performance in June 1932 was beginning to feel personal for Stoneham as well, affecting his pocketbook. Almost exclusively dependent on the earnings of the National Exhibition Company, he was extremely sensitive about the Giants' gate receipts. The dismal start to the 1932 season with the Giants languishing in last place was not lost on him. He could not afford to let the season slip away. McGraw's decision to step down not only was something that Stoneham accepted but was more than likely something that he sought.

Stoneham's central involvement in McGraw's resignation and Terry's hiring becomes more convincing in light of a conversation between Terry and Fred Lindstrom. Years after they had both left the game and were in a mood for reminiscing, Lindstrom mentioned that he was still angry about McGraw going back on his word when he offered the manager's job to Terry. According to Lindstrom, McGraw told Lindstrom that once the job was open—that is, when McGraw was ready to leave—Lindstrom would be McGraw's choice to fill the post. But Terry corrected him and explained that Stoneham, not McGraw, had offered Terry the job. Peter Williams recounts the conversation in his biography of Terry: "While Lindstrom thought McGraw chose Terry over Stoneham's objections, Terry was particularly firm in insisting it was the other way around. Considering McGraw's obvious loss of influence and his visible decline, plus the strong possibility that McGraw was either encouraged or forced to quit, Terry's version seems more likely."[15]

Terry's replacement of McGraw as the Giants' manager was only one of many changes that New York would see in 1932. There was the national presidential election, resulting in a change of administration. The presidential campaign also raised severe doubts across the country about the Eighteenth Amendment's prohibition on alcohol. Early in 1933 those doubts moved the Senate, on February 14, to approve the Twenty-First Amendment to the Constitution, repealing the Eighteenth Amendment; two days later the House of Representatives followed suit. By the end of the year, enough states had ratified the Twenty-First Amendment, and the country's thirteen-year experiment with Prohibition was over.[16] Locally, Samuel Seabury's corruption investigation would force a resignation in September from New York City mayor Jimmy Walker, signaling an end to Jazz Age politics in Gotham. Seabury's committee would sweep out many of Tammany Hall's politicos in other city positions as well.[17]

Change was coming, too, in the makeup of the 1933 Giants' roster. During the winter of 1932–33, Terry began a rebuilding campaign that would refashion the 1933 Giants as his team. Its primary purpose was to improve the ball club, but it was also a deliberate attempt to move out from under McGraw's shadow. Terry traded an unhappy Fred Lindstrom, one of McGraw's favorites, and brought back pitcher Roy "Tarzan" Parmelee (so named for his wildness on the mound) from Columbus, sent there by McGraw to work on his control. Then Terry pulled off a big trade with the Cardinals, getting catcher Gus Mancuso, one of the best in the league, for four players from the 1932 squad.[18] By the time Terry had finished dealing during the winter months, more than half of his 1933 team had never played for McGraw. The change was so pronounced that, in an article entitled "New Deal on the Diamond," *New York Times* sports columnist John Kieran compared Terry's moves to FDR's radical plans to reorganize and energize the nation's economy.[19]

The remaking of the 1933 Giants would never have happened without a green light from Stoneham, whose approval of the changes reflected the degree of confidence he had in his new manager. Indeed, that confidence was quick in coming, even before Terry began his remaking of the 1932 Giants. When Terry took the helm in June, the Giants were in last place; they finished the season in sixth place, a slight improvement. But Stoneham saw a big change in the Giants in the second half of the season. The team played better in July, August, and September. It was apparent to Stoneham that there was new energy on the field and a better mood in the clubhouse. Stoneham was impressed with this new managerial style—anti-McGraw, a manager who led his team rather than controlled it. The mood of authoritarian rule that hung over McGraw's teams had given way to a more open, relaxed, and tolerant style. F. C. Lane of *Baseball Magazine* described the contrast: "McGraw was the autocrat of the diamond. . . . Players to him were little beyond automata who batted and ran bases as he pulled the strings. . . . Terry is a player . . . the leading player on the team, and he manages not by driving nor even directing, so much as he does by leading."[20]

Terry treated his players as men who knew the game, who understood that they would have to compete and would have to prepare every day in order to do so. On Terry's watch, the door to the manager's office was always open, and players could drop in anytime to talk. The curfew set by McGraw at 11:30 p.m. was moved back to midnight; anyone who had a reason to come in later could always check with the skipper.[21] While the vibes were better under Terry and the players were playing hard, they could not do much to salvage the 1932 season. Nonetheless, Stoneham was greatly impressed, so much so that midway through September—only three months into Terry's managerial career—the Giants boss acknowledged the improvement by giving Terry a new two-year contract extension. It was also a strong vote of confidence to the new manager that would help him in building the 1933 team. Perhaps unknown to either man, a strong relationship between both of them was budding, one that, for Stoneham at least, would lead to a degree of trust that would have profound personal significance in the next two years.

The rebuilding process would reap great benefits. While few sports-writers and baseball pundits gave the Giants much of a chance for the

1933 season—most felt they would remain a second-division club—
Terry was quite optimistic, especially given the new players he had
assembled. The Giants opened the season quietly, winning some and
losing some, but found their rhythm in early June, when they took
over first place and never looked back. Sensing the prospects of a
good season, Terry decided to bring in some bench strength, nabbing
Lefty O'Doul, the reigning National League batting champion, in a
deal with Brooklyn on June 16.[22] With O'Doul coming off the bench
as a pinch hitter, or as a spot starter, the Giants added some offense
to their formidable pitching. Starters Carl Hubbell, Hal Schumacher,
Roy Parmelee, and Freddie Fitzsimmons combined for 71 wins in the
1933 season. Hubbell was particularly masterful, with a 23–12 record,
a 1.66 ERA, and 46 consecutive scoreless innings.[23]

The season was described as a run of nail-biter contests, with the
Giants prevailing in most one- and two-run games.[24] Two games in
midsummer stood out as characteristic. On July 2 the Giants played
a doubleheader at the Polo Grounds against the St. Louis Cardinals,
winning each game 1–0. But the real story was the pitching, especially
in the first game, when Hubbell went eighteen innings, struck out
twelve batters, gave up only six hits, and walked none. His opponent,
St. Louis pitcher Tex Carleton, went sixteen innings and gave way to
reliever Jesse Haines, who took the loss. The second game was between
Dizzy Dean of the Cardinals and Parmelee, both of whom went the
full nine innings. Parmelee struck out thirteen batters and gave up only
five hits; Dean struck out six and gave up just four hits. The second
game was decided by a Johnny Vergez solo home run. The combined
twenty-seven innings of both games featured two of the greatest days
of pitching in major league baseball history.

After moving to a comfortable six-game lead in mid-August, the
Giants were never threatened and clinched the National League pennant on September 19, when the second-place Pittsburgh Pirates lost.
On the road in St. Louis, Terry led his team to a postgame celebration
in the visitors' clubhouse, telling reporters that "this was my biggest

thrill in baseball."[25] The feeling must have grown when the Giants returned home the next day, September 20, and were met at Grand Central Station by a huge crowd of fans and two marching bands.[26] A beaming Charley Stoneham was among the dignitaries waiting for the team. He warmly greeted Terry and told him in an aside what a great job he did and how much the fans of New York appreciated it.[27]

The next morning the team was feted at City Hall in a public reception hosted by Mayor John P. O'Brien. Stoneham was one among others, including Mayor O'Brien, who offered his remarks. Stoneham's words were brief and pointedly effusive about the job Terry had done in his first full year as manager, but that Stoneham spoke at all—usually he assigned secretary Jim Tierney the role of club spokesman—was an indication of the pleasure he took in the Giants' achievement. It had been almost ten years since he had seen his team reach the top of the National League. Perhaps his public expression was motivated also by a sense of relief that he could now be fully absorbed in the sport he loved, that his attention was fixed on baseball and not on the legal troubles of the past few years or the front office squabbles that had plagued him recently with McGraw and, especially, McQuade. Something else was dramatically clear to him and probably extremely satisfying. He was now solely in charge of the organization and ready to enjoy the moment. His team had just won the National League pennant. And the best was yet to come.

The World Series against the powerful Washington Senators would be a rematch of the 1924 Fall Classic, when the Senators won in extra innings on a routine ground ball that struck a pebble and bounced over the third baseman's head for a game-winning base hit. This year sportswriters insisted that the Senators would need no help from the infield dirt. With their heavy-hitting lineup, they were huge favorites to beat the Giants.[28] But Terry was confident that his pitching would silence the Washington bats, and he proved to be prescient. Carl Hubbell was particularly dominant, winning Game One and Game Four; Hal Schumacher and Dolf Luque won the other two. For all their firepower, the Senators managed only one win in the best-of-seven series. After an eleven-year wait, the Giants were World Series champions once again.

It was a wild celebratory scene in the visitors' clubhouse at Washington's Griffith Stadium, with Terry running around embracing his players. Stoneham was present and gave some brief remarks, giving Terry credit and praising the players for a superb effort. McGraw was in the clubhouse as well but remained in the background, allowing Terry to bask in his achievement. American League president William Harridge and Senators manager Joe Cronin dropped in to congratulate the winners.[29] But the big celebration was yet to come. Their postgame clubhouse festivities over, the Giants boarded their special train taking them back to New York, where they were met at Pennsylvania Station by a crowd estimated at over two thousand and another round of impromptu speeches. Then it was on to the Hotel New Yorker, where Stoneham arranged a team reception that seemed at odds with the nation's economic and social predicament. The evening played to script; it was vintage Charley Stoneham as a Gatsby-like host, providing plenty of food and drink to establish a festive mood that carried on into the morning hours. One writer described the incongruity: "It may have been the Depression, but Charles Stoneham was both grateful and generous."[30] Characteristically, Stoneham took his pleasure essentially offstage, or on the edges of the action, letting others give the speeches and the toasts and sing the songs.

The hosting of the World Series victory celebration at the Hotel New Yorker is only one example of the joy that Stoneham took in the 1933 season and the exploits of his Giants ball club. Winning it all was in itself a great thing, as any owner would attest. But there was more significance to this pennant and this championship for Stoneham. For one thing, he had waited a long time and during that wait he had been mired in a number of legal distractions. All that was behind him now, which made the 1933 season all the more enjoyable. And his role in the success was significant. His decision to hire Terry as manager appeared not only to be a stroke of insight but also a full refutation of the criticism from those in the press who had questioned the appointment. Moreover, the admiration Stoneham held for Terry had grown during the year as they worked together. Stoneham's regard for Terry as manager exceeded his regard for him as a player. The two men had grown to respect one another, and Stoneham would continue to rely on Terry, both as the on-field leader of the ball club and as a trusted colleague in the franchise.

But there was something else that made the 1933 season so satisfying for Stoneham. He relished the achievement of this season particularly because of the recent changes in the front office ownership. With McGraw retired and McQuade effectively banished, Charley Stoneham was the last man standing from the original partnership. He took a certain amount of pride that he was now the singular head of the franchise. In this personal way, he did not have to share the year's accomplishment with anyone else. As it turned out, he would be right to celebrate the glory of this year for all of these reasons. It would be the last time he would enjoy such heights as a baseball man.

10

The Last Drop

He stretched out his hand desperately as if to snatch only a
wisp of air, to save a fragment. . . . But it was all going
by too fast now for his blurred eyes and he knew that
he had lost that part of it, the freshest and the best, forever.
— F. SCOTT FITZGERALD, *The Great Gatsby*

For Charley Stoneham 1934 was his last year as himself. A confirmed
Manhattanite, drawn to the city's restaurants and nightlife, a baseball
owner proud of his Giants' recent World Series championship as they
regained their lofty place in National League prominence, Stoneham
lived this year fully and, one would have to say, stubbornly, driven by
a conviction that his life was his own and that he could live it on his
terms. His stubbornness was made obvious during his midyear physical examination, when his doctor warned him to stop drinking. "Go
on the water-wagon, or you will not live very long" were the doctor's
words. Looking his doctor in the eye, Stoneham responded without
hesitation: "Listen, doctor. When Teddy Roosevelt was President he
had a tennis cabinet. Tennis was his obsession. One afternoon his doctor
examined him and gravely announced, 'Mr. President, you will have
to give up tennis or life itself.' Roosevelt said, 'I don't know which to
choose.' And so I say to you now, if life means no fun at all, I don't
know which to choose."[1]

But choose he did, and it was away from his doctor's admonition
and toward "fun," as he would call it, taking full advantage of city life,
hitting his convivial stride, and hosting parties and receptions at the

Waldorf or the Hotel New Yorker for baseball owners, officials, and friends of the ball club, as he did after the 1933 World Series championship. Even when the Giants finished second in the 1934 pennant race, having surrendered a seven-game lead in mid-September and losing out in the last two days to a surging St. Louis Cardinals team, Stoneham was generous in defeat, inviting players, club officials, and journalists to an open house at the season's end at the Hotel New Yorker. Rather than express publicly the disappointment he surely felt about his team's late collapse or second-guess his manager or suggest pay cuts for his players, he served drinks and provided food for his guests.

Perhaps playing the role of the gracious loser was a demonstration of something Stoneham had learned over the years about the game he loved: how difficult it was to win out consistently in Major League Baseball. Or perhaps all of this Gatsby-like hosting was simply another example of living large. At this stage of his life, with his doctor's warning running though his mind, he might have sensed how fleeting things are, that time allows so few and such moments to enjoy. If he did feel this way, he was right to seize the moment. In a little over a year, his doctor's words would ring true: Stoneham's illness (he would die of Bright's disease, a general and historical term for chronic nephritis) was gathering force and would soon become limiting. That year, 1934, would turn out to be his last full year for "fun."

The year was also one in which Stoneham could relish his associations with fellow owners. When he first became a member of baseball's House of Lords, he had more detractors than any owner in baseball, viewed by many as an interloper, a monied, shady businessman with a fondness for horses and gambling. But after fifteen years in the league, his peers had warmed to him, granting a sense of respect and even admiration; he was now regarded by his fellow owners as a wise senior counselor. He was elected vice president of the National League, voted onto different committees, and was a quiet but steady force in annual meetings. He spoke less often than others, but when he did, they listened, moved by his judgment, common sense, and rare ability to reconcile warring factions. "When the row had gone as far as he deemed necessary, in the interest of good fellowship Charley would pipe up with a witty remark, everybody would laugh and the tension was off," one National League owner remarked.[2] To settle a disagreement or bring matters to a voting consensus, Stoneham often would rise and deliver with a serious face what had become his famous quip, "Gentleman, the last one in buys the drinks."[3] His standing with his fellow owners in 1934 must have been a distinct pleasure for him, given the initial coolness and disdain with which they had received him in 1919.[4] While there is no evidence of a deep friendship with any single one of them, he did have pleasant relationships with every owner and, it appears, was regarded by them as good company.

Perhaps no clearer example of Stoneham's standing among his fellow lords, and his dedication to a life of fun, came during the National League owners' winter meetings of 1934—the final meeting he would attend due to failing health. Held in recently elected NL president Ford Frick's office in Manhattan, it was a lengthy affair that broke up at 11:00 p.m., at which point Stoneham invited his fellow moguls to join him for a late dinner and a night on the town. Always the convivial host, he held a reputation as a marathon reveler, and on this occasion he had the satisfaction of being the last man standing at six in the morning, when Cardinals owner Sam Breadon, the only one left lingering with him, curled up to sleep.[5] This episode adds to the Stoneham saga already crowded with stories of tremendous parties and spending, of someone with a boundless enthusiasm for squeezing the last possible drop of fun out of life.[6]

The year 1934 was the second of the midsummer classic All-Star Games between the American League and the National League. It was held on July 10, hosted by the Giants at the Polo Grounds. The occasion gave Stoneham yet another opportunity to entertain at the Hotel New Yorker, this time for the entire baseball world on the evening following the game. And he did not skimp, throwing a postgame reception for owners and players from both leagues and sports journalists as well, with everything to eat and drink that any of his guests could want. It was a grand celebration, and despite the National League's 9–7 loss, Stoneham could savor a great moment in All-Star Game history courtesy of his own Carl Hubbell. Hubbell, the NL starting pitcher, had struck out consecutively five of the AL's greatest hitters, all future Hall of Famers—Babe Ruth, Lou Gehrig, Jimmy Foxx, Al Simmons, and Joe Cronin—a feat that is still regarded as one of the game's legendary performances.

Determined to live fully, Stoneham was stubborn about doing so on his own terms. He celebrated in a particular, one might even say circumspect, manner, customarily out of the limelight, or at least as much as possible out of the public eye. Unlike some of his Jazz Age ostentatious contemporaries like Babe Ruth, F. Scott and Zelda Fitzgerald, Mayor Jimmy Walker, Broadway attorney William Fallon, or movie star Gloria Swanson, Stoneham felt no need to call attention to himself. As the generous host, he was often in the background, content to let his guests mingle on their own and have others do the toasting and the speech making. His choice of restaurants, favorites like Jack's and Billy the Oysterman's or the old Waldorf and the Hotel New Yorker, were calculated, knowing that as a regular he was assured a private table or a suite for his guests. In this sense he was an anomaly, a Jazz Age bon vivant who enjoyed the city's nightlife but never wanted to read his name in the newspaper social columns the following morning.[7] His discretion and penchant for privacy were marked even as the owner of the Giants, a storied and public enterprise in the city of New York and covered by a bevy of reporters. In almost all ball club matters, he avoided center stage, preferring that his managers—first McGraw and then Terry—function in the spotlight as the public face of the franchise or that club secretary Jim Tierney or Giants attorney Leo Bondy provide front office statements and interviews. His rift with fellow owner Frank McQuade was fueled in part by Stoneham's aversion to McQuade's flamboyant behavior and lack of discretion regarding Giants business. One writer remarked that sportswriters could cover the Giants for an entire season, be frequent guests at the Polo Grounds, and never lay eyes on Charley Stoneham.[8]

One thing that does seem apparent about Stoneham at this stage of his life was his increased personal involvement and interest in his ball club, certainly more than in previous years. Due in some part to the changes in the front office that were shaped by the managerial transition from McGraw to Terry, Stoneham became more active in the affairs of the club, especially with contracts and player acquisitions. But more important perhaps, he became an ardent baseball fan again. Stoneham took great pleasure in the 1933 championship and the oh-so close 1934 finish. He rarely missed a 1934 home game, watching almost all of them from the solitary confines of his office window, perched high above the center field bleachers. The rush of the pennant race that season was such that he decided to go on a few late-summer road trips, to Chicago, St. Louis, and Boston, the last season he would feel able to do so.

With the distance of time and Stoneham's known practice of secrecy, it is difficult to know with any certainty why this interest in baseball so concentrated his mind. His renewed joy with his ball club may have come because of the surprising success the Giants were enjoying with Terry's hand on the tiller. It also may have resulted naturally from the newfound attention he could give the game. Behind him and over with were the residue of his brokerage business, the legal entanglements of the last ten years, the strife with Frank McQuade, and the difficult managerial transition from John McGraw, whose recent death surely touched an emotional chord. McQuade was good riddance, but McGraw's absence was more complicated. Despite all their differences and difficulties, there had been a cooperative working relationship between the two men. On Stoneham's part, he felt enough connection and loyalty to his deceased former manager and partner that he attended both the wake at the McGraw home in New Rochelle and the funeral mass at Manhattan's St. Patrick's Cathedral, where he served as an honorary pallbearer. After the mass, he accompanied McGraw's widow, Blanche, taking the body to Baltimore for the burial.[9]

With McGraw gone, Stoneham was the last of the 1919 partners left within the organization, something that surely registered with him. Perhaps these considerations engendered a sense of renewal, prompting him to reconnect as a fan with the game he had fallen in love with first as a seventeen-year-old, playing right field for the semipro Jersey City Woodwards, and a year later with the Equitable Life Assurance Society New York City team.[10] It was during his playing days that he first developed deep affection for the Giants, and his fondness for the club was no small part of his motivation to buy the team many years later.[11]

It is tempting to imagine another explanation for his mood in 1934. Perhaps, at this stage of his life and with health issues troubling him, Stoneham chose to live to the utmost in the time he had remaining. He certainly was made aware of his physical condition not only by his doctor but also by telling bodily changes, especially a noticeable loss of weight, that were unmistakable.[12] In his stubborn attempt to squeeze every drop out of the moment, was there also an accompanying philosophical drive, or at least a reflective one? Did he look back on his decision to buy the Giants and forward to what might lie ahead? Sensing his mortality, did he consider what he had achieved and begin, in the proverbial sense, to settle his affairs? It is speculation to imagine the "inner life" of a man who tried so hard to live discreetly and cagily, who took privacy to an extreme level, and who continued to do so in the final year of his life.

But there is some evidence that informs and guides such speculation. Consensus from sportswriters at the time suggests that Stoneham was content with the progress of the Giants and optimistic about the future, especially now that Bill Terry was running the ball club.[13] The two had formed a congenial working relationship, and Stoneham had come to rely on Terry as one of his most trusted associates. This development had certainly seemed improbable, if not impossible, just two years earlier, when Terry held out in 1932 and Stoneham retaliated with a "take-it-or-leave-it" contract. After Terry became manager, however, their relationship changed. Stoneham began to warm to him. At the end of the 1933 world championship season, in appreciation of Terry's leadership and a reflection of the optimism in the club's future, Stoneham awarded his manager a new contract of forty thousand dollars—a hefty raise of ten thousand dollars in the midst of a national depression.[14] In turn, Terry appreciated the vote of confidence from his boss almost as much as the increase in salary.

There is also evidence that Stoneham's assessment of his son's ability as a baseball executive had become more positive and upbeat in recent years.[15] Horace Stoneham, now in his early thirties, had followed his father's regimen that he learn the business of baseball from the ground up, first in the mid-1920s, overseeing ticketing, then gradually progressing through travel arrangements, publicity, facility direction and operation, and finally, in the early 1930s, front office matters, including player contracts.[16] It was Horace's performance in these duties that eventually convinced Charley that his son would be capable as the ball club's chief executive.[17] The story has often been told that Stoneham bought the team so his son could take it over, but only in the last years of Stoneham's life did it appear that this legacy might become possible.[18] The father's early views of his son as a teenager and young adult did not inspire confidence that Horace could manage the responsibilities of running a business. Horace's biographer Steven Treder believes that it was only after Stoneham sent his son to work in the copper mines in California as a twenty-two-year-old, then brought him back to New York to work up through the Giants organization, that Horace matured and began to exhibit potential.[19] Charley's tough love had its effect.

Convinced that his son had matured and learned how the various levels of the organization functioned, Charley decided to hand down the National Exhibition Company to Horace, to keep it, as it were, a family business. But his decision did not quiet the rumors that the ball club was for sale. Stories of the sale of the Giants were rampant throughout the years that Charles Stoneham owned the team, but he was always quick with a qualified and quirky denial, saying that he wouldn't consider selling, "except at such a high price that no sane man could refuse."[20] With McGraw's death, new versions of this old tale surfaced—that with no partners to consult, Stoneham would now look to move the team for the right price. And with these rumors came the standard denials from Stoneham. This time, however, the denial had some support. By the end of 1934, the front office, led by attorney and club treasurer Leo Bondy, was preparing for the succession from father to son more or less as a foregone conclusion. No one in the front office could know how soon that future change would be upon the organization.[21]

Over the winter of 1934–35, declining health took its toll on Charley Stoneham. He went out less, cut back on evenings at his cherished restaurants and nightclubs, and put in only an occasional appearance at winter baseball events. Certainly, by the spring of 1935, his kidney disease had strengthened its grip; he no longer had the same zest for life nor much stamina. He did manage to attend the Giants home opener on April 23 and participate in the annual pregame stadium march, leading his baseball club to the center field flagpole. But just a cursory glance at the photos covering the events that day shows a pale and ashen Stoneham, a visible sign of his illness. Early in the 1935 season, he did watch some home games from his office seat window, undoubtedly feeling the need for privacy more than ever as he grew weaker. One of his last public appearances was to accept ringside seats from Yankees owner Jacob Ruppert for the Joe Louis–Primo Carnera heavyweight fight at Yankee Stadium on June 25.[22] By midsummer he began missing stretches of Giants home games—his family in Westchester remembers him resting in his room for two- and three-week periods in late summer and into the autumn. He gave up any thought of joining the team on a Midwest September road trip, passing that undertaking, as well as some club personnel matters, on to Horace.[23]

With the beginning of baseball's winter meetings in Chicago on December 8, the change in the Giants' operations was evidenced by the conspicuous absence of Charles Stoneham and the presence of

Horace Stoneham, representing the team, voting in meetings for the first time, and announcing trades.[24] Charley, home in New York and suffering, was in the last weeks of his life. By mid-December the situation had become dire. In a desperate move, Stoneham turned to the man he trusted most in the franchise, his manager Bill Terry. Stoneham phoned Terry at his home in Memphis, explained that he was gravely ill and weakened, and asked Terry to come immediately to New York and take him to Hot Springs, Arkansas, where he could be treated.[25] The Giants boss wanted no publicity, no reporters, no one from the Giants organization, not even his son Horace to know. He made it clear to Terry that he felt the necessity to go at once.

"When do you want to go?" Terry asked.

"As fast as we can get the tickets," Stoneham said.[26]

Terry was then told to contact Stoneham's doctor, W. M. Blackshare, and to ask him to get to Hot Springs as soon as possible. Stoneham had one other request. He wanted his African American butler, Alfred, to accompany him, and asked Terry to arrange a suite at one of the segregated hotels to accommodate Alfred. Terry did as he was asked; he came to New York and took his weakened and dying boss south by train to Arkansas.[27]

It must have been a particularly grueling trip for all three of them, considering the time of year, with all the complications of travel with a sick man, not to mention the hectic pace and crowding of a holiday season. Undoubtedly, having Alfred along was a great help to Terry. They arrived just before Christmas, and Stoneham's doctor was there to meet them. The treatment was palliative, consisting mostly of draining significant amounts of fluid from the terminal patient and making him as comfortable as possible. Terry remembered Stoneham's suffering vividly, watching the doctor extract enough fluid to fill a two-gallon bucket, and listening to Stoneham gasping and calling out for a drink a number of times. Just after the new year and knowing that the end was near—Stoneham was lapsing in and out of consciousness—Terry disregarded his boss's demand for secrecy and placed a call to Horace.

Terry explained that Stoneham was gravely ill and that if Horace wanted to see his father, he should come to Arkansas immediately. Terry then left for his home in Memphis.[28] An astonished Horace arrived a day later and was at the bedside, along with Stoneham's physician, Polo Grounds supervisor Ernie Viberg, and personal servant Alfred, when Stoneham died.[29] The following day Horace took his father's body back to New Jersey and arranged for a small, private requiem mass to be celebrated in Jersey City. Bill Terry was among the five Giants officials who joined Horace and his mother, Hannah, at the mass. Burial at Holy Name Cemetery followed.

Stoneham's attachment to secrecy was so strong that it outlived him, exerting its pressure on his survivors. His wish that his funeral and burial service be private and restricted—"no fanfare, no eulogy, no pall bearers, no excitement"—were closely respected by his family.[30] No one from baseball was invited; indeed, quite the opposite. The Commissioner's Office, the league presidents, fellow owners, the players and coaches from the Giants, all were asked by the family not to attend, and not to send flowers or notes. Similarly, the New York chapter of the Baseball Writers' Association and the local press were not informed about arrangements until the services were over. For obvious reasons of schedule and ceremony, only the clergy at All Saints Church were informed, and they were only four in number. The family requested that no one except the invited mourners be allowed inside the church during the mass. The total number who attended Stoneham's funeral, including the priests on the altar, was twelve.[31]

That Stoneham's desire for privacy regarding both his illness and his funeral rites were scrupulously followed might be taken as a strong indication of deference and respect from Terry and from Stoneham's immediate family, especially Horace. But the shroud placed on Stoneham's death and the speedy last rites that quickly followed raise intriguing questions. Why did Stoneham, satisfied at last with his son's capacity to run the Giants organization, turn to Bill Terry to reveal the extent of his illness, to arrange his treatment, and to manage the last days of his life? Why did Stoneham urge Terry to keep all the details of the illness, of the travel and the treatment quiet, even from those in the front office, including his son? Why did Stoneham insist on a private funeral? Why did Horace and his mother, Hannah (she had a right under law as a surviving widow to some say in these matters), adhere so faithfully to Stoneham's demand that all of baseball be prevented from attending or sending flowers? Where was Stoneham's daughter Mary in all of this?[32] And what of Stoneham's other family in Westchester County— Margaret Leonard Stoneham and son Russell Stoneham and daughter Jane Stoneham—who were excluded from the services?[33] The existence of a second family raises even more questions about Charley's life, not the least of which is how he managed two households simultaneously. What were the costs on the man, emotionally and psychologically, to live with these two families as both husband and father?

There are, of course, no definitive answers to these questions. But one conclusion that can be drawn is that Charley Stoneham lived a compartmentalized life, dividing affection, attention, and concentration. Long involved in extramarital flings, he lived both within and without his marriage.[34] By the time he started a second family with Margaret Leonard, a showgirl he had met after the war, his relationship with Hannah had become more distant, and his familial responsibilities had lessened: both daughter Mary and Horace were on their own. While his motivations remain unknown, one can guess why he could neither leave one wife nor completely live with the other. As an Irish Catholic, in a cultural sense at least, Stoneham wanted to avoid the social stigma of a divorce. Moreover, a divorce settlement with Hannah would come with huge financial costs, likely requiring him to liquidate his holdings in the Giants. This, in turn, would end all possibilities of Horace's succession as Giants boss. Exposure of his family with Margaret Leonard would raise questions of misrepresentation in the 1930 U.S. Census and possible bigamy charges.[35] These reasons leave aside the emotional toll of a life with two families with children. So he kept a Jersey City residence with Hannah and a Westchester County address with Margaret Leonard. Presumably, he could explain his absence from either address by the frequent demands of travel and late nights with baseball, but one wonders about the thoughts and feelings of each wife. Perhaps it was a case with both women of live and let live. It was, after all, the Jazz Age, when traditional Victorian mores were being challenged by a demand for freedom of lifestyle by a younger generation and when various Jazz Age celebrities and socialites had liaisons and arrangements that called for flexibility in domestic matters. In this sense Charley was a man of his time.[36]

This divided self might explain the degree to which he sought release in drinking and late-hour revelry, as a temporary escape from familial responsibilities, which in his case were extreme. His complicated family life might also account in another way for his intense desire for privacy and a feeling that he wanted to be guarded, even mysterious, about aspects of his personal life. The insistence upon privacy seems to have had an effect. No mention of Stoneham's complicated family life appears in the press during his lifetime nor in any of the testimony from the many appearances Stoneham made in New York courts over the years. Indeed, the only evidence appears in the 1930 U.S. Census, showing Stoneham living in two places with two separate families.[37] It appears that in Stoneham's case at least, history reveals men's deeds and outward accomplishments but nothing about the secret self, the life of the mind and heart.[38]

While the inner life of Charles Stoneham remains enigmatic, his outward life—his public deeds, his work, his business activities—is less so. There is a substantial body of commentary on him as a businessman, a ruthless one at that, and highly successful. Writers point to his various companies, offices, and connections. They comment on his drive, his intelligence, and his risk taking as reasons for his prominence in the brokerage and investment business. None of the writers who describe his business activities mistake him for a choirboy. Stoneham dealt primarily in unscrupulous bucket shop trading, in which the rules and procedures were more flexible and loose than those of the more traditional and established Wall Street brokerage houses. The terms *cutthroat* and *aggressive* were often applied to him.

Much has been made of Stoneham as a gambler, not only his attraction to gaming and horse racing but also his reputation as a high-stakes player in New York City. There are stories of sensational bets that he made (one evening he bet $70,000 over the phone) and those that might have happened but didn't (once he continued to raise the stakes of a side bet with Yankees owners Ruppert and Huston to $700,000, until a third party intervened and called off the bet).[39] There are also accounts of how gambling facilitated him in the investment market. "Stocks and games were one coin to Charles Stoneham," as one writer put it.[40] Gambling dictated his business style, especially in risk taking and timing, two essentials when dealing with stocks. Stoneham's sense of timing was generally good throughout his business career, particularly in 1920, when he made the decision to leave the investment business and to buy the Giants. With the 1920 market heating up and showing no signs of stopping—Stoneham's strategy depended upon a falling market to maximize profits—he got out while he could still make gains, leaving many other bucket shop firms to take big losses.

Given the profligate and somewhat mysterious life of Charles A. Stoneham and views of him as a ruthless business type and self-gratifying playboy, two essentially conflicting views have emerged concerning his stewardship of the New York Giants. One view gives him negative marks as the head of the ball club and the organization. Those who hold this view argue that in 1919 Stoneham bought the premier baseball franchise in all of Major League Baseball and let it slide over the years from its vaulted perch to become the second-best team in New York City. This happened chiefly because of Stoneham's decision to milk the cash cow that was the National Exhibition Company in order to sustain his high-spending Jazz Age lifestyle and to distribute the annual dividends the Giants earned, rather than reinvest them to enhance the team's future.[41] An opposing view admits Stoneham's reckless and self-indulgent lifestyle, "cut-throat businessman by day, boozy bon vivant by night," but argues that in spite of this behavior, Stoneham's years as the New York Giants' owner were among the most successful in team history.[42]

Stoneham might have drawn some satisfaction from this conflicting view of him as a baseball man, adding to the mystery and complexity of his life. Judging his success as an owner, one might argue that in the Stoneham years, 1919–35, the Giants' record does not compare to the Yankees' totals during the same period, in World Series championships, in pennants in attendance, and in fan base. And in the two years immediately following Stoneham's death, 1936 and 1937, the Yankees again beat the Giants in the World Series. But more than a comparison with the Yankees is needed to measure Stoneham's achievements in baseball. He had a good run as an owner and eventually was respected overall by his peers as a trusted colleague and as someone who contributed to the general welfare of the game.[43] His leadership posts and responsibilities in the National League testify to that. Moreover, the Giants were successful at the gate under his watch, and they won their fair share of pennants and World Series championships, twice beating the Yankees. During the Stoneham years, the Giants' revenue posted higher annual profits than in all other previous years in the club's history. The matter of judging his effectiveness as an owner, therefore, depends on what is being measured: competition with the Yankees or an overall career as a baseball owner. If Stoneham's time with the Giants is weighed with the second category in mind, it was a success. But that there is even the possibility of contrasting views of a life in baseball seems appropriate and apt for a man so hard to assess and understand as a person, a man who spent most of his life creating an aura of mystery about his behavior, his actions, and his thinking and, it seems, even his achievements.

Epilogue

"Who is he?" I demanded. "Do you know?"
"He's just a man named Gatsby."
"Where is he from, I mean? . . . And what does he do?"
"Well—he once told me he was an Oxford man . . .
 However I don't believe it."
"Why not?"
"I don't know . . . I just don't think he went there."
—F. SCOTT FITZGERALD, *The Great Gatsby*

Charley Stoneham had been buried only a day or two before the New York journalists went to their typewriters to tell his story. Articles appeared regularly for the next three weeks, both obituaries and features, giving historical background and providing anecdotes about his activities and contributions as a baseball owner. But it was a strange turn of practice. Largely having neglected him for the past sixteen years—most of the reporting on Stoneham during his lifetime had been perfunctory, mainly confined to brief remarks on him attending to the business side of baseball or hosting a meeting—the reporters now felt compelled to render an account of his life. And the life that they described revealed the shortcomings of their efforts due to their earlier decision to narrow the focus. As a kind of *caveat lector*, one writer explained, "In so far as his biography is concerned, we are to busy ourselves only with the things he did in baseball."[1]

Some journalists portrayed Stoneham's love of baseball as a lifelong obsession. In these articles all events in his life, including his connections with Tammy Hall as a young man, his subsequent stormy business career as an investment broker, and his life as a Broadway playboy, were seen as a prelude to his ownership of the Giants. Other writers characterized Stoneham's purchase of the Giants as a paternal gesture, a gift to his son Horace, turning the National Exhibition Company into a family business. These articles were consistent in their concentration on a baseball life, depicting someone devoted to the sport and to the running of his team, a "forceful and progressive owner," a "respected member of baseball's ruling fraternity," "a great fan of the game." Those commenting on Stoneham's life were also consistent in what they chose not to consider. There was no treatment of Charley Stoneham the man, whose private and personal life involved complexities and contradictions and whose pursuit of money and pleasure embodied the paradox of his age: full enjoyment of a Jazz Age lifestyle encouraged, if not necessitated, straddling both sides of the law. None of this appeared in the New York articles on Stoneham in early January 1936.

Part of this crabbed approach had to do with the times and the journalistic codes governing the writers who followed baseball: the focus was to be placed on the players as participants in the game and on owners as leaders and executives of the sport. Personal matters, especially those that bordered on the scandalous or the unseemly, were to pass unnoticed and unmentioned. There was a tacit agreement between writer and subject that certain behavior—excessive drinking, rowdy antics at a restaurant or bar, a player's indiscretion with a female fan—was off the record and unprintable.

There were practical reasons for adherence to this writerly code. For most writers with the New York newspapers of the 1920s and 1930s, covering baseball was a cushy assignment, involving travel (including spring training in Florida during the cold late winters in the city), freedom away from the office, hanging out with celebrity players, and better salaries. Meals, drinks, ballpark admission, and often even hotel rooms were covered by the clubs that they followed. Baseball writers were aware of these special circumstances and appreciated that their livelihood depended on access to the players. Players were unlikely to give interviews to writers whom they did not trust. Also, the perks the writers enjoyed while covering baseball depended on the largesse of the ball clubs. Club officials could deny access to teams (and to the writers' lounge where food and drink were available) if miffed by what they deemed unfavorable coverage. So the writers walked a fine line. They wanted to provide insight and even be entertaining, but they had to be careful about putting anything unflattering, salacious, or overly personal in their columns. This was especially true of covering teams on road trips, when players and club official had plenty of spare time to congregate at hotel bars and seek out downtown amusements.[2]

The versions of Stoneham's life that appeared immediately following his death conformed to the 1936 sports writing ethic, concentrating on the professional and ignoring the personal. No mention was made of family life, friendships, or religious or political interests. Most of the big-name beat writers weighed in. Frank Graham of the *Sun*, Sid Mercer of the *New York American*, Bill Corum of the *New York Evening Journal*, John Drebinger and John Kieran of the *New York Times*, and Daniel M. Daniel of the *World-Telegram* all contributed articles summing up Stoneham's life in New York baseball. These were not obituaries— they also appeared in most of the major newspapers and followed the standard anonymous form of the genre—but, rather, reflections on an individual, written from a baseball writer's perspective. Only days after Stoneham's funeral service and burial, Daniel devoted two lengthy articles laced with heavy doses of purple prose, offering some background on Stoneham's life in baseball. The death of the Giants' boss was the culmination of an epic struggle, he wrote: "For more than a year Stoneham had faced the outstretched grasp of the Grim Reaper." Regarding Stoneham's early attraction as a boy to the New York Giants, readers were informed that "even in the somewhat bedraggled, rarely successful Giants of the '90s Stoneham saw sports Olympians to whose comparatively humble station he aspired with the fervor of a Moslem pilgrim struggling on the hot and barren road to Mecca," an extravagant ecumenical reflection on Irish-Catholic Stoneham's motivation for having bought the Giants.[3] Daniel's articles on Stoneham's life were also nostalgic, depicting Good Time Charley as a free spender among his fellow owners, picking up checks and hosting dinners.

In their attempts to busy themselves only with matters of a baseball life, the writers were mostly, but not completely, successful; intimations of the personal would seep through. More than one writer commented on Stoneham's penchant for privacy, his attempts at remaining offstage, out of the public eye, even when watching his team at the Polo Grounds. The *New York Herald Tribune*'s Richards Vidmer saw Stoneham's quest for privacy as a lifelong preoccupation: "To the public and the players, the late Mr. Stoneham was a name often seen in print but seldom heard on the street; a face that frequently appeared in the newspapers but seldom where the fans gathered. He was an unseen power in baseball; a figure that moved about behind closed doors in conference, and though he got as much enjoyment out of the game and the Giants as the most frenzied fan, he cheered silently and celebrated privately."[4] Although his focus was on a baseball life, Vidmer hinted at a larger and important problem in biography: what to do with a subject who led a mysterious life and tried so desperately to cover his tracks? It is possible that the New York baseball writers decided to eschew the personal when reflecting on Stoneham not only because of journalistic convention but also because they may not have known much of his life beyond the game itself.

One is left with the problem of writing a life of an individual who lived as if he wished to make that effort severely difficult, a public figure who strove to live as a guarded, private man. Consider the dilemma of the *New York Times* columnist who reported on Stoneham's funeral: "In accordance with the expressed desire and wishes of Mr. Stoneham, no one was present at the services except the immediate family and the baseball family of the New York Giants." The subject is privacy, again, but there is no reliable information available about Stoneham's "expression." To whom did he express this? And what exactly are "desires" and "wishes"? Are they offhand remarks—"I would like something . . ." or "I wish it were cooler"—or are they strict imperatives, as the *New York Times* article seems to suggest? And what about "family," given that there are at least two sets of children with mothers involved? This funeral reporting is just one example of the perplexing challenge one faces in a consideration of the uncertainties of Stoneham's life. Without any real evidence, how does one describe the life of an individual when so much of it remains murky or confusing? None of these sports writers seems to have worried about this difficulty.

When faced with an obscure or secretive subject, there is, however, another route to understanding: to place that subject within the context of the time in which he lived. It is this second consideration, rather than the one followed by the sportswriters, that has guided the approach of the previous chapters. While his work as a baseball owner undoubtedly defined certain aspects of his life, the era in which he owned the team weighs more heavily in developing a portrait of Stoneham, both as an organizational man and as an individual personality.

Chasing enjoyment and fun was the goal of the Jazz Age generation. Stoneham joined that pursuit and lived large during the 1920s because his earlier business practice provided him the means to do so.[5] Intelligent, savvy, and ruthless in the unregulated markets of the early twentieth century, he thrived in the tough, dog-eat-dog atmosphere of Wall Street and profited spectacularly. Stoneham cut corners, took accounts on margin, and worked the edges of legality, always putting profit over concerns for his clients and fighting back fiercely when dragged into court. Tenacious and driven, with deep pockets and the willingness to hire top attorneys, he stood up to federal prosecutors and financial regulators. Charley Stoneham was one tough and determined customer, as those who prosecuted him found out. Hardly a saint—more than likely the sheer number of his civil accusations and criminal charges led many who read the New York newspapers in the early 1920s to assume a "where-there-is-smoke" attitude about his guilt—he was indifferent to what was whispered about him and focused only on his success in business and survival in court.[6]

The wealth that Stoneham accumulated gave him the means to join in the Jazz Age swim. And Good Time Charley dove in. His reputation as a party boy and skirt chaser is deserved, although his talent in the latter category is somewhat surprising. The photos of Stoneham in the early 1920s—he was short, stout, and jowly—controverted any resemblance to the image of a dashing Lothario. But he seemed to have no problem attracting and romancing numerous women. During his thirty-five years of marriage to second wife, Hannah, he carried on with widows, married women, and Broadway showgirls. He even started a second life with one of them, chorus girl Margaret Leonard, who bore him two children. Even as he shuttled between Hannah and Margaret, maintaining two families and households simultaneously, it would be naive to imagine that there were no other women in his life during that time. Stoneham's position as Giants owner, with all of the attendant meetings, hosting duties, and travel, gave him ample time and plenty of cover to indulge such appetites.

In his relationships with women, especially with the two who seemed to be closest to him, Charley Stoneham was an incontestable cad. But in his own fashion, he was a caring father. He was a strict and demanding disciplinarian with son Horace, patiently grooming him for stewardship of the ball club. He took care of daughter Mary by bestowing upon her a sizable share of the National Exhibition Company.[7] He established a trust fund for Russell Stoneham and Jane Stoneham, children from his relationship with Margaret Leonard.[8] Yet the concept of paternal care seemed to have a limit for this complex man. There is little evidence that he was affectionate or personally close to any of his children.[9]

The impersonal relationships Stoneham had with his children extended to others. Indeed, it appears that Stoneham had no real friends and remained detached from those he knew, even from those with whom he worked closely. Instead, he had a wide array of acquaintances. His long, twenty-plus-year association with Arnold Rothstein linked them in many social and business settings. But their relationship was not a friendship. The same holds for the men he partnered with to buy the Giants in 1919. Charley Stoneham had a professional and collaborative relationship with John McGraw over the thirteen years they worked together, but respect for McGraw's baseball acumen did not translate into a real friendship. Stoneham's relationship with his other Giants junior partner, Frank McQuade, was even more distant, shaped as it was early in their collaboration by rancor and intense ill will. None of his fellow baseball owners, all of whom respected his work as a baseball executive and enjoyed his company socially, felt close enough to Stoneham to view him as a friend. Even with Giants manager Bill Terry, whom Charley trusted enough to keep secret his illness and, in his last days, to arrange his final journey to Hot Springs, he did not have a relationship that could be called a friendship. Rather, Charley Stoneham was a self-sufficient loner, whose detachment and impenetrable privacy bear an uncanny resemblance to Jay Gatsby—Jazz Age bon vivant, socially prominent and wealthy business tycoon, but a man without close friends, a generous host whose parties attracted hundreds every weekend but whose funeral was attended only by a handful.

These character traits that underlay the Charles Stoneham personae—unscrupulous and ruthless businessman, serial philanderer and quasi-bigamist, guarded socially and without even one close friend—reveal Stoneham to be an isolated individual, one who had to take risks to find enjoyment and satisfaction. Perhaps deep down that is the gambler's personality: risk something—money, reputation, relationships—to gain something. This penchant for risk taking applied as much to Stoneham's business and playboy lifestyle as it did to the gaming table or the racetrack. He could go all in for the moment and feel the adrenaline rush in the confidence of his success, with little concern for what anyone else thought.

Nonetheless, behind all of this reckless and selfish behavior—indeed, sustaining it—is a considerable strength of personality and conviction, characteristics that make Charley Stoneham, even in his roguishness, a fascinating and intriguing man. That sense of conviction and focus allowed Stoneham to achieve considerable success in his life, find some enjoyment, and endure the many challenges that came as a result. He allowed little to bother him or get in the way of where he wanted to go, whether it was a business deal, a legal issue, a player's contract, or a mistress's company. Indifferent to gossip or public opinion, he lived life on his own terms, even rejecting the advice of his personal physician to be more moderate and abstemious. He had an enormous appetite for "fun," as he called it, and he tried to grab as much of it as he could. He paid the price, not reaching his sixtieth year and suffering an agonizing death, but it is difficult to imagine him changing his behavior to gain a few more years. Spirited and complicated, Charley Stoneham epitomized his Jazz Age era.

Appendix

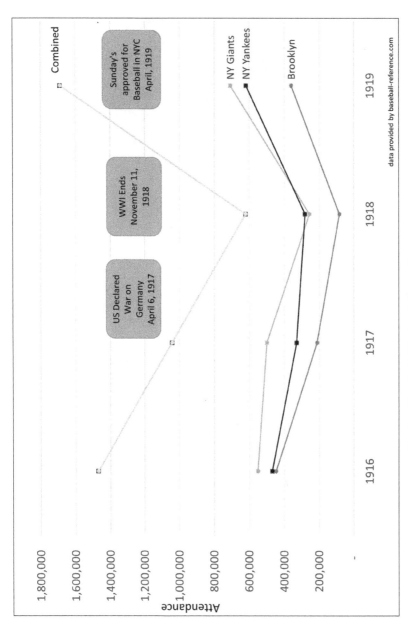

Graph 1. New York City baseball attendance, 1917–1919

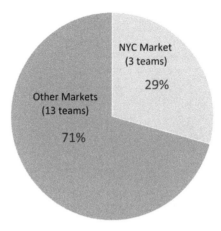

data provided by baseball-reference.com

Graph 2. New York City's share of baseball attendance, 1930–1935

Notes

Preface

1. The phrase appears in Ernest Hemingway's *The Sun Also Rises* and was attributed to Gertrude Stein, an American expatriate living in Paris in the 1920s, describing the young writers of the decade, including Hemingway, F. Scott Fitzgerald, John Dos Passos, and e. e. cummings, among others.
2. Faulkner, *Requiem for a Nun.*
3. Barry, *Great Pandemic.*
4. The 1920 election was also a reaction against decades of progressive campaigns against big business, corruption, and international policing. See Parrish, *Anxious Decades,* 3–10.
5. Corrigan, *So We Read On,* 23–25.
6. Corrigan, *So We Read On,* 4–6.
7. I was not the only reader returning to *The Great Gatsby*. In early 2021 the novel entered into the "public domain," when the ninety-five-year copyright expired (*Gatsby* was first published by Charles Scribner's Sons in 1925). As a result, no fewer than six new editions flooded the current market, prompting a number of reviews, some of which identified the work as the most important twentieth-century American novel. See John Williams, "The *Great Gatsby* Glut," *New York Times,* January 14, 2021.
8. Although no Fitzgerald scholar has proposed Stoneham as the direct model for Gatsby, there are many aspects of Stoneham's life that connect them. Like Gatsby's, the source of Stoneham's wealth is ambiguous, to say the least. Stoneham was connected to illicit bonds sales, as was Gatsby. Stoneham hosted many flamboyant parties. Fitzgerald also knew many of Stoneham's associates, including Arnold Rothstein and Edward Fuller (Fuller's trial for business fraud in 1923 ensnared Stoneham in serious legal difficulties). See Bruccoli, *F. Scott Fitzgerald,* 91n.

9. Stoneham was a successful "bucket shop" broker, a quasi-legal investment business that speculated with customer money. He is rumored to have partnered with Rothstein in the bootlegging business. Pietrusza, *Rothstein*, 195–96; Katcher, *Big Bankroll*, 235–36. Jane Leavy, author of biographies of Babe Ruth, Mickey Mantle, and Sandy Koufax, suggested that her grandfather partnered with Stoneham in the bootlegging business in the 1920s. Interview with the author, March 4, 2019.

10. Bradley, *Such Was Saratoga*, 300–301.

11. See, for example, Graham, *New York Giants*, 220; Hynd, *Giants of the Polo Grounds*, 297; Williams, *When the Giants Were Giants*, 193.

12. In the final draft and published version of the novel, the standoff between Tom and Gatsby occurs in the Plaza Hotel in Manhattan. Fitzgerald, *Great Gatsby*, 217–21.

13. Piper, *F. Scott Fitzgerald*, 119–20.

14. Piper, *F. Scott Fitzgerald*, 119–20. For an account of Fitzgerald's interest in the Fuller-McGee trial, see Churchwell, *Careless People*, 133–35.

15. Fitzgerald, *Tales of the Jazz Age*; and *Jazz Age*.

16. See, for example, Parrish, *Anxious Decades*, 183, 193; Waldo, *Baseball's Roaring Twenties*, ix.

17. Seymour and Seymour Mills, *Baseball*, 389–90; C. Alexander, *John McGraw*, 289; Pietrusza, *Rothstein*, 195–96; Tosches, *King of the Jews*, 277.

18. Graham, *New York Giants*, 220.

19. From 1922 through 1926, for example, Stoneham was associated with a number of bankruptcy cases and investment fraud trials that were covered in most of the city's newspapers.

20. Stoneham's name was connected to two women who took their lives because of unhappy love affairs. See *New York Times*, May 7, 1905, and February 11, 1920.

21. I have been guided here by Aristotle's *Poetics*, sec. 9, in which Aristotle argues for the superiority of poetry over history in depicting general truths, since "its [poetry's] statements are of the nature rather of universals, whereas those of history are singulars. By a universal statement I mean one as to what such or such a man will probably or necessarily say or do." Stoneham's character, a composite of his actions and opinions that are known to us, will probably or necessarily determine an action and behavior that would be consistent with that person.

Introduction

1. Wesley Morris describes Gatsby as the perfect Jazz Age overreacher, where "merely being oneself wouldn't suffice." Gatsby wanted Daisy, and the world, to see him as the realization of the American dream: someone who could rise from nothing to become enormously wealthy. "Introduction," *Great Gatsby*.
2. Garrett, *La Guardia Years*, 55.
3. The history of the United State census is available at the U.S. Census website, census.gov.
4. "Top 100 Biggest U.S. Cities in the Year 1920," Biggest U.S. Cities, last updated May 11, 2022, https://www.biggestuscities.com/1920; Mordden, *That Jazz*, notes that Chicago had its own Jazz Age moment, another example of the urban characteristics of the music, nightlife, and Prohibition in the 1920s. See especially 137–41.
5. Quoted in O'Meara, *Lost City*, 211–12. In a 1931 letter to his editor, Max Perkins, Fitzgerald reminded Perkins that back in 1922, he (Fitzgerald) had coined the phrase *Jazz Age*.
6. Mordden, *That Jazz*, 83.
7. Burns, *1920*, 89–91.
8. Douglas, *Terrible Honesty*, 64.
9. *New Yorker*, November 14, 1925.
10. Tosches, *King of the Jews*, 37.
11. Fitzgerald, "Echoes of the Jazz Age," *Jazz Age*, 6.
12. Allen, *Only Yesterday*, 95.
13. Mordden, *That Jazz*, 153.
14. O'Meara, *Lost City*, 24.
15. Douglas, *Terrible Honesty*, 74.
16. Quoted in Douglas, *Terrible Honesty*, 15.
17. Douglas, *Terrible Honesty*, 75.
18. Paul Whiteman was white, and his orchestra was not integrated, but he wanted to hire Black musicians until persuaded of the financial consequences of doing so. However, Whiteman did rely frequently on Black arrangers. DeVeaux and Giddins, *Jazz*, 116–17.
19. Okrent, *Last Call*, 208.
20. Block, "Melody (and the Words) Linger On," 133.
21. Smith, *Babe Ruth's America*, 179.

22. Parrish, *Anxious Decades*, 160.
23. Fowler, *Beau James*, 189. Part of Walker's appeal was his understanding of the city's nightlife and the importance of leisure and drinking as true cosmopolitan values. See Lerner, *Dry Manhattan*, 164.
24. The so-called Seabury Investigation was the result of an action by the New York State Legislature to investigate corruption in New York City politics. In 1930 a committee headed by state senator Samuel Hofstadter appointed Judge Seabury to lead the investigation. The result of this work by Seabury led to a number of resignations of magistrate judges (among them Francis X. McQuade) and politicians. See Fowler, *Beau James*, 288–327.
25. "Any American who wanted a drink during prohibition could get one." Editors of the *New York Times*, "Roaring Twenties", 42.
26. Allen, *Only Yesterday*, 100.
27. Quoted in Burns, *1920*, xiv.
28. Fitzgerald, "Echoes of the Jazz Age," 6.
29. Okrent, *Last Call*, 206.
30. Geoffrey Perrett suggests a refinement in his argument against the view that Prohibition caused the rise in organized crime in the 1920s: "Organized crime did not begin with Prohibition; instead, it was given a powerful incentive to become better organized" (*America in the Twenties*, 393–411).
31. Walker, *Night Club Era*, 142.
32. Lerner, *Dry Manhattan*, esp. 61–95.
33. F. Scott Fitzgerald, "My Lost City," *Jazz Age*, 25–26.
34. Allen, *Only Yesterday*, 100.
35. Mordden, *That Jazz*, 134.
36. Quoted in Okrent, *Last Call*, 333.
37. Okrent, *Last Call*, 373.
38. Walker, *Night Club Era*, 159–60.
39. Lerner, *Dry Manhattan*, 81–84.
40. Morris, *Incredible New York*, 340.
41. Like many things in Charles Stoneham's life, his place of residence was complicated. A 1906 Jersey City directory has Stoneham living at 134 Claremont Avenue, Jersey City, with his wife, Hannah, children, brother, and mother. He probably moved to Manhattan with Hannah, son Horace C., and daughter Mary by 1909, residing at the Bretton Hall Hotel at Eighth

and Broadway for at least fifteen years. He moved back to Jersey City with Hannah sometime in the late 1920s but maintained another residence in Westchester County with a second family.

42. *Sporting News*, November 2, 1922.

43. F. Scott Fitzgerald may have modeled Gatsby's Long Island parties on Swope's gatherings. See Alfred Allan Lewis's biography of Swope, *Man of the World*, 128; and Churchwell, *Careless People*, 93–94.

44. The business partnerships between Rothstein and Stoneham have been mentioned by a number of writers. See, for example, Tosches, *King of the Jews*, 277; Pietrusza, *Rothstein*, 181; Seymour and Seymour Mills, *Baseball*, 388–89. According to one of his biographers, Rothstein took advantage of Stoneham's connections in Cuba to offload Scotch whisky in Havana. Stoneham then made arrangements for the whisky to be sent to the United States in small boats. See Katcher, *Big Bankroll*, 235–36.

45. Burns, *1920*, 52–53.

46. The 1930 U.S. Census lists Charles Stoneham living in Jersey City with wife Hannah Stoneham and in Greenburgh (Westchester County), New York with wife Margaret Leonard Stoneham and children Russell and Jane.

47. Compare Gene Fowler's remarks on Mayor Walker's life to Stoneham's situation: "The 1920s were not conducive to the repair of marriage relationships once the ties began to fray. As did many other men of personality, position and the means with which to enjoy the carnival, Walker danced with the throng and shook the bells of self-indulgence. Wine flowed illegally. Women, 'freed' from conventions, nosedived from their pedestals. Songs took on primitive overtones; the Congo River usurped, then overflowed, the banks of the Danube." Fowler, *Beau James*, 112.

48. Fallon died at forty-one, shaken and drained at the end. See Fowler, *Great Mouthpiece*, 388–400. Walker was forced out of office because of scandals in both his political and personal lives. Rothstein, age forty-six, was shot in November 1928 over an unpaid gambling debt. Rudolph Valentino died in 1926 at the age of thirty-one. The intensity and the brevity of the lives of some Jazz Age figures is aptly described in Edna St. Vincent Millay's 1920 poem "First Fig":

My candle burns at both ends;
    It will not last the night;
But, ah, my foes and, oh, my friends—
    It gives a lovely light!

49. According to Peter Williams, the dying Stoneham asked Bill Terry, the man Stoneham considered "the most reliable and discreet man in the organization," rather than his son Horace, to take him to Hot Springs, Arkansas, for treatment (*When the Giants Were Giants*, 192–93). Charles's daughter Jane, from his relationship with Margaret Leonard, says she saw very little of her father in the last three years of his life; when he did stay with them, he was "more or less like a guest, who confined himself to his room." Jane Gosden, interview with the author, July 21, 2019.

50. See Burns, *1920*, xi–xviii; Perrett, *America in the Twenties*, 147–78; Susman, *Culture as History*, 105–21.

1. Endgames

1. All Saints Catholic Church was established in 1896 to accommodate the growing Irish Catholic community in Jersey City. Stoneham was baptized in St. Patrick's Church, established in 1869. His family eventually joined the All Saints Parish. He was married in All Saints in 1898 to his first wife, Alice Rafter, who died in childbirth in 1899. Stoneham married his second wife, Hannah, in 1901 in All Saints.

2. *New York Times*, January 7, 1936.

3. Hill, *Vapors*, 4–8.

4. Jane Gosden (Charles A. Stoneham's daughter), interview with the author, July 9, 2019.

5. Stoneham's personal physician, W. M. Blackshare, had been with Stoneham for almost two weeks, treating him. Stoneham's manservant, Alfred, had accompanied him from New York to Hot Springs. New York Giants manager Bill Terry joined the train in St. Louis and accompanied the Stoneham party to New Jersey. *Sporting News*, January 16, 1936.

6. *New York Times*, January 9, 1936.

7. *New York Times*, January 10, 1936. Stoneham's widow Hannah was identified as Kate by reporters covering the funeral.

8. *New York Times*, April 29, 1924.

9. Foley's requiem mass, held at St. James Catholic Church, overflowed with guests, including Stoneham, New York governor Al Smith, and many Manhattan political VIPs. Three hundred motorcycle policemen led the cortege from the church to the cemetery. One reporter noted that the mourners also included many from ordinary walks of life. "The great majority, ranging from persons prominent in the political life of the city

to humble neighbors who knew the dead leader as a benefactor, stood massed in the thousands for blocks in every direction from the church and home." *New York Times*, January 17 and 18, 1925.

10. Mordden, *That Jazz*, 179.

11. The solemn high requiem mass was celebrated on August 26, 1926, at the intimate St. Malachy's Church on West Forty-Ninth Street, the church of Manhattan show business Catholics like George M. Cohan and Jimmy Durante. Only five hundred could attend the service, most of them film stars, including Douglas Fairbanks and Mary Pickford, or city officials. *New York Times*, August 31, 1926.

12. Mordden, *That Jazz*, 181.

13. NewYorkPress.com/Strausmedia, February 16, 2015.

14. Fallon was also known as a great raconteur, drinker, and party boy, the toast of the town, who openly strayed from his wife, often with Broadway showgirls, and had a long romance with the actress and dancer Gertrude Vanderbilt. Fowler, *Great Mouthpiece*, 255–63, 319–21, 341–72.

15. *New York Times*, May 3, 1927.

16. *New York Times*, November 7, 1928; M. Alexander, *Jazz Age Jews*, 57–58; Pietrusza, *Rothstein*, 291–92.

17. *New York Herald Tribune*, November 7, 1928; *New York Times*, November 8, 1928.

18. Hernandez, *Manager of the Giants*, 193; *New York Times*, March 1, 1934.

19. *New York Times*, February 28, 1934; *New York Herald Tribune*, March 1, 1934; *New York Times*, March 1, 1934.

20. Ebbets's funeral took place at Holy Trinity Episcopal Church in Brooklyn April, 21, 1925. "Thousands at Rites for Chas. H. Ebbets," ran the headlines of the *New York Times*, April 22, 1925.

21. Aside from the four house servants, Gatsby's father, the postman from West Egg, and Nick Carraway, Gatsby's neighbor and the novel's narrator, only one partygoer came. Fitzgerald, *Great Gatsby*, 136.

22. Lamb, "Charles A. Stoneham."

23. Mrs. Olivia Gray took her life on May 6, 1905, claiming Stoneham had jilted her. See Lamb, "Suicide at the Imperial Hotel," 26–29; *New York Times*, May 7, 1905. Mrs. Claire James took her life on May 17, 1920, and left a note and ten thousand dollars to Stoneham. *New York Times*, May 18, 1920.

24. Lamb, "Charles A. Stoneham."

25. Stoneham was listed as married to Hannah Stoneham and living in Jersey City, New Jersey, and married to Margaret Stoneham and living in Westchester County, New York. There were two children, Russell and Jane, listed at the Westchester address.

26. Jane Gosden, Charles Stoneham's daughter, interview with the author, July 9, 2019.

27. Charles Stoneham's estate provided for his widow Hannah, his son Horace, and daughter Mary to inherit his shares of the National Exhibition Company, making them principal owners of the New York Giants baseball team. See *New York Times*, January 11, 1936. Apparently, a trust fund was set up for Russell and Jane, Charles Stoneham's children by putative second wife, Margaret Leonard Stoneham. See *New York Times*, April 16, 1936.

2. Go East, Young Man

1. Charley Stoneham grew up in an Irish-Catholic neighborhood of Jersey City and belonged to All Saints Parish. It is likely that Charley's father, Bartholomew Stoneham, a bookkeeper, had some links to financial companies. His mother, Mary Howells, an Irish immigrant, would have had associations with other Irish immigrant families of All Saints Parish, some of whom, undoubtedly, had political connections.

2. Hochfelder, "'Where the Common People Could Speculate,'" 342.

3. *New York Times*, September 9, 1923. See also Katcher, *Big Bankroll*, 192.

4. Lamb, "Charles A. Stoneham"; *New York Times*, January 16, 1908.

5. Bartholomew Stoneham served in Company B, Second Regiment, New Jersey Calvary, and fought in the battles of Petersburg and Fredericksburg. He was mustered out on June 19, 1865, in Trenton, New Jersey. Bartholomew Stoneham was buried with military honors on January 9, 1894, in Jersey City.

6. Ancestry.com. Alice Rafter Stoneham was buried in Holy Names cemetery in Jersey City.

7. Charles A. Jr., Stoneham's firstborn son from the marriage with Hannah McGoldrick Stoneham, drowned in a Jersey City canal when he was four years old. *New York Times*, May 7, 1905.

8. David Hochfelder identifies Haight and Freese as one of the most pronounced brokerage houses that practiced highly speculative margin trading. See "'Where the Common People Could Speculate,'" 344.

9. M. Alexander, *Jazz Age Jews*, 41–43.

10. C. Alexander, *John McGraw*, 210.

11. Guenther, "Pirates of Promotion," 29.

12. Allen, *Tiger*, 194–206; Katcher, *Big Bankroll*, 27–29.

13. Allen, *Tiger*, 204.

14. According to Ancestry.com, Bartholomew Stoneham (Charles's father) was born in 1847 in New York to Irish immigrant parents; Mary Howells Stoneham (Charles's mother) was born in 1843 in Dublin.

15. Foley helped Stoneham secure legal advice in 1908 and would appear as a friendly witness in legal proceedings against Stoneham in the early 1920s. *New York Times*, February 12, 1908; *New York Herald Tribune*, February 18, 1922.

16. *Duluth Tribune*, March 26, 1909.

17. *Boston Herald*, April 25, 1909; *Salt Lake Telegraph*, December 17, 1909.

18. Hochfelder, "'Where the Common People Could Speculate,'" 336.

19. Guenther, "Pirates of Promotion," 30–32. See also *New York Times*, September 9, 1923.

20. Murphy, *After Many a Summer*, 30.

21. For a description of bucket shops, see M. Alexander, *Jazz Age Jews*, 12–13; Tosches, *King of the Jews*, 274–75. Another practice by the bucketeers involved executing an order but immediately creating a dummy account to trade against the purchase, balancing and washing the transaction. See Fowler, *Great Mouthpiece*, 318; Ferber, *I Found Out*, 144–45. It should be noted that in the early 1920s, bucket shops, while risky and highly speculative, were not illegal nor regulated by the Security and Exchange Commission.

22. See *New York Herald Tribune*, February 18, 1922, for a detailed description of bucket shop practices and a warning to investors.

23. Gatewood v. North Carolina, 203 U.S. 531, 536 (1906).

24. Allen, *Only Yesterday*, 8–9.

25. While Stoneham's sense of timing was generally remarkable, occasionally he misjudged the direction of the market when managing an account. An early miscalculation resulted in a lawsuit from a client obliging Stoneham to make good personally on a thirteen hundred–dollar withdrawal. *New York Times*, February 2, 1909. See also Murphy, *After Many a Summer*, 28.

26. *New York Times*, September 9, 1923. According to dollartimes.com $10 million in 1920 is the equivalent of $157,766,303 in 2020. In the "most

wealthy Americans" list in *Forbes* in 1919, Stoneham would not make
the top thirty, all of whom had a personal worth of $50 million or more.
Nonetheless, Stoneham was considered a wealthy man in his time.

27. Ferber, *I Found Out*, 142.

28. Murphy, *After Many a Summer*, 27–28; Fetter, *Taking on the Yankees*, 87–88; Seymour and Seymour Mills, *Baseball*, 389–91.

29. Lamb, "Charles A. Stoneham."

30. See, for example, *New York Times*, October 18, 1919; January 21 and June 21, 1921; *New York Sun*, April 13, 1919.

31. *New York Times*, October 18, 1919. For background on McGraw's role in getting Stoneham to buy the track, see Graham, *McGraw of the Giants*, 129–31.

32. Seymour and Seymour Mills, *Baseball*, 389; Murphy, *After Many a Summer*, 27.

33. Probably the most sensational of all of Rothstein's brushes with the law was the June 1919 grand jury indictment accusing him of shooting three policeman in a raid on one of his dice games. One month later these charges were dismissed due to lack of sufficient evidence. According to his biographers, Rothstein did shoot the police, inflicting minor wounds, but none of the victims would testify against him. Tosches, *King of the Jews*, 288; Pietrusza, *Rothstein*, 140–44.

34. The accounts of Rothstein's connection with the 1919 World Series are many and varied. See, among others, Pietrusza, *Rothstein*, 147–92; Fountain, *Betrayal*, especially 80–89, 194–96. The fictionalized story of the Black Sox scandal by Asinof, *Eight Men Out*, includes a version of Rothstein's part in betting on the Series.

35. Tosches, *King of the Jews*, 316–17; Pietrusza, *Rothstein*, 284–93.

36. The "permanent floating crapgame" was featured in *Guys and Dolls*, a musical by Frank Loesser, based on Damon Runyon's stories about Broadway characters in the Jazz Age. *Guys and Dolls* opened on Broadway in 1950 and won the Tony Award. One of the musical's principal characters, and the organizer of the floating crapgame, is gambler Nathan Detroit, modeled on Arnold Rothstein.

37. Pietrusza, *Rothstein*, 94.

38. Tosches, *King of the Jews*, 259–65. *Redstone* is the English translation of the German word *Rothstein*.

39. *New York Times*, May 17 and 24 and October 6, 1918.

40. Yellow Hand won the Empire City handicap, the Pelham handicap, the Hyde Park handicap, and the Hanover handicap, among others; Dry Moon also won a number of races, including the Mahopac handicap. See the *New York Times*, June 15 and 21; July 10, 13, and 15; and October 18, 23, and 30, 1921.
41. *New York Times*, July 12 and September 26, 1923.
42. *New York Times*, August 20, 1921.
43. Bradley, *Such Was Saratoga*, 310.
44. Pietrusza, *Rothstein*, 124–29.
45. Pietrusza, *Rothstein*, 129; Katcher, *Big Bankroll*, 112.
46. According to Seymour and Seymour Mills, *Baseball*, 389; M. Alexander, *Jazz Age Jews*, 43, 49; Tosches, *King of the Jews*, 277.
47. Katcher, *Big Bankroll*, 235.
48. See, for example, Murphy, *After Many a Summer*, 29.
49. His son Horace, who inherited the team, remarked that Charles Stoneham's boyhood idol was Giants outfielder Mike Tiernan, who, like Stoneham, was from Jersey City: "When my pop bought the club, he liked to say that he'd followed Tiernan over to the Giants." Quoted in Angell, *Five Seasons*, 267.
50. Fetter, *Taking on the Yankees*, 63.
51. Editors of the New York Times, *Roaring '20s*.
52. Okrent, *Last Call*, especially 227–89; Editors of the New York Times, *Roaring '20s*, 46–70.
53. C. Alexander, *John McGraw*, 217.

3. The House of Lords

1. Schott and Peters, *Giants Encyclopedia*, 90.
2. For a history of the upstart Federal League and the challenges it presented to Major League Baseball, see Seymour and Seymour Mills, *Baseball*, 196–213.
3. Hempstead was one of the leaders among baseball owners dealing with the Federal League crisis. Hempstead said he would always listen to offers to buy the team and set the price at two million dollars; Sinclair declined. *Sporting News*, January 20, 1916.
4. Seymour and Seymour Mills, *Baseball*, 250.
5. *Sporting News*, September 26, 1918. The 1918 total attendance of 128,483 was down from the 1917 World Series total of 186,654.

6. The United States declared war on Germany and its allies on April 6, 1917.

7. Zinn, *Charles Ebbets*, 175–76.

8. The Cubs drew 360,218 in 1917 and 337,256 in 1918; the White Sox drew 684,521 in 1917 and 195,081 in 1918. Thorn, Palmer, Gershman, and Pietrusza, *Total Baseball*.

9. C. Alexander, *John McGraw*, 178.

10. Lamb, "New York Giants Ownership History"; Graham, *New York Giants*, 109.

11. In an email to the author, New York Giants historian Bill Lamb writes, "After researching the organizational history on the NY Giants for more than 30 years, I cannot say confidently just how events went down."

12. Fowler, *Beau James*, 175.

13. *New York Times*, January 15, 1919.

14. C. Alexander, *John McGraw*, 209.

15. Stoneham was a fan of New Jersey native Mike Tiernan, who played for the Giants in the 1890s. See Angell, *Five Seasons*, 266. Many Tammany New Yorkers were Giants fans. See C. Alexander, *John McGraw*, 210.

16. Graham, *McGraw of the Giants*, 113.

17. Fetter, *Taking on the Yankees*, 63. Bill Lamb, author of the SABR BioProject entry on Charles Stoneham, has found no evidence of a Stoneham financial connection to the Newark ball club.

18. *New York Times*, January 15, 1919.

19. *New York Times*, January 15, 1919.

20. There are multiple figures given for the exact amount of the purchase of the National Exhibition Company. Newspapers, such as the *New York Times*, report the sale at $1 million. Court documents in McQuade v. Stoneham, 189 N.E. 234 N.Y. 323 (1934) (McQuade's suit against Stoneham and McGraw for unlawful dismissal as club treasure) state the amount at $939,500. Tom Schott and Nick Peters, in *Giants Encyclopedia*, claim the amount was 1.3 million dollars. Eleanor Brush, a daughter of John Brush, refused to part with her shares until 1924. But without the rest of the family's shares, which were sold to Stoneham, she had no controlling interest in the team. See Lamb, "New York Giants Team Ownership."

21. Tosches, *King of the Jews*, 277; Pietrusza, *Rothstein*, 39, 181. A Stoneham family legend, however apocryphal, has the inveterate gambler Charles Stoneham winning the Giants at a poker game. Jaime Rupert, great-

granddaughter of Charles Stoneham, interview with the author, July 12, 2019.

22. Seymour and Seymour Mills, *Baseball*, 140; M. Alexander, *Jazz Age Jews*, 49. Alexander mistakenly claimed that Rothstein brokered the 1919 sale for Stoneham with Andrew Freedman, who had died in 1915.

23. C. Alexander, *John McGraw*, 208–9.

24. Fetter, *Taking on the Yankees*, 63.

25. Fetter, *Taking on the Yankees*, 407.

26. See Lamb, "Frank McQuade." Lamb points out that in a 1917 case that involved John McGraw violating Sunday blue laws by playing baseball at the Polo Grounds, Judge McQuade did not recuse himself from hearing the case "despite his personal friendship with defendant McGraw."

27. Quoted in Graham, *McGraw of the Giants*, 114–15; and the *Sun*, January 8, 1936. See also *Sporting News*, November 2, 1922.

28. Lamb, "Frank McQuade." Lamb suggests the political motive on Stoneham's part, perhaps as a sop to Tammany Hall.

29. The Stoneham group was not the sole holder of Giants stock. Eleanor Brush held onto her shares until 1924; Ashley Lloyd (Brush's junior partner) also held a small amount. Details of other small holdings are cited in McQuade v. Stoneham, 189 N. E. 234 N.Y. 323 (1934).

30. Contractional details and agreements between parties are set forth in McQuade v. Stoneham, 189 N. E. 234 N.Y. 323 (1934).

31. Lamb, "New York Giants Team Ownership."

32. McQuade was known as the "father of Sunday baseball" for his role in overturning the blue laws in New York City that forbade games on Sunday. See, among others, Fetter, *Taking on the Yankees*, 69.

33. *New York Herald Tribune*, February 17, 1919.

34. *New York Tribune*, January 15, 1919.

35. *Sun*, January 15, 1919.

36. A rumor reported in a Boston newspaper that he bankrolled George Washington Grant's 1919 purchase of the Boston Braves would have violated baseball's rule of interest in more than one team. *Boston American*, September 9, 1923.

37. He opposed the $11,000 monthly club expenditure and favored returning to a 154-game schedule for the 1919 season. He lost both votes. *New York Herald Tribune*, January 16, 1919.

38. *Sun*, January 19, 1919.

39. Helyar, *Lords of the Realm*, 1994.
40. Literature on the Federal League challenge is vast. See Seymour and Seymour Mills, *Baseball*, 196–234. For a quick summary, see Surdam and Haupert, *Age of Ruth and Landis*, 8–13.
41. Eventually, the case made its way to the U.S. Supreme Court, where Justice Oliver Wendell Holmes, writing for the majority, concluded famously that baseball was not "interstate commerce" and left the reserve clause intact. For this, at least, the owners could breathe a sigh of relief. See, among others, Surdam and Haupert, *Age of Ruth and Landis*, 12–13.
42. The Black Sox scandal has been covered widely. For a general account, see Seymour and Seymour Mills, *Baseball*, 274–310; for a quick summary, see Vecsey, *Baseball*, 58–64. For more detailed discussion, see, among others, Carney, *Burying the Black Sox*; Pietrusza, *Rothstein*, 147–92; M. Alexander, *Jazz Age Jews*, 48–54; Fountain, *Betrayal*, especially 80–89, 194–96; SABR, "Eight Myths Out," https://sabr.org/eight-myths-out. The fictionalized story of the Black Sox scandal, Asinof's *Eight Men Out*, has been made into a popular movie and takes some liberty with the facts of the scandal.
43. The National Agreement joined the National League with the American League in all matters of oversight regarding player contracts, territorial rights, and the World Series. The intensity of the rivalry in the early years can be seen in McGraw's refusal in 1904 to have the Giants participate in the World Series "against a team from the minor leagues." Seymour and Seymour Mills, *Baseball*, 14–15; C. Alexander, *John McGraw*, 108–9.
44. Heyler, *Lords of the Realm*, 8.
45. Seymour and Seymour Mills, *Baseball*, 311.
46. The National League owners joined with Charles Comiskey of the Chicago White Sox, Harry Frazee of the Boston Red Sox, and Jacob Ruppert and Tillinghast Huston, co-owners of the New York Yankees, to push for an early version of the Lasker plan, advocating administrators from outside baseball. See, among others, Spink, *Judge Landis*, 65–67.
47. A sample of the accounts include Burk, *Much More than a Game*, 3–17; Seymour and Seymour Mills, *Baseball*, 311–23; Surdam and Haupert, *Age of Ruth and Landis*, 25–40; Spink, *Judge Landis*, 48–79; Fountain, *Betrayal*, 176–93.
48. For an interesting take on the drama behind this change, see Veeck, "Harry's Diary," 252–99.

49. While Landis's authority was far-reaching, it applied mostly to player personnel, disputes between owners, and monetary disputes over three hundred dollars. Owners control salaries of ballplayer. See Burk, *Much More than a Game*, 12–13; Surdam and Haupert, *Age of Ruth and Landis*, 28–29.

50. *New York Herald Tribune*, November 12, 1920.

51. *New York Herald Tribune*, November 21, 1920.

52. Veeck, "Harry's Diary," 288–89. Veeck said his nephew found the diary hidden behind an old desk in a storage room at Comiskey Park in 1963. The diary has been a controversial source for baseball historians ever since Veeck's rather detailed account of it in *The Hustler's Handbook* (252–99). Lost for over forty years, it has gone missing again, and apparently the only one to have seen it was Veeck. It does not appear among Veeck's papers at the Chicago History Museum.

53. *New York Times*, January 24, 1920. Overall Major League (ML) attendance in 1918 was 3,080,126; 1919 overall ML attendance was 6,532,439. Giants attendance in 1918 was 256,618 and, in 1919, 708,857. Attendance figures cited from Thorn, Palmer, Gershman, and Pietrusza, *Total Baseball*. Stoneham was not the only owner to raise salaries. Charles Ebbets gave his Dodgers a pay raise, but given his long association with baseball ownership, his fellow NL peers did not extend the same pique to him that they did to Stoneham. See Zinn, *Charles Ebbets*, 181–82.

54. *New York Times*, October 26, 1922; *Sporting News*, November 2, 1922.

55. Lamb, "Frank McQuade."

56. The Eighteenth Amendment to the U.S. Constitution was ratified on January 16, 1919, and became known as the Volstead Act, after Minnesota congressman Andrew John Volstead, who served as chairman of the Judiciary Committee responsible for its enforcement. See Okrent, *Last Call*, 108–14.

4. A Fresh Scent of Scandal

1. The definitive account of the year 1921 in New York baseball is Spatz and Steinberg, *1921*.

2. Durso, *Days of Mr. McGraw*, 162–63.

3. Graham, *McGraw of the Giants*, 146.

4. The 1921 World Series was the last to be played under a best-of-nine games format.

5. Graham, *McGraw of the Giants*, 148.

6. Spink, *Judge Landis*, 130; *New York Times*, October 2, 1924.

7. Bucky Weaver is the prime example of someone who did not participate in the Black Sox fix but who knew about it and did not report it. Landis put Weaver on the permanently ineligible list. See Carney, *Burying the Black Sox*, 209–17.

8. Graham, *New York Giants*, 151–54. A *Sporting News* writer stated that Landis was impressed by Frisch's, Youngs's, and Kelly's "straightforwardness," while Dolan was evasive (October 9, 1924). O'Connell was completely candid with Landis and admitted his guilt. Landis eventually released the testimony of his interviews with all the parties in order to establish his credibility with newspaper writers (*New York Times*, January 11, 1925).

9. *New York Times*, October 2, 1924. See also the accounts in Graham, *New York Giants*, 154; Spink, *Judge Landis*, 132–33; C. Alexander, *John McGraw*, 257.

10. Seymour and Seymour Mills, *Baseball*, 379–80.

11. *Sporting News*, January 21, 1925.

12. Durso, *Days of Mr. McGraw*, 187.

13. *Sporting News*, November 6, 1924.

14. Numerous historians claim that Fallon "represented" Stoneham, despite the fact that there is no evidence to prove this. For most of his life, Stoneham's personal attorney was Leo J. Bondy, a board member of the National Exhibition Company. Those who name Fallon as Stoneham's legal representative include Seymour and Seymour Mills, *Baseball*, 380; and Spink, *Judge Landis*, 138. Stoneham was acquainted with Fallon, who did represent McGraw and advised Rothstein on his testimony before the grand jury in Chicago regarding the 1919 Black Sox scandal. See Pietrusza, *Rothstein*, 175.

15. *Sporting News*, January 15, 1924.

16. Spink, *Judge Landis*, 140; Fowler, *Great Mouthpiece*, 389.

17. *Sporting News*, January 22, 1925.

18. Spink, *Judge Landis*, 140. Joe Vila published a story that Fallon had told him that McGraw was footing Dolan's legal fees. Graham, *New York Giants*, 156.

19. *New York Times*, January 12, 1925.

20. *Sporting News*, January 29, 1925.
21. Hal Chase and Heinie Zimmerman were suspended by McGraw at the end of the 1920 season for throwing games. Benny Kauff was suspended by Landis for alleged involvement with stolen cars (Kauff was acquitted of the charges). Phil Douglas was suspended by Landis for offering to throw games in 1922. Much has been written about all of these cases. See, for example, Graham, *New York Giants*, 115–16, on Chase and Zimmerman; C. Alexander, *John McGraw*, 229–29, on Kauff; Seymour and Seymour Mills, *Baseball*, 375–76, on Douglas.
22. C. Alexander, *John McGraw*, 258; Murphy *After Many a Summer*, 30–31; *New York Times*, October 10, 1924; *Sporting News*, January 15, 1925.
23. In addition to the various accounts in Graham, Spink, and Alexander, see Seymour and Seymour Mills, *Baseball*, 378–82. Lowell Blaisdell underscores the unresolved aspects of the event in his 1982 *Baseball Research Journal* article "Mystery and Tragedy: The O'Connell-Dolan Scandal."
24. Blaisdell, "Mystery and Tragedy."
25. Spink, *Judge Landis*, 136.
26. Quoted in Spink, *Judge Landis*, 137.
27. "Baseball Men Want Stoneham to Sell," *New York Times*, September 3, 1923; *Sporting News*, January 14, 1925.
28. *New York Times*, May 7, 1905, and February 14, 1920; Pietrusza, *Rothstein*, 127–29.
29. Spink, *Judge Landis*, 87–88; C. Alexander, *John McGraw*, 229–30; Seymour and Mills Seymour, *Baseball*, 389–90. All of these sources indicate that Landis did not try to interfere with Stoneham's private business dealings with Rothstein.
30. Coverage of Stoneham's legal entanglements was widespread in the newspapers of 1922–25, especially the *New York Times* and the *New York Herald Tribune* and even tabloids like the *New York Mirror*.
31. New York State, McQuade v. Stoneham (230 A.D. 57) 1930.
32. *Sporting News*, March 12, 1925.
33. *New York Times*, December 23, 1931.
34. A conclusion drawn by both Fetter, *Taking on the Yankees*, 93–97; and Murphy, *After Many a Summer*, 28–33.
35. *Sporting News*, March 12, 1925.

5. See You in Court

1. Fetter, *Taking on the Yankees*, 90.
2. Most of Stoneham's clients, 85 percent of them, were mailed letters identifying Hughes & Dier as the firm that would handle the clients' accounts. The remainder of his clients were mailed letters designating the transfer to E. M. Fuller & Company and E. H. Clarke & Company. *New York Times*, August 31, 1923.
3. *New York Times*, February 25, 1922; *New York Herald Tribune*, March 27, 1922.
4. *New York Herald Tribune*, February 18, 1922.
5. *New York Times*, March 15 and 21, 1922; *New York Herald Tribune* March 15, 1922.
6. *New York Herald Tribune*, March 12, 1922.
7. *New York Times*, July 9, 1922.
8. *New York Times*, January 18, 1922.
9. *New York Times*, March 25, 1922.
10. *New York Times*, June 3, 1922; June 20, 1922.
11. *New York Times*, August 3, 1923. The letter to the clients was dated March 1, 1921. Stoneham explained that Hughes & Dier was a large and substantial firm with a strong history of broker trading.
12. Fetter, *Taking on the Yankees*, 91.
13. *New York Herald Tribune*, January 12, 1924.
14. See, for example, *New York Herald Tribune*, June 6 and July 11, 1922.
15. *New York Times*, June 28, 1922.
16. *New York Times*, June 12, 1923.
17. *New York Herald Tribune*, July 25, 1923.
18. *New York Times* August 31, 1921; September 9, 1923. See also Fowler, *Great Mouthpiece*, 326–40.
19. Hays, *City Lawyer*, 110–15.
20. The court set up an account to pay off the creditors, removing E. M. Fuller from the process. *New York Times*, June 28, 1922
21. Fowler, *Great Mouthpiece*, 339–40.
22. *New York Times*, May 29 and November 30, 1924.
23. *New York Times*, June 30, 1927.
24. Pietrusza, *Rothstein*, 259.
25. Fowler, *Great Mouthpiece*, 326–403.
26. Bruccoli, *F. Scott Fitzgerald*, 91.
27. Piper, *F. Scott Fitzgerald*, 119.

28. *New York Herald Tribune*, January 12, 1924; *New York Times*, February 25, 1925. In addition to Stoneham, the indictment also names members of Charles A. Stoneham and Company, including Leo J. Bondy, Stoneham's attorney, and board members Horace A. Stoneham, Charles's brother, and Ross F. Robertson, named by various newspapers as Charles's brother-in-law. All are charged with alleged fraud for having used the mails to obtain money "by false and fraudulent pretenses, representations and promises."

29. *Sporting News*, September 18, 1924.

30. *Collyer's Eye*, November 10, 1923. See also *New York Times*, February 25, 1925.

31. *New York Times*, December 26, 1922, and September 3, 1923.

32. C. Alexander, *John McGraw*, 253. For Stoneham's resolve to stay in baseball, see *Sporting News*, June 21, 1923.

33. There were twelve counts in the indictment, each one charging a particular unlawful act by sending through the mails to the customers of the Stoneham company letters that allegedly contained false statements, in particular that Dier was solvent. *New York Times*, January 12 and 16, 1924.

34. *New York Times* February 10, 1925.

35. *New York Times*, February 5, 1925.

36. *New York Herald Tribune*, January 16, 1924. House may have felt strongly about prosecuting the Dier case and may have harbored a personal animus toward Stoneham. He presented the Dier case to the grand jury in October 1923 and then left the U.S. Attorney's office for private practice. He returned to prosecute Stoneham as a specially appointed staff attorney. I am indebted to Bill Lamb for information on House's legal career.

37. *New York Times* February 20, 1925.

38. *New York Times*, February 19, 1925.

39. *New York Times*, February 27, 1925.

40. *New York Times*, February 28, 1925.

41. Murphy, *After Many a Summer*, 32.

42. Fetter, *Taking on the Yankees*, 93.

43. Surdam and Haupert, *Age of Ruth and Landis*, 208.

44. *Sporting News*, November 15, 1923.

45. *Sporting News*, January 31, 1924.

46. The following exchange takes place in the Holmes mystery "The Adventure of Silver Blaze":

INSPECTOR GREGORY: Is there anything to which you wish to draw my attention?

SHERLOCK HOLMES: To the curious incident of the dog in the nighttime.

GREGORY: The dog did nothing in the nighttime.

HOLMES: That was the curious incident.

Doyle, "Adventure of Silver Blaze," 397.

47. *New York Times*, July 14, 1921.
48. Spink, *Judge Landis*, 87–88.
49. See, for example, *New York Herald Tribune*, May 19, 1927.
50. *New York Times*, February 1928.
51. Walker, *Night Club Era*, 60–62.
52. *New York Times*, June 12, 1925, and April 8, 1927.
53. Bill Lamb, email exchange with the author, November 8, 2020. On the background and the specifics of both the Dier case and the Fuller-McGee hearings and proceedings, I am indebted to Bill Lamb for his insights and his knowledge of the New York courts.

6. The Battle for New York

1. The Giants and the Yankees met in an all–New York World Series three straight years, from 1921 through 1923. The Giants won the first two (both games were played at the Polo Grounds). The Yankees won the third series in 1923, when the games alternated between the Polo Grounds and the new Yankee Stadium in the Bronx.
2. The Yankees drew 1,289,422 in 1920, 1,230,698 in 1921, and 1,026,134 in 1922, all in the Polo Grounds. In the same years the Giants drew 929,609, 973,477, and 945,809. Curiously, when the Yankees moved into their own ballpark in 1923, their attendance dropped from the previous year to 1,007,069. Thorn, Palmer, Gershman, and Pietrusza, *Total Baseball*, 106–7.
3. The story of the Yankees' eviction from the Polo Grounds has been told often and varies in plotline. Some see it as a failed attempt by Ban Johnson to oust Ruppert and Huston from American League ownership. Others present it as the Giants' failed attempt to assert their leadership. See Steinberg and Spatz, *Colonel and Hug*, 118–23; Fetter, *Taking on the Yankees*, 68–80.
4. *New York Times*, April 19, 1998, in an article on the history of Yankee Stadium.
5. Durso, *Days of Mr. McGraw*, 160.

6. Fitzgerald, *Great Gatsby*, 75.

7. Corrigan, *So We Read On*, 113.

8. Surdam and Haupert, *Age of Ruth and Landis*, 145.

9. Williams *When the Giants Were Giants*, 75.

10. Barthel, *Babe Ruth and the Creation of the Celebrity Athlete*, 119–23.

11. Stoneham's and McGraw's nostalgic yearning for past glory is another echo of *The Great Gatsby*. Gatsby, trying to recapture his lost love life with Daisy, now a married woman, was cautioned that it was futile to try to recapture a lost love. But he was adamant. "Can't repeat the past?" he cried incredulously. "Why of course you can!" (86).

12. *Sporting News*, July 24, 1924.

13. Lowenfish, *Branch Rickey*, 115.

14. Nor was the competition for the public's money confined just to baseball. Boxing and college football were big draws, and general entertainment beyond the sporting world was available to New Yorkers, especially theater, music, and film. See Surdam and Haupert, *Age of Ruth and Landis*, 74 and 116.

15. C. Alexander, *John McGraw*, 227–28.

16. Quoted in Graham, *New York Giants*, 126.

17. Durso, *Days of Mr. McGraw*, 189.

18. *New York Times*, November 17, 1923.

19. Rogers, "Ross Youngs."

20. There are many accounts of the rupture between McGraw and Frisch. See, for example, Hernandez, *Manager of Giants*, 159; Durso, *Days of Mr. McGraw*, 189; C. Alexander, *John McGraw*, 273–74; Graham, *McGraw of the Giants*, 209–13; Waldo, *Baseball's Roaring Twenties*, 174–75.

21. In addition to the fallout with Frisch, McGraw suffered the loss of longtime friend and assistant manager Hughie Jennings, who developed tuberculous and was confined to a sanitorium in North Carolina. Hernandez, *Manager of Giants*, 158.

22. *Sporting News*, July 24, 1924.

23. See C. Alexander, *Rogers Hornsby*, 124–25.

24. *New York Times*, December 21, 1926.

25. *Los Angeles Times*, December 21, 1926.

26. Hynd, *Giants of the Polo Grounds*, 267.

27. Hornsby received a total of $122,000 for the sale of his stock. See C. Alexander, *Rogers Hornsby*, 128–32, for an account of the issue.

28. Quoted in C. Alexander, *Rogers Hornsby*, 127.

29. Sports Reference website, baseball-reference.com.

30. Leavy, *Big Fella*, 219–20.

31. Tygiel, "New Ways of Knowing," *Past Time: Baseball as History*, 74.

32. Tygiel, "New Ways of Knowing," 76.

33. *New York Times*, March 1, 1927.

34. Lowenfish, *Branch Rickey*, 172.

35. Allen, *National League Story*, 185.

36. C. Alexander, *Rogers Hornsby*, 136–37.

37. *New York Times*, January 13, 1928.

38. Durso, *Days of Mr. McGraw*, 202.

39. C. Alexander, *Rogers Hornsby*, 142; Graham, *McGraw of the Giants*, 225.

40. *St. Louis Post-Dispatch*, December 19,1927; *New York Times*, December 22, 1927.

41. See, for example, *New York Times*, January 12, 1927.

42. *Los Angeles Times*, January 12, 1928.

43. C. Alexander, *Rogers Hornsby*, 141–42.

7. Götterdämmerung

1. The agreement, dated February 21, 1919, was attached to the court documents in McQuade v. Stoneham, 142 Misc. 842, 256 N.Y.S. (Sup. Ct. 1932). On the specifics of the sale agreement, see *New York Times*, February 24, 1929. I am indebted to Dan Levitt, who shared material on the McQuade court hearings, and Bill Lamb, who explained structural matters of the New York Appellate courts and provided a chronology of the McQuade v. Stoneham litigation.

2. *Sporting News*, January 16, 1936.

3. *New York Tribune*, January 15, 1919.

4. Originally a theory of personality developed in the 1950s by cardiologists Meyer Friedman and Ray Rosenman, "type A" has entered into popular psychology as a description of high achievers who are impatient, highly status conscious, unlikely to take the advice of others, and have a strong sense of competitiveness. See Elizabeth Scott, "What It Means to Have 'Type A' Personality," verywellminded.com; and Dr. Saul McLeod, "Type A and Type B Personality," SimplyPsychology.org, for general descriptions.

5. McQuade v. Stoneham, 230 A.D. 57, 248 N.Y.S. 548 (1st Dept. 1930).
6. McGraw once said that he only fought when he was drunk. Stoneham was also known as a heavy drinker, so the brawl between them probably amounted to a few punches. It took place at one of Havana's famous watering holes, Carmela's Roof Garden, and one reporter proclaimed Stoneham as the winner. See Hernandez, *Manager of the Giants*, 118; *New York Herald*, February 23, 1920; *Evening Star*, February 23, 1920. Stoneham described the fight in his testimony in the McQuade suit. McQuade v. Stoneham, 230 A.D. 57, N.Y.S. 548 (1st Dept. 1930).
7. *New York Evening Post*, February 23, 1920.
8. C. Alexander, *John McGraw*, 210–11.
9. Seymour and Seymour Mills, *Baseball*, 363.
10. *New York Times*, April 30 and May 5, 1919.
11. According to the Sports Reference website, baseball-reference.com, the Giants drew 256,618 in 1918.
12. *New York Times*, April 7, 1955.
13. An unforeseen consequence of McQuade's success and a milestone in the history of New York City baseball involved the Yankees building Yankee Stadium in the Bronx. The contractual commitment to rent their ballpark to the Yankees in the early 1920s deprived the Giants of many lucrative Sunday playing dates at the Polo Grounds. In 1922 the Giants gave the Yankees notice that they would have to find their own ballpark. See Fetter, *Taking on the Yankees*, 74–80; Steinberg and Spatz, *Colonel and the Hug*, 118–23.
14. The phrase *Sic transit gloria mundi* traces to fifteenth-century German theologian Thomas a Kempis's *Imitation of Christ* and asserts the fleeting and temporary nature of worldly achievement and success.
15. In 1923 McGraw, having grown tired of McQuade's constant bickering, pleaded with Stoneham to raise McQuade's salary so there would be peace among the owners. See McQuade v. Stoneham, above at 142 Misc. 842.
16. *New York Times*, December 22, 1931. See also the transcripts of court testimony, McQuade v. Stoneham, 230 N.Y. 323, 189 N.E. 234 (Ct. App. 1934).
17. Details of McGraw's contentious relationship with McQuade can be found in the transcripts of McQuade v. Stoneham, above at 230 A.D. 57. See also C. Alexander, *John McGraw*, 302–3.

18. *New York Times*, December 19, 1931; McQuade v. Stoneham, above at 142 Misc. 842.

19. *New York Times*, December 25, 1929; January 7, 1930. I am indebted to Bill Lamb for clarifying matters on the Kenny suit.

20. McQuade v. Stoneham, above at 263 N.Y. 323; *New York Times*, December 31, 1929; *New York Herald Tribune*, January 7, 1930.

21. McQuade v. Stoneham, above at 230 A.D. 57.

22. McQuade v. Stoneham, above at 230 A.D. 57.

23. McQuade v. Stoneham, above at 230 A.D. 57; *New York Herald Tribune*, January 13, 1932.

24. For Stoneham's fight with McGraw, see n. 5 in this chapter. Stoneham was more prone to intervene in fights started by McQuade. See McQuade v. Stoneham, above at 263 N.Y. 323 for McQuade's fight with Leo Bondy; see private papers, "Discussion at the Office of the New York National League Baseball Club," September 10, 1931, Harris and Stacy, Certified Shorthand Reporters, Stoneham Family Private Papers, Hillsborough CA, for McQuade's fight with Harry Frazee of the Boston Red Sox. See Hernandez, *Manager of the Giants*, 118, for a list of McGraw's brawls, most of which, according to Hernandez's list, McGraw lost.

25. McQuade v. Stoneham, 230 A.D. 57, 248 N.Y.S. 548 (1st Dept. 1930).

26. *New York Times*, December 23, 1931.

27. McQuade v. Stoneham, above at 142 Misc. 842.

28. *New York Times*, March 18, 1933; McQuade v. Stoneham, 238 App. Div. 827, 262, N.Y.S. 966 (1st Dept. 1933).

29. An interesting aside to the McQuade v. Stoneham legal process is the continuing relevance and interest it holds for contemporary legal study. Just a cursory internet search of the case shows a number of cites that use the case as an example for law students preparing for courses and examinations in corporate law.

30. Coverage of the Court of Appeal's ruling is in *New York Times*, January 19, 1934. Two members of the court concurred in the reversal but limited their rationale to McQuade's disqualification for sitting on a corporate board while a magistrate. I am indebted to Bill Lamb for his clarifications of the ruling.

31. C. Alexander, *John McGraw*, 289, 297.

32. *New York Herald Tribune*, December 10, 1930.

8. Crash Time

1. Robert S. McElvaine remarks that Black Tuesday, October 29, is *the* day most economists and historians credit as "the crash." *Great Depression*, 48.

2. Smith, *Babe Ruth's America*, 206.

3. Perrett, *America in the Twenties*, 377.

4. Parrish, *Anxious Decades*, 233.

5. Parrish, *Anxious Decades*, 204.

6. Parrish, *Anxious Decades*, 233; Smith, *Babe Ruth's America*, 207.

7. See McElvaine, *Great Depression*, 48–50, for a summary of the views.

8. McElvaine, *Great Depression*, 73.

9. Parrish, *Anxious Decades*, 235.

10. Tosches, *King of the Jews*, 37.

11. Tygiel, *Past Time*, 87.

12. Sports Reference website, baseball-reference.com.

13. Rabinowitz, "Baseball in the Great Depression," 49–50.

14. Surdam, *Wins, Losses, and Empty Seats*, 30.

15. Leavengood, "Baseball Gets a Taste of the Depression," 216–20. See also Tygiel, *Past Time*, 89–90.

16. C. Alexander, *Breaking the Slump*, 62–64; Surdam, *Wins, Losses, and Empty Seats*, 66–68.

17. C. Alexander, *Breaking the Slump*, 59.

18. Tygiel, *Past Time*, 87–88.

19. The Cardinals drew only 325,056, down considerably from their 1931 World Series year. Thorn, Palmer, Gershman, and Pietrusza, *Total Baseball*, 107.

20. The Cubs drew 1,086,422 in 1931, and the White Sox drew 403,550. Thorn, Palmer, Gershman, and Pietrusza, *Total Baseball*.

21. A number of economists see the winter of 1932–33 as the bottom of the economic downturn. See, for example, McElvaine, *Great Depression*; Friedman and Schwartz, *Great Contraction*; Jensen, "Causes and Cures of Unemployment," 553–83.

22. Brooklyn drew 434,188 in 1934 and 470,517 in 1935; the Yankees drew 848,682 in 1934 and 657,508 in 1935. See Sports Reference website, baseball-reference.com.

23. Stoneham used the Polo Grounds as a moneymaker when baseball season was over or when the Giants were out of town, hosting boxing events, such as the Dempsey-Firpo fight in 1923, and college football games with teams such as Columbia, Fordham, Army, Navy, and Notre Dame.

24. See, for example, Murphy, *After Many a Summer*, 27–30; Lamb, *Charles Stoneham*.

25. Allen, *Giants and the Dodgers*, 161.

26. Fetter, *Taking on the Yankees*, 89.

27. Surdam, *Wins, Losses, and Empty Seats*, 22.

28. It is unclear how much Stoneham lost. According to Bill Corum, Stoneham began selling some of his holdings in 1928. Roger Kahn claims a "family member" told him that in the 1929 crash, Stoneham lost "scores of millions of dollars" (*Era*, 20). Kahn does not identify the family member. Jane Gosden, Stoneham's daughter, said her father was hurt somewhat by the crash but that it did not affect his (or her) lifestyle. Interview with the author, July 9, 2017.

29. Jane Gosden remembers her father, a few months before his death, staying in his room for weeks at a time, resting and recuperating from illness. Interview with the author, July 9, 2019.

9. The Last Hurrah

1. C. Alexander, *Breaking the Slump*, 1.

2. For a description of Depression life for workers, clerks, and farmers, see McElvaine, *Great Depression*, 170–95.

3. The date of President Roosevelt's inauguration was March 4, 1933.

4. Graham, *New York Giants*, 193–95; C. Alexander, *John McGraw*, 305–7.

5. Stein, *Under Coogan's Bluff*, 11.

6. *Sporting News*, June 16, 1932.

7. Over the years as manager, McGraw would single out certain players to bear the brunt of his criticism for the entire squad. Larry Doyle and Frank Frisch were early targets before Lindstrom. See C. Alexander, *John McGraw*, 232–33.

8. *Sporting News*, June 23, 1932.

9. The full text of McGraw's statement is quoted in the front-page article on McGraw's resignation in the *New York Times*, June 4, 1932.

10. Williams, *When the Giants Were Giants*, 120.

11. Williams, *When the Giants Were Giants*, 121–22.

12. C. Alexander, *John McGraw*, 307–8.
13. Frank, Graham, *McGraw of the Giants*, New York: G. P. Putnam's Sons, 260.
14. Stoneham was blunt and hardnosed in his dealings with Terry's 1932 holdout, telling Terry he could sign for what the club offered or he could quit baseball. Stoneham was not going to trade or sell Terry to another club. Williams, *When the Giants Were Giants*, 114.
15. Williams, *When the Giants Were Giants*, 127–28.
16. The Senate's vote to approve the Twenty-First Amendment was 62–23; the House vote was 281–121 in favor of the new amendment. On December 5, 1933, Utah was the thirty-sixth state to ratify the repeal, ending Prohibition. See Okrent, *Last Call*, 344–54.
17. Allen, *Tiger*, 242–51.
18. Terry traded catcher Bob Farrell, outfielder Ethan Allen, and pitchers Jim Mooney and Bill Walker for Mancuso. Sports Reference website, baseball-reference.com.
19. *New York Times*, April 8, 1933.
20. *Baseball Magazine*, October 1933.
21. Terry allowed beer in the clubhouse after the games. Williams, *When the Giants Were Giants*, 123–24.
22. McKenna, "Lefty O'Doul"; Snelling, *Lefty O'Doul*, 110–15.
23. Hubbell's streak extended from July 13 to August 1. Sports Reference website, baseball-reference.com.
24. Williams, *When the Giants Were Giants*, 152; Graham, *New York Giants*, 205–6.
25. Williams, *When the Giants Were Giants*, 153.
26. Fred Stein estimates the welcoming crowd at ten thousand (*Under Coogan's Bluff*, 23).
27. *New York Times*, September 21, 1933.
28. *New York Times*, October 1, 1933.
29. *New York Times*, October 8, 1933.
30. Hynd, *Giants of the Polo Grounds*, 290.

10. The Last Drop

1. Daniel M. Daniel, *World Telegram*, January 9, 1936.
2. Quoted in Sid Mercer, "Memory of Stoneham Will Long Remain with Ball Fans," *New York American*, January 19, 1936.
3. Mercer, "Memory of Stoneham."

4. See the details in chapter 3, "The House of Lords."

5. New York newspaper clipping, January 7, 1936, Charles Stoneham File, San Francisco Giants Archives.

6. New York newspaper clipping, January 7, 1936.

7. But not always successfully. As Bill Lamb points out in his SABR biography, "Charles A. Stoneham," Stoneham wished to remain out of the limelight, but due to various business problems and personal scandals, his name would often appear in the press.

8. Graham, *New York Giants*, 220.

9. There is some dispute about the number of Giants officials who accompanied Blanche McGraw on the train from New York to Baltimore, but all accounts mention Charles Stoneham being present. In *When the Giants Were Giants*, Peter Williams remarks that only Stoneham and Terry were with Mrs. McGraw (171); in his biography of McGraw, Charles Alexander identifies a party of thirty people accompanying Mrs. McGraw, including Stoneham, Terry, and Leo Bondy from the Giants, 315. See also *New York Times*, March 1, 1934, in which Stoneham and Terry are mentioned. A *Times* article on February 27, 1934, mentions Stoneham as an honorary pallbearer at the funeral mass.

10. Daniel M. Daniel, *Sporting News*, January 16, 1936.

11. Horace Stoneham was fond of telling the story that his father's favorite Giants player was New Jersey native Mike Tiernan, who played in the 1890s. Horace said that his dad simply followed Tiernan from New Jersey to the Polo Grounds. See Shaplen, "Lonely, Loyal Mr. Stoneham."

12. New Jersey newspaper, January 7, 1936, Charles Stoneham File, San Francisco Giants Archives.

13. Stoneham had every confidence in Terry as a manager and judge of player personnel. He also saw Terry as one of the most reliable and discreet members of the front office. *World Telegram* January 9, 1936; see also Williams, *When The Giants Were Giants*, 173. *New York Times*, September 23, 1935.

14. *New York Times*, October 10, 1933; Stein, "Bill Terry."

15. *New York Times*, January 8, 1936; *Sun*, January 8, 1936.

16. *New York Times*, January 8, 1936.

17. Treder, *Forty Years a Giant*, 39–40, 46–65.

18. On Stoneham's purchase of the team for his son, see Shaplen, "Lonely, Loyal Mr. Stoneham"; Daniel, *World Telegraph*, January 8, 1936; Graham, *New York Giants*, 221.

19. Treder, *Forty Years a Giant*, 34–36.

20. New York newspaper clippings, January 6, 1936, Charles Stoneham File, San Francisco Giants Archives.

21. On the passing of the ball club from father to son, see New York newspaper clipping, January 7, 1936, Charles Stoneham File, San Francisco Giants Archives; Frank Graham, *Sun*, January 8, 1936; *Sporting News*, January 16, 1936.

22. *New York Times*, June 26, 1935.

23. Interview with Jane Gosden, Charles Stoneham's daughter, July 9, 2019; *Sporting News*, October 23, 1935; *New York Times*, January 8, 1936. See also Treder, *Forty Years a Giant*, 86.

24. *New York Times*, December 8, 1935, and December 9, 1935; Allen, *Giants and the Dodgers*, 161–62.

25. For a description of the medicinal attractions of Hot Springs, see Hill, *Vapors*, 3–6.

26. Quoted in Williams, *When the Giants Were Giants*, 193.

27. Williams, *When the Giants Were Giants*, 193.

28. Williams, *When the Giants Were Giants*, 192–93.

29. New Jersey newspaper, January 7, 1936, Charles Stoneham File, San Francisco Giants Archives.

30. Daniel M. Daniel, *Sporting News*, January 16, 1936.

31. See chapter 1 for the names of the priests and the mourners.

32. Mary Aufderhar is Stoneham's daughter by Alice Rafter, Stoneham's first wife, who died giving birth to Mary. Mary's name does not appear in any of the accounts of those attending the funeral mass and burial.

33. Russell Stoneham was born in 1920 and Jane Stoneham in 1925. According to Jane, Horace never met either Russell or Jane. Interview with Jane Gosden, July 9, 2019.

34. Two of his affairs made the papers as suicides. *New York Times*, May 7, 1905, and February 11, 1920. See also Lamb, "Suicide at the Imperial Hotel," 26–29.

35. I am grateful for exchanges with Bill Lamb on these matters.

36. The list of Jazz Age celebrities with complicated marital arrangements and multiple relationships is long and includes both sexes, including Stoneham's acquaintances Arnold Rothstein, Broadway attorney William Fallon, Mayor Jimmy Walker, Babe Ruth, newspaper mogul William Randolph Hearst, and various movie stars and musicians. Louise Brooks,

Gloria Swanson, Bessie Smith, and Zelda Fitzgerald were among the many women who pursued open relationships.

37. Certainly Stoneham's brother, Horace A. Stoneham, and attorney Leo Bondy knew of a second family since they were legal designates of a trust fund Stoneham had set up for his children by Margaret Leonard. This trust was made public three months after Stoneham's death, when Margaret went to court to guarantee payments through the trust to her children, Russell and Jane. *New York Times*, April 2 and 16, 1936.

38. Victorian writers, precursors to the Freudian age, were fascinated with the possibility that people might hold an inner life that is different from the outward personality one brings to the social world. Robert Louis Stevenson posed this idea with an extreme example of a dual personality in *The Strange Case of Dr. Jekyll and Mr. Hyde*; Oscar Wilde portrayed the inner life of a public man in *The Portrait of Dorian Gray*; and Edward Bulwer-Lytton described it as a human characteristic in *Pilgrims of the Rhine*: "There are two lives to each of us, the life of our actions, and the life of our minds and hearts. History reveals men's deeds and their outward characters, but not themselves. There is a secret self that has its own life, unpenetrated and unguessed" (22).

39. The $70,000 phone bet was with Arnold Rothstein and has been reported widely. See, for example, Pietrusza, *Rothstein*, 129. The bet with the Yankee owners occurred during the negotiations over a proposed "city series" between the Giants and the Yankees in 1920. Stoneham started out at a $100,000 bet with Jacob Ruppert, Yankees owner, and over the next few hours Stoneham had raised his wager to $700,000. A Yankees club official intervened and called off the bet. Reported by Sid Mercer, *New York American*, January 19, 1936.

40. Murphy, *After Many a Summer*, 30.

41. This is the view of Fetter, *Taking on the Yankees*, 84–97.

42. Lamb, "Charles A. Stoneham."

43. American League president Will Harridge said that some of Stoneham's decisions helped advance baseball in general, even when they came at some immediate costs to the National Exhibition Company. Quoted by Daniel M. Daniel, *World Telegraph*, January 8, 1936.

Epilogue

1. Daniel M. Daniel, *Sporting News*, January 16, 1936.
2. Richard Ben Cramer argues that Babe Ruth set the standard for the press, that his off-the-field exploits were ignored by the sportswriters, and this practice spread throughout baseball coverage. *Joe DiMaggio*, 82–83.
3. "By Daniel," *New York Telegram*, January 8, 1936.
4. "Down in Front," *New York Herald Tribune*, January 9, 1936.
5. I am grateful to both Bill Lamb and Gabriel Schechter for their email exchanges that helped sharpen my thinking on Charles Stoneham.
6. Robert E. Murphy believes few who read the newspapers would have doubted Stoneham's guilt. *After Many a Summer*, 29.
7. In Stoneham's will he gave ownership of the Giants to his wife Hannah, daughter Mary, and son Horace, in equal portions.
8. See the *New York Times*, April 2 and 16, 1936.
9. In this regard it is telling that a dying Charley turned not to Horace, his son, but rather in secret to Bill Terry, the Giants manager, to arrange treatment at Hot Springs, Arkansas. Jane Stoneham remarked that her father was quite distant with both her and her brother Russell. Interview with Jane Gosden, July 9, 2017.

Selected Bibliography

Archives and Collections

Bill Veeck papers, Chicago History Museum
Branch Rickey papers, 1890–1969, Library of Congress
Charles A. Stoneham papers, Rupert Family Private Collection
Charles A. Stoneham papers, San Francisco Giants Archives
Kenesaw Mountain Landis papers, Chicago History Museum
Museum of the City of New York
Newspaper Archive Room, New York Public Library
Prints & Photographs Division, Library of Congress
San Francisco History Center, San Francisco Public Library

Published Sources

Alexander, Charles C. *Breaking the Slump: Baseball in the Depression Era*. New York: Columbia University Press, 2002.

———. *John McGraw*. Lincoln: University of Nebraska Press, 1988.

———. *Rogers Hornsby*. New York: Henry Holt, 1995.

Alexander, Michael. *Jazz Age Jews*. Princeton NJ: Princeton University Press, 2001.

Allen, Frederick Lewis. *Only Yesterday*. New York: Harper & Brothers, 1931.

Allen, Lee. *The Giants and the Dodgers: The Fabulous Story of Baseball's Fiercest Feud*. New York: G. P. Putnam's Sons, 1964.

———. *The National League Story*. New York: Hill & Wang, 1961.

Allen, Oliver E. *The Tiger: The Rise and Fall of Tammany Hall*. Reading MA: Addison-Wesley, 1993.

Asinof, Eliot. *Eight Men Out*. New York: Henry Holt, 1963.

Barry John. *The Great Pandemic*. New York: Penguin Books, 2005.

Barthel, Thomas. *Babe Ruth and the Creation of the Celebrity Athlete*. Jefferson NC: McFarland, 2018.

Block, Geoffrey. "The Melody (and the Words) Linger On: American Musical Comedies of the 1920s and 1930s." In *The Cambridge Companion to the Musical*, edited by William A. Everett and Paul R. Laird. 3rd ed. Cambridge University Press, 2017.

Bradley, Hugh. *Such Was Saratoga*. New York: Arno Press, 1975.

Bruccoli, Matthew J., ed. *F. Scott Fitzgerald: A Life in Letters*. New York: Charles Scribner's Sons, 1994.

Burk, Robert F. *Much More than a Game*. Chapel Hill: University of North Carolina Press, 2001.

Burns, Eric. *1920: The Year That Made the Decade Roar*. New York: Pegasus Books, 2015.

Carney, Gene. *Burying the Black Sox: How Baseball's Cover-Up of the 1919 World Series Fix Almost Succeeded*. Washington DC: Potomac Books, 2007.

Chandler, Lester. *America's Great Depression*. New York: HarperCollins, 1970.

Chavez, Henry. *Play the Devil: A History of Gambling in the United States from 1492 to 1955*. New York: Bonanza Books, 1960.

Churchwell, Sarah. *Careless People: Murder, Mayhem and the Invention of* The Great Gatsby. New York: Penguin Press, 2014.

Clark, Tom. *The World of Damon Runyon*. New York: Harper & Row, 1978.

Corrigan, Maureen. *So We Read On: How* The Great Gatsby *Came to Be and Why It Endures*. New York: Little, Brown, 2014.

Cramer, Richard Ben. *Joe DiMaggio: The Hero's Life*. New York: Simon & Schuster, 2000.

D'Emilio, John, and Estelle B. Friedman. *Intimate Matters: A History of Sexuality in America*. New York: Harper & Row, 1988.

DeVeaux, Scott, and Gary Giddins. *Jazz*. New York: W. W. Norton, 2009.

Douglas, Ann. *Terrible Honesty: Mongrel Manhattan in the 1920s*. New York: Noonday Press, Farrar, Straus & Giroux, 1995.

Doyle, Arthur Conan. "The Adventure of Silver Blaze." *Memoirs of Sherlock Holmes, The Complete Sherlock Holmes*. New York: Doubleday, 1953.

Durso, Joseph. *The Days of John McGraw*. Englewood Cliffs NJ: Prentice-Hall, 1969.

Editors of the *New York Times*. *The Roaring '20s*. New York: Meredith, 2019.

Elder, Donald. *Ring Lardner*. New York: Doubleday, 1956.

Everett, William A., and Paul R. Laird, eds. *The Cambridge Companion to the Musical*. 3rd ed. Cambridge: Cambridge University Press, 2017.

Fabian, Ann. *Card Sharps, Dream Books, and Bucket Shops: Gambling in Nineteenth-Century America*. Ithaca: Cornell University Press, 1999.

Fass, Paula. *The Damned and the Beautiful*. New York: Oxford University Press, 1977.

Faulkner, William. *Requiem for a Nun*. New York: Random House, 1951.

Ferber, Nat. *I Found Out: A Confidential Chronicle of the Twenties*. New York: Dial, 1939.

Fetter, Henry D. *Taking on the Yankees: Winning and Losing in the Business of Baseball, 1903–2003*. New York: W. W. Norton, 2003.

Finlay, John M. *People of Chance: Gambling in American Society from Jamestown to Las Vegas*. New York: Oxford University Press, 1986.

Fitzgerald, F. Scott. *The Great Gatsby. The Cambridge Edition of the Works of F. Scott Fitzgerald*. Edited by Matthew J. Bruccoli. Cambridge: Cambridge University Press, 1991.

———. *The Jazz Age*. New York: New Directions, 1969.

———. *Tales of the Jazz Age. The Cambridge Edition of the Works of F. Scott Fitzgerald*. Edited by James L. W. West III. Cambridge University Press, 2002.

Fitzgerald, F. Scott, and Maxwell E. Perkins. *Dear Scott / Dear Max: The Fitzgerald-Perkins Correspondence*. Edited by John Kuehl and Jackson Bryer. London: Cassell, 1973.

Fountain, Charles. *The Betrayal: The 1919 World Series and the Birth of Modern Baseball*. New York: Oxford University Press, 2016.

Fowler, Gene. *Beau James: The Life and Times of Jimmy Walker*. New York: Viking Press, 1949.

———. *The Great Mouthpiece*. New York: Grosset & Dunlap, 1931.

Friedman, Milton, and Anna Jacobson Schwartz. *The Great Contraction, 1929–1933*. Princeton NJ: Princeton University Press, 2009.

Garrett, Charles. *The La Guardia Years*. New Brunswick NJ: Rutgers University Press, 1961.

Ginsberg, Daniel E. *The Fix Is In*. Jefferson NC: McFarland, 1995.

Gioia, Ted. *The History of Jazz*. New York: Oxford University Press, 1997.

Graham, Frank. *McGraw of the Giants*. New York: G. P. Putnam's Sons, 1944.

———. *The New York Giants: An Informal History*. New York: G. P. Putnam's Sons, 1952.

Guenther, Luis. "Pirates of Promotion." *World's Work*, November 1918.

Hamilton, Nigel. *How To Do Biography*. Cambridge: Harvard University Press, 2008.

Hays, Arthur Garfield. *City Lawyer: The Autobiography of a Law Practice*. New York: Simon & Schuster, 1942.

Heimer, Mel. *Fabulous Bawd: The Story of Saratoga*. New York: Henry Holt, 1952.

Hernandez, Lou. *Manager of the Giants*. Jefferson NC: McFarland, 2018.

Hill, David. *The Vapors: A Southern Family, the New York Mob, and the Rise and Fall of Hot Springs, America's Forgotten Capital of Vice*. New York: Farrar, Straus & Giroux, 2020.

Hochfelder, David. "'Where the Common People Could Speculate': The Ticker, Bucket Shops, and the Origins of Popular Participation in Financial Markets." *Journal of American History* 93, no. 2 (September 2006):335–58.

Hynd, Noel. *The Giants of the Polo Grounds: The Glorious Times of Baseball's New York Giants*. New York: Doubleday, 1988.

Jensen, Richard J. "The Causes and Cures of Unemployment in the Great Depression." *Journal of Interdisciplinary History* 19, no. 1 (Spring 1989).

Kahn, Roger. *The Era: 1947–1957*. Lincoln: University of Nebraska Press, Bison Books, 2002.

Katcher, Leo. *The Big Bankroll: The Life and Times of Arnold Rothstein*. New York: Da Capo, 1994.

Lamb, Bill. "Charles A. Stoneham." SABR BioProject. Society for American Baseball Research. N.d. https://sabr.org/bioproj/person/charles-a-stoneham.

———. "Frank McQuade." SABR BioProject. Society for American Baseball Research. N.d. https://sabr.org/bioproj/person/frank-mcquade.

———. "New York Giants Team Ownership." SABR Team Ownership History Project. Society for American Baseball Research. N.d. https://sabr.org/bioproj/topic/new-york-giants-team-ownership-history.

———. "Suicide at the Imperial Hotel." *Inside Game* 14, no. 1 (February 2014): 26–29.

Leavengood, Ted. "Baseball Gets a Taste of the Depression." *The Winter Meetings, Vol. 1: 1901–1957*. Edited by Steve Weingarden and Bill Nowlin. Phoenix: Society of American Baseball Research, 2016.

Leavy, Jane. *The Big Fella*. New York: HarperCollins, 2018.

Lerner, Michael A. *Dry Manhattan: Prohibition in New York City.* Cambridge: Harvard University Press, 2007.

Lewis, Alfred Allan. *Man of the World: Herbert Bayard Swope, a Charmed Life of Pulitzer Prizes, Poker and Politics.* New York: Bobbs-Merrill, 1978.

Lowenfish, Lee. *Branch Rickey: Baseball's Ferocious Gentleman.* Lincoln: University of Nebraska Press, 2009.

McElvaine, Robert S. *The Great Depression: American, 1929–1941.* New York: Three Rivers Press, 2009.

McKenna, Brian. "Lefty O'Doul." SABR BioProject. N.d. https://sabr.org/bioproj/person/lefty-odoul.

Millay, Edna St. Vincent. *A Few Figs from Thistles.* New York: Harper Brothers, 1922.

Mordden, Ethan. *That Jazz! An Idiosyncratic Social History of the American Twenties.* New York: G. P. Putnam's Sons, 1978.

Morris, Lloyd. *Incredible New York.* New York: Random House, 1951.

———. *Postscript to Yesterday: America: The Last Fifty Years.* New York: Random House, 1947.

Morris, Wesley. "Introduction." *The Great Gatsby.* New York: Modern Library, 2021.

Murphy, Robert E. *After Many a Summer.* New York: Union Square Press, 2009, 30.

Nasaw, David. *The Patriarch.* New York: Penguin Press, 2012.

Okrent, Daniel. *Last Call: The Rise and Fall of Prohibition.* New York: Scribner, 2010.

O'Meara, Lauraleigh. *Lost City: Fitzgerald's New York.* New York: Routledge, 2002.

Parrish, Michael E. *Anxious Decades: America in Prosperity and Depression, 1920–1941.* New York: W. W. Norton, 1992.

Perrett, Geoffrey. *America in the Twenties.* New York: Simon & Schuster, 1982.

Pietrusza, David. *Judge and Jury: The Life and Times of Judge Kenesaw Mountain Landis.* South Bend IN: Diamond Communications, 1998.

———. *Rothstein: The Life, Times, and Murder of the Criminal Genius Who Fixed the 1919 World Series.* New York: Basic Books, 2011.

Piper, Henry Dan. *F. Scott Fitzgerald: A Critical Portrait.* New York: Holt, Reinhart & Winston, 1962.

Rabinowitz, Bill. "Baseball in the Great Depression." In *Baseball History*, edited by Peter Levine. Westport CT: Meckler, 1989.

Riess, Steven A. "The Baseball Magnates and Urban Politics in the Progressive Era: 1895–1920." *Journal of Sports History* 1, no. 1 (1974): 41–62. *Scholarly Journals Bulletin Proceedings Collection*. Digital Library Collection.

Riley, Glenda. *Divorce: An American Tradition*. New York: Oxford University Press, 1991.

Rogers, C. Paul, III. "Ross Youngs." SABR BioProject. Society for American Baseball Research. Last updated October 4, 2020. https://sabr.org /bioproj/person/ross-youngs.

Runyon, Damon. *Guys and Dolls*. Franklin Center PA: Franklin Library, 1979.

SABR. "Eight Myths Out." Society for American Baseball Research website. https://sabr.org/eight-myths-out.

Schott, Tom, and Nick Peters. *The Giants Encyclopedia*. Champaign IL: Sports Publishing, 2003.

Seymour, Harold, and Dorothy Seymour Mills. *Baseball: The Golden Age*. New York: Oxford University Press, 1971.

Shaplen, Robert. "The Lonely, Loyal Mr. Stoneham." *Sports Illustrated*, May 5, 1958.

Spink, J. G. Taylor. *Judge Landis and 25 Years of Baseball*. New York: Thomas Y. Crowell, 1947.

Smith, Robert. *Babe Ruth's America*. New York: Thomas E. Crowell, 1974.

Snelling, Dennis. *Lefty O'Doul: Baseball's Forgotten Ambassador*. Lincoln: University of Nebraska Press, 2017.

Stein, Fred. "Bill Terry." SABR BioProject. N.d. https://sabr.org/bioproj /person/bill-terry.

———. *Under Coogan's Bluff*. Glenshaw PA: Chapter & Cask, 1981.

Steinberg, Steve, and Lyle Spatz. *1921: The Yankees, the Giants, and the Battle for Baseball Supremacy in New York*. Lincoln: University of Nebraska Press, 2010.

———. *The Colonel and the Hug*. Lincoln: University of Nebraska Press, 2015.

Surdam, David George. *Wins, Losses, and Empty Seats: How Baseball Outlasted the Great Depression*. Lincoln: University of Nebraska Press, 2011.

Surdam, David George, and Michael J. Haupert. *The Age of Ruth and Landis*. Lincoln: University of Nebraska Press, 2018.

Susman, Warren I. *Culture as History: The Transformation of American Society in the Twentieth Century*. New York: Pantheon Books, 1973.

Thorn, John, Peter Palmer, Michael Gershman, and David Pietrusza. *Total Baseball*. 6th ed. New York: Total Sports, 1999.

Tosches, Nick. *King of the Jews*. New York: Ecco, 2005.

Treder, Steven. *Forty Years a Giant: The Life of Horace Stoneham*. Lincoln: University of Nebraska Press, 2021.

Turnbull, Andrew, ed. *The Letters of F. Scott Fitzgerald*. New York: Charles Scribner's Sons, 1963.

Tygiel, Jules. *Past Time: Baseball as History*. New York: Oxford University Press, 2000.

Vecsey, George. *Baseball*. New York: Modern Library, 2006.

Veeck, Bill. "Harry's Diary—1919." *The Hustler's Handbook*. Chicago: Ivan R. Dee, 1985.

Waldo, Ronald T. *Baseball's Roaring Twenties*. Lanham MD: Rowman & Littlefield, 2017.

Walker, Stanley. *The Night Club Era*. New York: Blue Ribbon Books, 1933.

Waller, George. *Saratoga: Saga of an Impious Era*. New York: Prentice-Hall, 1966.

Weingarden, Steve, and Bill Nowlin, eds. *Baseball's Business: The Winter Meetings, Vol. 1: 1901–1957*. Phoenix: Society for American Baseball Research, 2016.

Williams, Peter. *When the Giants Were Giants: Bill Terry and the Golden Age of New York Baseball*. Chapel Hill NC: Algonquin Books of Chapel Hill, 1994.

Zinn, John G. *Charles Ebbets: The Man behind the Dodgers and Brooklyn's Beloved Ballpark*. Jefferson NC: McFarland, 2019.

Index

Haight and Freese Company, 26, 27
Hammerstein, Oscar, II, 5
Harding, Warren, xiv
Harlem, 4
Harridge, Will, 16, 143
Harris, Sam, 44
Harrison, James R., 99
Hart, Larry, 5
Havana, Cuba, 32
Hays, Arthur Garfield, 115–16
Hearst, William Randolph, 197n36
Hempstead, Harry, 41–43, 45–46, 55
Herrmann, Garry, 50
Heydler, John, 64, 66–67, 68
Hogan, James "Shanty," 103
Hoover, Herbert, 122
Hornsby, Rogers, 92–104, 137
Hot Springs AR, 13, 15–16, 153–54, 164
House, Victor, 84, 187n36
Hubbell, Carl, 133, 141, 142, 148
Hughes & Dier. See E. D. Dier and Company
Huston, Tillinghast, 52, 54, 83, 90, 157, 182n46
Hylan, John, 109

Jack's restaurant, 107, 147
Jacobson, Isaac N., 115–16
Jamaica Racetrack, 32, 34
Jay Gatsby (*The Great Gatsby*), as dreamer, 90; funeral of 20; as Jazz Age prototype, xv, 10, 90; as suggestive of Charles Stoneham's behavior, xv–xvi, 10, 165
jazz, 3–4, 124
Jazz Age, xii, xvii, 1, 3–9, 11, 13, 17,

91–92, 100–101, 121, 125; 129, 156, 160; characteristics of, 91; depiction in *The Great Gatsby*, xvii; funerals in, 17–19; music of, 3–5; phrase coined by Fitzgerald 4; prohibition and, 6–9
jazz journalism, 100–101
Jersey City NJ, 9–10, 15, 25–26, 27, 45, 54, 130, 150, 155
Johnson, Ban, 52, 54, 63, 67, 90
Johnson, Walter, 67

Kauff, Benny, 70, 85–86, 185n21
Kelly, George, 65, 97
Kenny, William, 113–14, 118
Kern, Jerome, 5
Kieran, John, 101, 139, 161
Knickerbocker hotel, 34
Knowles, "Doc," 135–36

LaGuardia, Fiorello, 6
Lamb, Bill, 21, 87
Landis, Kenesaw Mountain, 20, 53, 64–71, 83, 85–86, 126
Lane, F. C., 140
Lasker, Albert D., 53
Lasker Plan, 53–54, 182n46
Leavy, Jane, 100
Lindstrom, Fred, 133, 135, 138
Loft, George, 44
Lowden, George H., 11
Lowenfish, Lee, 95, 101
Luque, Dolf, 142

Mancuso, Gus, 139
Mathewson, Christy, 109
McCook, Philip, J., 114, 116–17